Access 97

Answers!
Certified Tech Support

Access 97

Answers!
Certified Tech Support

Edward Jones
Jarel Jones

Osborne **McGraw-Hill**
Berkeley • New York • St. Louis • San Francisco
Auckland • Bogotá • Hamburg • London • Madrid
Mexico City • Milan • Montreal • New Delhi
Panama City • Paris • São Paulo • Singapore
Sydney • Tokyo • Toronto

Osborne/**McGraw-Hill**
2600 Tenth Street
Berkeley, California 94710
U.S.A.

For information on translations or book distributors outside the U.S.A., or to arrange
bulk purchase discounts for sales promotions, premiums, or fundraisers, please contact
Osborne/**McGraw-Hill** at the above address.

Access 97 Answers!
Certified Tech Support

4567890 DOC 99

ISBN 0-07-882382-X

Publisher	**Editorial Assistant**
Brandon A. Nordin	Gordon Hurd
Editor-in-Chief	**Copy Editor**
Scott Rogers	Jerome Colburn
Acquisitions Editor	**Production Coordinator**
Joanne Cuthbertson	Kathryn Mikulic
Technical Editor	
Leigh Yafa	

Nikki Jones, for just being there.

—Jarel Jones

To all my family at UFC New York. We've come this far . . .

—Edward Jones-Mack

Contents @ a Glance

Contents

Acknowledgments

We would like to thank the staff at Stream International, who willingly committed much time and knowledge to this effort. Many of the support specialists spent untold hours searching the Stream data banks for the top questions and answers and reviewing manuscript and pages. Without all of their hard work, this book would not be the encompassing source of answers that it is. We would like to thank personally each of the following people for their assistance: Denise Boudreau, Ceci Chamorro, John Kelley, Greg Walker, Angela Santos, and Wiley Mallet.

The staff at Osborne was also a vital part of this book. Everyone worked hard to help us meet the important deadlines necessary in bringing this book to market. We would like to extend special thanks to Joanne Cuthbertson, Acquisitions Editor, for giving us the chance to do this project and for those important suggestions that helped us refine the book's structure; Scott Rogers, Editor-In-Chief, for his work in bringing the overall series concept in cooperation with Stream International to reality; Nancy McLaughlin, Project Editor; and Gordon Hurd, Editorial Assistant, whose work helped organize all the components of the project; Leigh Yafa, Technical Reviewer, for an outstanding tech edit; and all of the Production staff, who contributed, in ways too numerous to count, toward the goal of making this book the best source of technical support available.

Introduction

There is no good time to have a problem with your computer or the software you are using. You are anxious to complete the task you started and do not have time to fumble through a manual looking for an answer that is probably not there anyway. You can forget about the option of a free support call, since most software vendors now charge as much as $25 to answer a single question.

Access 97 Answers: Certified Tech Support can provide the solutions to all of your Access questions. It contains the most frequently asked Access questions, along with their solutions to get you back on track quickly. The questions and answers have been formulated with the assistance of Stream International, the world's largest provider of third-party technical support. Since they answer over one million calls a month from users just like you, odds are high that your problem has plagued others in the past and is already part of their data bank. *Access 97 Answers: Certified Tech Support* is the next best thing to having a Stream International expert at the desk right next to you. The help you need is available seven days a week, any time you have a problem.

Access 97 Answers: Certified Tech Support is organized into 16 chapters. Each chapter contains questions and answers on a specific area of Access. Within each chapter, you will find the questions organized alphabetically, based on a highlighted key phrase. With this organization, you can read through questions and answers on particular topics to familiarize yourself with them before the troubles actually occur. An excellent index makes it easy for you to find what you need even if you are uncertain which chapter would cover the solution.

Throughout the book you will also find elements that help you sail smoothly through Access tasks, whether you are a novice or a veteran user.

1 Answers!

Top Ten
FAQs

Answer Topics!

How can I save a database in Access 97 to Access 95?

Why do i see "#Name?" in some controls instead of my data?

Why do I get the message "You can't add or change a record because a related record is required"?

In my form, how can I give my fields a raised appearance as on a button?

How do I change a field in a form to a list box or a combo box?

How can I break the link to an attached table?

What does the Make MDE file option do to my database?

Can I use a value typed into a text box on a form to filter my query?

How can I create a form that initially appears every time I open a database?

How can I bring in data from a data source other than Access?

Top Ten FAQs
@ a Glance

In this chapter, we've presented step-by-step solutions for the problems that have given rise to the ten most frequently asked questions (FAQs) that users have had with Access 97. Thousands of users have encountered these problems. They received expert help from Stream Corporation, and now you can, too!

   You might not have to ask these questions at all if you review this chapter now. Later, if any of these problems should still arise, you'll know what to do.

1 How can I save a database in Access 97 (version 8.0) to Access 95 (version 7.0)?

You can't save a database backwards to a previous format in Access, as you can with documents in Microsoft Word or Microsoft Excel. There is no feature for converting a database as a whole to an earlier version of Access. However, you can export the tables to a file format that you can then import into Access 95. You can use the following steps to do this:

1. In the Database window, right-click the table you want to export, and choose Save As/Export from the shortcut menu.

2. In the Save As dialog box which appears, leave the To an External File or Database option selected, and click OK.

3. In the next dialog box that appears, under Save As Type, change the type to a format that your earlier version of Access can import, such as Text, Excel, FoxPro, or dBASE IV.

4. Choose a destination drive and folder in the upper portion of the dialog box, enter a name under File Name, and click Export to export the table.

5. Repeat steps 1 through 4 for each table that you need to import into the earlier version of Access.

6. Launch the earlier version of Access, and use the File/Import procedure appropriate to that version of Access to import the tables.

After importing the tables into the earlier version of Access, you'll need to recreate manually any queries, forms, reports, macros, or modules needed.

•••••• *Tip:* If the table you are bringing into the earlier version of Access contains memo fields or OLE Object fields, FoxPro 2.6 is a recommended choice as the export format, because the complete contents of the memo fields and the OLE Object fields will be retained, and all but the earliest version of Access can import FoxPro 2.6 files. (Excel does not handle OLE Object fields, and it will not let you store more than 255 characters in a cell, so any memo fields will lose all characters after the 255th character if exported to Excel.) On the other hand, if the table contains currency fields but no memo fields or OLE Object fields, Excel is a recommended choice because the formatting of the currency fields will be retained.

2 When I open my form or report, I see "#Name?" in some controls. What happened to my data?

"#Name?" is the error message that appears in a control when it can't find the data it is supposed to display. *Controls* are the elements of a form or report that can display data. Each control has many *properties* that define how it works. The Control Source property defines the source of the data that the control displays. If this property is set to a source that Access can't find or that doesn't exist, the "#Name?" error message appears instead of the missing data.

•••••• *Tip:* The idea behind properties may be confusing at first, but it is actually quite simple. Properties modify controls the same way that adjectives modify the meaning of a noun. An adjective can't change the basic definition of the noun, but it does provide more information. Properties can't change the kind of control in your form or report, but they can provide clarifying information, such as what data the control displays.

Figure 1-1 shows a form with several controls that have invalid Control Source property settings. You want these controls to show meaningful data, so you need to make the Control Source property setting valid. To change the Control Source property setting, open the form or report in Design view. (You can select the form or report in the

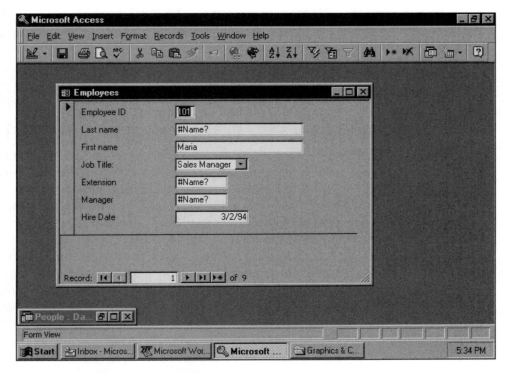

Figure 1-1   A form with invalid data

Database window and then click the Design button, or you can right-click the form or report in the Database window and choose Design from the shortcut menu that appears.) Right-click the problem control (the one that displayed the "#Name?" error message while in Form view), and choose Properties from the shortcut menu that appears to open the Properties window. Click the Data tab, and examine the entry in the Control Source property. The current setting may be a mistyped field name, or it may refer to a field that you have removed from the underlying table or query. Set the property to an existing source of data. After you fix the entry, your form or report should work correctly.

Tip: You can show either some or all of the properties for a control in the Properties window. To show all of the properties, click the All tab in the window. To show some of the properties, click the appropriate tab (Format, Data, Event, or Other).

•••••• *Tip:*   You can also change the Control Source property for a text box by clicking once within the text box, and typing the new entry for the property.

3 Why do I get the message "You can't add or change a record because a related record is required in table 'tablename'" when I try to add a record using my form?

When you set up a *relationship* between the table the form is based on and another table, you chose to enforce *referential integrity.* Relationships between tables indicate how records in the two tables relate. For example, you could set a one-to-many relationship between the Employee ID field in your Employees table and the Sales Representatives field in your Invoices table. When you enforce referential integrity, Access makes sure that all new and edited records in the tables keep the type of relationship you set. For example, in this one-to-many relationship, you can enter ID numbers for the Sales Representatives field only if they already exist in the Employee ID field in the Employees table.

When you try to save a record, Access checks to make sure that the record doesn't violate referential integrity. For example, after you enter a record in your Invoices table, Access checks that the entry in the Sales Representatives field already exists in the Employees table. If it doesn't, Access won't save the record and displays the message you saw.

Enforcing referential integrity protects you against incorrect entries. If you mistype an employee's ID in the Sales Representative field, Access stops you. Obviously, your sales representative can't be someone who isn't already an employee. This lets you fix the mistake immediately instead of discovering it much later.

4 In my form, how can I give my fields a raised appearance as if they are on a button, not a flat appearance as if they have been typed on a sheet?

You can do this by adding a special effect of your choice to the field's appearance. Open the form in Design view, and right-click the field. From the shortcut menu that appears, choose Special Effect. A submenu will appear as shown here, from which you can choose the desired effect.

You have a choice of flat, raised, sunken, etched, shadowed, or chiseled for the possible special effects.

5 How do I change a field in a form to a list box or a combo box?

Open the form in Design view, right-click the field, and choose Change To from the shortcut menu. From the next menu that appears, choose List Box or Combo Box, as desired. Depending on the size of the entries in the original field, you may want to resize the control to add space for the down arrow at the right of a combo box or the scroll bar in a list box.

Tip: Once you've changed the field, you will need to modify the Row Source Type and Row Source properties for the list box or combo box, depending on what you want the box to display. If you're not sure about how to do this, you may be better off adding the list box or combo box as a new field and letting the Control Wizards automate the process. You can delete the existing field, and make sure that the Control Wizards are turned on in the Toolbox (the Control Wizards button should appear depressed). Next, click the List Box tool in the Toolbox (if you want a list box) or click the Combo Box tool in the Toolbox (if you want a combo box). Finally, click in the form where you want to place the list box or combo box. The wizard will ask you a series of questions. Depending on your answers, the wizard will fill in the Row Source and Row Source Type properties for you.

6 How can I break the link to an attached table?

In the Database window, select the attached table. Open the Edit menu and choose Delete, or press the DEL key. In the dialog box that appears asking for confirmation, click Yes. This deletes the link and removes the name of the attached table from the list of tables in the Database window. Note that when you delete an attached table, you are deleting only the information that Access uses to open that table. You are not deleting the table itself. You can reattach the same table again.

7 Under the Database Utilities option of the Tools menu there's an option for Make MDE file. What does this do to my database?

Saving a database as an MDE file results in a copy of the database that does not allow changes to forms, reports, or any Visual Basic for Applications (VBA) code stored in that database. (You can make changes to tables, queries, and macros in a database that has been saved as an MDE file.) If your database contains VBA code, saving it as an MDE file compiles all modules, removes all editable source code, and then compacts the destination database. Any VBA code will continue to run, but it cannot be viewed or edited. In addition to preventing changes by unauthorized users, saving a database as an MDE file has performance benefits. The size of your database will be reduced due to the removal of the code, and memory usage is optimized, improving performance.

■■■ *Caution:*   If you save a database as an MDE file, be sure to maintain a copy of the original database (.MDB) file in a secure location. You will need it if you want to make any changes to the forms, reports, or code that are stored in the database.

8 How can I type something into a text box on a form and use that value to filter my query?

There is a technique called *query-by-form* that you can use to accomplish this. You enter an expression in the Criteria row of the query that refers back to the text box on the form, and you add a Search button to the form that, when clicked, runs the query. As an example, Figure 1-2 shows a form used to enter query criteria, and the resulting query when the Search button is clicked.

You can use the following steps to implement query-by-form:

1. Create a form with text boxes you want to use to supply the desired criteria to the query. You will need one text box for each cell in the query that you want to provide criteria for. As an example, if you wanted to fill in the City and State fields of a query based on entries in a form, you would add two text boxes to the form.

2. Turn on the Control Wizards in the Toolbox, if they are not already on.

3. Add a command button to the form. The Command Button Wizard dialog box will appear. Under Categories, choose Miscellaneous. Under Actions, choose Run Query. Then click Next.

4. In the next dialog box, choose your query that will accept the values entered into the form, then click Next.

5. In the next dialog box, click Text and enter an appropriate caption for the button, such as "Search." Then click Finish to add the button to the form.

6. Save the form.

7. Open the query in Design view. In the Criteria row for each field that has a corresponding text box on the form, you will need to enter an expression like this:

Forms![Form Name**]![**Control Name**] OR**
Forms![Form Name**]![**Control Name**] Is Null**

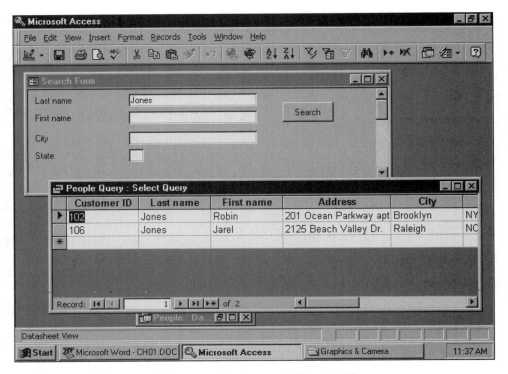

Figure 1-2   A form used for query-by-form and the resulting query

where *Form Name* is the name of your form, and *Control Name* is the name assigned to the text box control. For example, if you named the form "Query People" and the form contained a text box named "AskLastname," you would have an expression like this one in the Criteria row of the Last Name field of the query grid:

```
[Forms]![Query People]![AskLastname] OR [Forms]
![Query People]![AskLastname] Is Null
```

After saving the query, you can open the form, enter criteria in one or more of the text boxes, and click the button to run the query using the criteria supplied.

9 How can I create a startup form, or a form that initially appears every time I open a database?

In earlier versions of Access, this was commonly done with an Autoexec macro containing an Open Form argument that opened the desired form. You can still do it this way, but Access 97 provides an easier technique with more options. With the Database window active, open the Tools menu, and choose Startup. You will see the Startup dialog box, shown here.

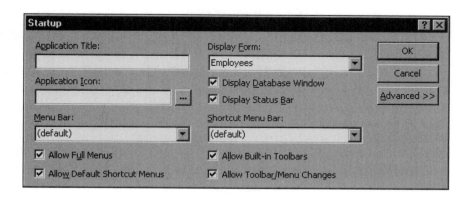

Click the down arrow at the right of the Display Form list box, and choose the form by name that you want to open when the database is opened. You can use the other options in this dialog box to hide the Database window, to provide a title for the Application title bar, to display or hide the full menus and built-in toolbars, to name any custom menus and menu bars used by the database, and to specify an icon that appears in place of the default Access icon in the Application title bar and in the Windows Taskbar.

10 How can I bring in data from a data source other than Access?

You can use the following steps to bring in data from an external data source:

1. Open the database where you want to store the data, or create a new database if you want the data stored in that database.

2. Open the File menu and choose Get External Data.

3. From the next menu that appears, choose Import.

4. In the Import dialog box that appears, choose the type of file under the Files of Type box.

5. Enter a name and path for the file under File Name. (Alternately, you can use the Drive and Folder icons at the top of the dialog box to navigate to a folder where the file is stored, and select it.)

6. Click Import to bring the data into your Access database.

7. Depending on the type of data you are importing, Access may launch an Import Wizard to help you complete the process. If that happens, answer all of the questions in the Wizard.

2 Answers!

Access Basics

Answer Topics!

Access Basics
@ a Glance

Although Access is a powerful database management program, it is designed to be easy to use. Many of the problems encountered with the package occur because of the vast array of features and the new ways that Access provides to use all of the graphical features that Windows offers.

Even in simple tasks such as installation and basic database creation, there are numerous potential problem areas. Some users experience difficulty installing Access on networks. Others find that a database becomes unmanageable with graphics. This chapter provides the answers to these and other basic questions, letting you overcome these problems and focus on more advanced options.

The questions you'll find answers to in this chapter deal with the following areas:

☞ **Installation** The questions in this part of the chapter deal with specifications and with problems that arise when installing Access.

☞ **Opening and Converting Files** Here you'll find information on opening and converting data between Access 97 and other database software, including earlier versions of Access.

> **Managing the User Interface**   The questions in this portion of the chapter help you control the overall appearance of Access as you work with different databases.

> **Security**   This portion of the chapter provides answers to questions about Access security: the methods used to control rights to data used by multiple users.

> **Troubleshooting**   This portion of the chapter provides information relating to error messages and other problems that may arise in regard to the general operation of Access.

The Basics of Access

One of the more challenging aspects of starting to use Access is learning the terms and concepts behind organizing your data. Whether you are upgrading from another database management program or using a database manager for the first time, you'll find that the following definitions will help you work with the features of Access.

In Access, a *database* is a single file that contains the various Access "objects"—tables, queries, forms, reports, macros, and modules—that you work with on a regular basis. When you open a database, the Database window appears as shown here, containing the objects in the database.

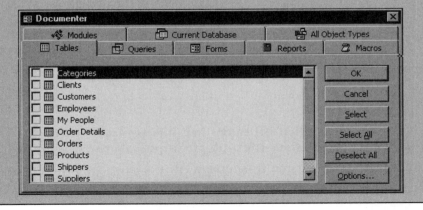

You use the six tabs at the top of the window to choose which objects currently appear in the window.

Tables are the containers that store your data. They are arranged in a row-and-column format, similar to that of spreadsheets. Each column, or *field*, holds a specific type of information, such as last names or phone numbers. Each row, or *record*, holds all the information related to a single entry, such as the last name, first name, address, city, state, ZIP code, and phone number for a particular customer. With relational database managers such as Access, a database often includes a number of different tables that contain related data. For example, in a database designed to track videos rented from a small video rental store, you might have one table for customers and another table for the names of the tapes rented by those customers.

Queries are Access objects that ask questions about the data in your database. Based on the way that the query is designed, the query can retrieve and combine data from different tables in the database. For example, you might design a query to tell you how many customers have overdue accounts or how many employees have been with the company for five years or more. Queries can also perform actions on groups of data, such as updating or deleting a certain group of records.

Forms are windows that provide an easy way to view existing records or to add new records to the tables in your database. In Access, you can create forms that let you work with a single table or with multiple tables simultaneously, and you can print forms as well as display them.

Reports are designed to show data, like forms, but they are designed primarily to be printed, and cannot be used for data entry.

Macros are stored sequences of actions in Access. They can be used to automate many everyday tasks and to simplify your work in Access.

Modules are procedures written in Visual Basic for Applications (VBA), the programming language that lies beneath Access. Using VBA, you can write program code that accomplishes specialized tasks not possible with Access macros.

INSTALLATION

 **I reinstalled Access to fix corrupted program files, but I still have the same problems. What's wrong?**

A reinstallation of Access won't fix corrupted files. What you'll need to do is to uninstall Access, then reinstall it. When you reinstall Access over an existing version of the program, the Setup routine detects the existing copy of Access and simply replaces any missing files. Hence, any corrupted program files are still there. To completely remove the existing program files, run Setup and choose Remove All to completely remove the existing copy of Access. Then reinstall Access using the Setup program. If you know precisely which program files are corrupted, you can delete those files, and then start Access Setup and choose Reinstall to replace them.

Note: If you are tempted to remove Access by dragging the folder where the program is stored to the Recycle Bin (or by deleting the program's directory under DOS), avoid this temptation. Many of the files used by Access aren't stored in the directory with the program files. Using Setup removes all the Access program files regardless of their location.

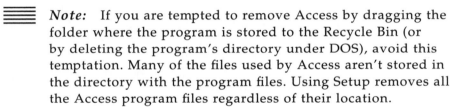 **What are the hardware requirements for installing Access 97?**

To run Access 97, you'll need a PC with a 486 or better processor; Windows 95 or Windows NT Workstation 3.51 Service Pack 5 or later; 12MB of memory (if using Windows 95) or 16MB of memory (if using Windows NT); and between 28MB and 60MB of hard disk space. You'll also need a VGA or higher resolution video adapter (Super VGA recommended), and a Microsoft mouse or compatible pointing device. While these are the "official" requirements stated by Microsoft, we found ourselves able to run Access 97 on a machine with 8MB of installed RAM; just don't expect stellar performance. If you plan on using multiple programs simultaneously, consider installing 32MB of RAM. The disk space requirement will vary between the 28MB minimum and the 60MB maximum, depending on which options you choose to add during the installation process (a typical installation uses 40MB). If you're using Windows NT, you should be aware that you can't run Access 97 on versions of NT prior to version 3.51.

Can I use a variety of **language conventions** for my database?

No, you cannot. The language conventions that Access uses for currency, list separators, date and time formats, and other settings are not controlled by Access. They are set by the options in the Windows Control Panel. These same settings are used by all Windows applications. Since you can select only one language setting at a time in Windows, you can use only one set of language conventions at a time in Access.

What's the **maximum size** for an Access database?

In theory, an Access database is limited to one gigabyte in size. But since tables in a database can be linked to tables stored in other Access databases or tables stored as external files, the total amount of data is limited only by available disk space.

How do I install Access 97 on a **network file server**?

You want to run the Administrative installation of Access, which provides the various options for installation on a network. You do this by including the /A option after the word "Setup." Insert the CD-ROM or Program Disk 1 in the drive, and from the Windows desktop, click Start and choose Run. In the Run dialog box that appears, enter **X:\ SETUP /A** (where **X** is the letter of your CD-ROM or diskette drive).

> ≡ *Note:* Network installations can be involved and potentially troublesome. If you are not the Network Administrator, you should contact the Network Administrator before attempting this.

 ## What **networks** can I install Access 97 on?

Access 97 is supported on the following networks. (It may operate satisfactorily on other network operating systems, but Microsoft isn't making any guarantees.)

▷ Microsoft Networks (LAN Manager 2.*x*, Windows NT 3.5*x* and 4.*x*, and Windows 95)

▷ Novell® 3.*x* and 4.*x* (32-bit client)

▷ Banyan Vines® 5.52 or higher (32-bit client)

▷ LANtastic® 6.*x* or higher (32-bit client)

▷ DEC PATHWORKS™ 6.2

▷ IBM™ LanServer

Can I install Access 97 simultaneously on a machine that has an **older version of Access** installed?

You can install and run multiple versions of Access on the same computer, as long as each version of Access is installed in its own folder (directory). If you are going to run Access 97 on a machine with an earlier version of Access installed (and you want to keep the earlier version of Access), be sure to install Access 97 in a separate folder. Also, keep in mind that Windows 95 will associate or "link" the .MDB extension used by all Access databases to the last version of Access you installed. So, double-clicking an .MDB file in Windows Explorer or in My Computer will cause the last version of Access that was installed to be launched. If you want to change the version of Access that's associated with .MDB files, you'll need to change the file association under Windows; search Windows Help under "associating" for details on how to do this.

? **I installed Access 97, and now my old applications written in the run-time version of Access 2.0 don't work. What happened?**

When you run the Setup program for Access 97, at some point you are asked whether you want to remove the components for older versions of Access. (If you installed Access as part of Office 97, you are asked whether you want to remove components for Office 4.*x* and Office 95.) If you answered Yes to either of these questions, the Setup routine for Access 97 deleted certain files that are used by applications written in the run-time versions of Access 2.0 or Access 95. To resolve this problem, you'll have to reinstall your custom run-time applications. Rerun Setup for your custom applications, and click Reinstall in the Maintenance Program dialog box.

? **My Access 97 installation didn't create a Workgroup Administrator icon for administrating workgroups on a network. Why not?**

Unlike earlier versions of Access, Access 97 does *not* automatically create a Workgroup Administrator icon for the Windows desktop. This behavior is intentional; Microsoft intended for you to manage workgroup security from within Access. But if you liked doing things the old way with a separate icon, you can still add one to your Programs menu on the Windows 95 Taskbar. Perform these steps to do this:

1. Click the Start button, and choose Settings, then Taskbar.
2. In the Taskbar Properties dialog box that appears, click the Start Menu Programs tab.
3. Click the Advanced button.
4. In the Explorer window that opens, double-click the Programs folder to show its contents.
5. Choose New from the File menu, then choose Shortcut.

6. In the Create Shortcut dialog box that appears, click Browse.

7. Find the file titled **Wrkgadm.exe**. If you accepted the default options during installation, the file is located in the Windows System folder.

8. Select **Wrkgadm.exe** and click Open.

9. Click Next.

10. Enter the name you want to assign to the shortcut, such as "Access Workgroup Administrator"; then click Finish.

11. Close the Explorer window and the Taskbar Properties dialog box.

12. Click the Start button, and choose Programs. You'll see the icon for the Workgroup Administrator added to your Programs menu.

OPENING AND CONVERTING FILES

? **Is there any way to open an Access 97 database in an earlier version of Access?**

You can't directly open an Access 97 database in an earlier version of Access, because Access 97 uses a file format that's different from the one used by all earlier versions. You can, however, choose Save As/Export from the File menu to export tables to an earlier version of Access. If you are faced with a situation where users of different versions of Access are on a network and they must all use the same database, there's a solution:

1. Store the tables in a database that's created in the earliest version of Access you are using.

2. Then create a "front-end" database in each version of Access that contains the queries, forms, and reports you'll need (but no tables).

3. Then, from within each of these "front-end" databases, attach to the tables that are stored in the database created in the earliest version of Access.

? How many **network users** can have the same database open simultaneously?

On a network, up to 255 users can have the same database open at the same time.

? Can I **open or convert databases** from earlier versions of Access?

When you want to work with databases created in earlier versions of Access, you have two choices: you can *open* the database and work with the data it contains, or you can *convert* the database into the file format used by Access 97. If you open a database created in an earlier version of Access, you can make changes to the data stored in the tables, and you can use the other objects (the queries, forms, reports, and macros), but you can't make design changes to any of the objects in the database. If you convert the database to the format used by Access 97, you can then make any changes you wish to the database. However, you will not be able to open the converted database in an earlier version of Access.

To open or convert a database from an earlier version, choose Open Database from the File menu, and select a database in the Open dialog box that appears. The next dialog box that appears (Figure 2-1) will give you a choice

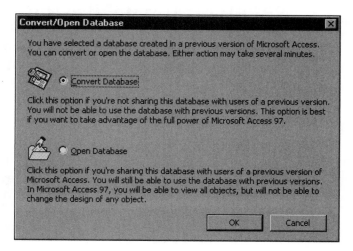

Figure 2-1: The Convert Database dialog box

of converting or opening the database. If you click Convert Database and click OK, Access will convert the older database into Access 97 file format. If you click Open Database and click OK, Access will open the database while preserving it in the old file format.

Caution: Before converting a database, you may want to make a copy of the database in case, for any reason, you aren't happy with the conversion.

I'm having trouble opening a Paradox table in Access. Why don't I see any database drivers for **Paradox or Lotus 1-2-3**?

If you're trying to import or link to a Paradox or a Lotus 1-2-3 file, you won't see these names as valid file types in the Link or Import dialog boxes. This is because the database drivers used for working with Lotus and Paradox files aren't installed with the standard installation of Access 97. The drivers are contained in the Office 97 ValuPack, which is provided on your installation CD-ROM. Insert the CD-ROM in your compact disc drive, open the \ValuPack\DataAcc folder on the CD, and double-click DataAcc.exe to run the Setup program to install the drivers.

MANAGING THE USER INTERFACE

Whenever I delete an object such as a table or a form, Access always asks me for confirmation of the deletion. I find this annoying. Can I make Access stop **asking for confirmation**?

This could be dangerous, but yes, you can tell Access to stop asking. Choose Options from the Tools menu, and click the Edit/Find tab in the Options dialog box that appears (Figure 2-2). In the Confirm portion of the dialog box, turn off the Document Deletions option, then click OK.

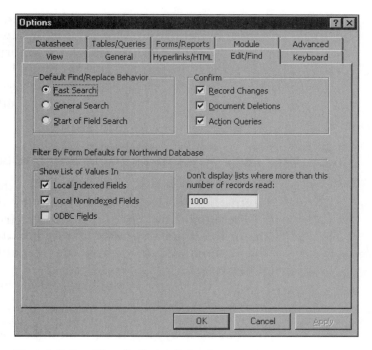

Figure 2-2:   The Options dialog box

? Is there a shortcut for entering the **current date and time**?

Yes, Access has shortcut keys for entering the current date and time. They can be used while entering data in tables, queries, or forms.

Press CTRL-; (semicolon) to enter the current date.
Press CTRL-: (colon) to enter the current time.

? Can I create a **custom menu** that appears when I open a form or report?

You can change the Access menus you see when working on a form or report. (This can prove helpful when you want to give users a form that doesn't have the standard Access menu options on it.) You add a custom menu to a form or report by attaching a macro that creates a custom menu bar to the MenuBar property of the form or the report. The easiest way to create a custom menu bar macro is to use the Menu Builder. See Chapter 12, "Access Macros," for more information about macros in general and about creating macros.

How can I **customize toolbars** in Access?

You can add or remove buttons from the existing toolbars. Right-click on any blank space in the toolbar you want to customize, and choose Customize from the shortcut menu that appears. In the dialog box that opens, click the Commands tab to show the available commands (Figure 2-3).

Click the desired category, and at the right side of the dialog box, drag any command button you want onto the toolbar. You can remove a button you've added to any toolbar by dragging it off the toolbar onto any blank portion of the dialog box.

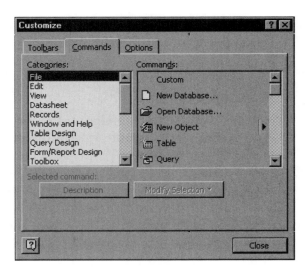

Figure 2-3:   The available commands in the Customize dialog box

? How can I obtain a list of the **definitions of objects** in my database?

Access has a feature called the Database Documentor that produces a report that details the objects in your database. Using the Database Documentor, you can select any or all objects in your database and then produce a report documenting those objects. You can use the following steps to produce this report:

1. Open the database you want to document.

2. Open the Tools menu and choose Analyze, then choose Documentor from the next menu that appears. In a moment, the Documentor window appears as shown here. In appearance, this window resembles the Database window.

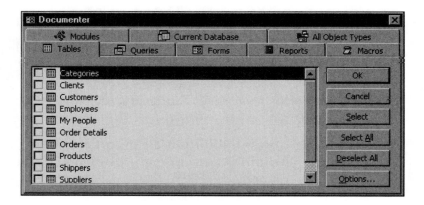

3. Click on each desired tab to select a different area (tables, queries, forms, reports, macros, modules, or all object types), and in each area, click the check boxes beside the objects you want to print definitions for.

4. For each object type that you want to include in the report, click the Options button and click the checkboxes on or off to specify which types of information should be included in the report; then click OK.

5. When done selecting all the desired objects, click OK.

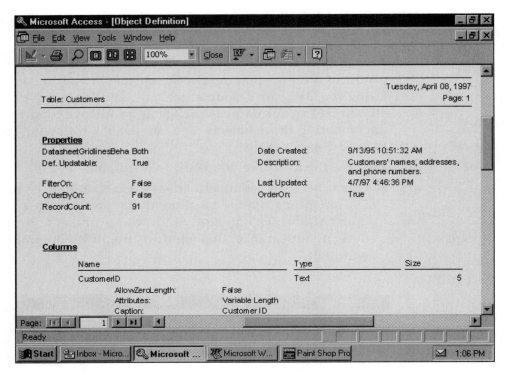

Figure 2-4:   A report containing object definitions from a database

Access will produce a report containing the object definitions. An example of such a report is shown in Figure 2-4.

❓ Can I **disable certain keys** such as F1?

Yes, you can disable keys so that other users cannot use them in your database. This can be useful in an application where you want to limit the users' options. To do this, create an AutoKeys macro that tells Access what to do when you press a certain key. The AutoKeys macro executes automatically each time a database is opened. You disable a key by telling Access to do nothing when the key is pressed. You can use these steps to create an AutoKeys macro:

1. Create a macro with the name AutoKeys.

2. Choose Macro Names from the View menu to display the Macro Names column if you do not already see it.

3. Assign macro names using the SendKeys code of the key you want to disable.

4. Add the SendKeys action and leave the Keystrokes argument empty.

5. Close and save the macro.

6. Save and close the database.

The next time you open the database, Access performs the AutoKeys macro. The effect of the AutoKeys macro remains as long as the database is open.

For example, you could create an AutoKeys macro to disable the F1 key. Enter {**F1**} in the Macro Name column, and choose **SendKeys** in the Action column. Leave the Keystrokes argument for the SendKeys action empty. The next time you open the database, Access will perform this macro every time you press F1. Since the Keystrokes argument is empty, no keystroke is sent to Access. Therefore, pressing F1 has no effect.

❓ Can I **hide a table** so that it doesn't appear in the Database window?

If you want to hide a table in the Database window so that other users can't select it, there is a neat but little-known trick for doing this. Rename the table, and give it any name that starts with the letters **Usys**. For example, if you want to hide a table named **Salaries**, you might rename it to **Usyssalaries**. (A quick way to rename the table is to right-click it in the Database window, choose Rename from the shortcut menu that appears, and enter a new name in the dialog box that appears.) Access considers all tables with names that begin with the letters **Usys** to be system objects, and system objects are normally hidden in the Database window.

If you want to see this table again later, open the Tools menu and choose Options. When the Options dialog box appears, click the View tab, and turn on the System Objects option. Click OK, and you will be able to see the previously hidden table. (When done working with the hidden table, remember to turn the option off so that the appearance of system objects in the Database window doesn't confuse users.)

■■■ *Caution:*   If you are going to use the View tab of Tools/Options to see the system objects in the Database window, be careful not to modify the actual system objects. These tables are used by Access for its internal operations, and you can cause major problems in the program's operation if you change or delete data stored in these tables.

❔ How do I get Access to **maximize the Database window** upon startup?

You can do this by creating an Autoexec macro that maximizes the active window. Since the Database window is the active window when Access starts, it is the window that will be maximized by the macro. Use these steps to create the macro:

1. Click the Macros tab in the Database window.
2. Click New, to open a new macro window.
3. In the Action column for the first row, click the down arrow and choose **Maximize** from the list.
4. Choose Save from the File menu.
5. Enter **Autoexec** as the macro's name and click OK. Access automatically executes any macro named Autoexec when you open a database.

Opening the database after creating this macro maximizes the Database window, as shown in Figure 2-5.

••••• *Tip:*   You can prevent this or any Autoexec macro from running if you hold the SHIFT key down while opening the database.

❔ Can I create a **new toolbar** with my favorite buttons?

Yes, you can create new toolbars containing any buttons you desire. Use the following steps to create a custom toolbar:

1. Right-click on any existing toolbar, and choose Customize from the shortcut menu that appears.
2. In the Customize dialog box that appears, click the Toolbars tab, then click New.

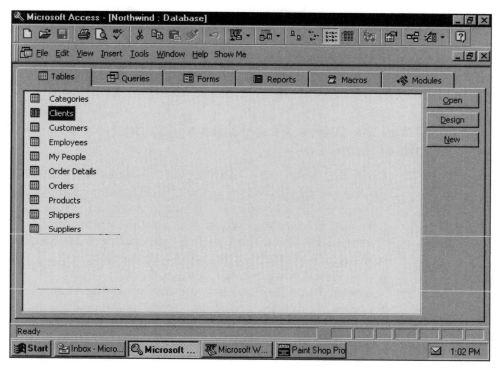

Figure 2-5:   Maximizing the Database window

3. Enter a name for the custom toolbar in the New Toolbar dialog box that appears, and click OK. The new toolbar appears, containing no buttons.

4. Drag the new toolbar to one side so you can see the new toolbar and the Customize dialog box at the same time.

5. In the Customize dialog box, click Commands.

6. At the left side of the dialog box, click the Category that contains the button you want to add to the new toolbar.

7. At the right side of the dialog box, find the desired button in the list, and click and drag it onto the new toolbar.

8. Repeat steps 6 and 7 for each toolbar button you want to add.

9. Click Close to put away the Customize dialog box.

10. Drag the new toolbar to the desired location on the screen.

? I find the **Office Assistants** annoying. How do I get rid of them?

Click the Office Assistant button in any toolbar to bring up the Office Assistant. If the Office Assistant menu does not automatically appear, click the Assistant, then click Options, to display the Office Assistant dialog box (Figure 2-6). Click the Options tab, and turn off the Respond to F1 Key option, the Display Alerts option, and all the Show Tips About options. Click OK.

Some Office Assistants are more annoying than others. You can change the character used for the Assistants by clicking on the Gallery tab in the same dialog box, and using the Next and Back buttons to select a different Assistant.

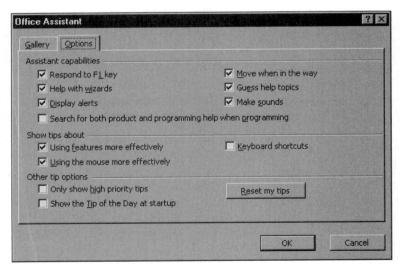

Figure 2-6:   The Office Assistant dialog box

? **What does the Send command on the File menu do, and why is it dimmed?**

> The Send command in the File menu saves the output of the selected database object as a file and attaches that file to an e-mail message. If the command is dimmed on your system, then you do not have an e-mail system that's supported by Access installed. You must be using an e-mail system that's compatible with Microsoft Office 97, or you must install Windows Dial-Up Networking, to send objects from within Access. If you installed your e-mail system after you installed Access, you may need to reinstall Access so the program will recognize your e-mail provider.

? **My toolbars have disappeared. How do I get them back?**

> If another user (or an application written in Access) turns off a specific toolbar, it will remain off until you turn it back on. Open the View menu, and choose Toolbars. In the next menu that appears, select the toolbar that you want to turn back on.

SECURITY

? **I secured my database, but it's still possible to get at the data using Visual Basic or another front-end utility program. What do I have to do to prevent that?**

> Access security provides password protection, but it doesn't prevent others from reading your database with utilities or from opening it in other software. To provide this level of protection, you'll need to *encrypt* the database. When you encrypt a database, the database file gets saved in an encoded format that can be read only by Access. Use these steps to encrypt an Access database:
>
> 1. Close any database that is open.
> 2. Open the Tools menu and choose Security. Then choose Encrypt/Decrypt from the next menu that appears.

3. In the dialog box that opens, specify the database you want to encrypt and click OK.

4. Specify the name and location (drive and folder) for the encrypted database, and click OK.

Keep in mind that the performance of Access while working with encrypted databases is slower than with normal databases, because Access must translate the data as you retrieve it.

Note: You can save an encrypted version of the database to the same filename and folder as the previous (unencrypted) version. When you use the same filename and folder and the database is encrypted successfully, Access then replaces the original database file with the encrypted version. If the encryption process fails for any reason, Access will not delete your original file.

I want to **reassign permissions** in a database, but someone else created it. How can I make myself the owner so I can assign permissions?

You can in effect transfer ownership of an entire database to yourself (or to another user). To do this, you must create a new database, and import all of the objects in the other database into the new database. Here are the steps you'll need to do this:

1. Start Access, using a workgroup containing the user account that should be the owner of the new database.

2. Create a new database by choosing New Database from the File menu.

3. Choose Get External Data from the File menu. From the next menu that appears, choose Import.

4. In the dialog box that appears, make sure Microsoft Access is chosen as the file type, select the database you want to import in the list, and click OK.

5. In the next dialog box that appears, select each tab (Tables, Queries, Forms, Reports, Macros, and Modules) one at a time, and click the Select All button after clicking each tab.

6. Click OK.

≡ *Note:* Before you can import a database that has security applied, you must have Open/Run permission for the database, Read/Design permission for its objects, and Read/Data permission for its tables. If you have permission for some (but not all) objects, Access will import only objects for which you have permissions.

TROUBLESHOOTING

 I get the error message "Can't update. Database or object is read-only (Error 3027)." What does this mean?

Access reports this message when you try to make changes to objects in a database that has been marked as read-only by your network operating system. You may not have network rights to the file, or it may be stored on a read-only drive (such as a CD-ROM drive). You should contact your network administrator for help in getting full rights to the file.

How did my Access database become corrupted? Can I fix it?

Access database files can become corrupted on occasion, for the same reasons Word documents and other Windows files become corrupt: power surges, exiting Windows improperly, viruses, or network servers crashing. Any abnormality that affects the stability of your computer system can cause one of your database files to become corrupt. If Access shuts down unexpectedly for any reason, a database file can become corrupt.

Because file corruption can happen with databases, Access includes a repair utility as part of the program. To repair a database:

1. Close any open database.

2. Open the Tools menu and choose Database Utilities, then choose Repair Database from the next menu that appears.

3. In the Repair Database dialog box that appears, select the database that is to be repaired.

4. Click Repair.

You may lose some data when repairing a database. The best safeguard against serious data loss is to back up your database files on a regular basis.

■■■ *Caution:*   If you were editing data in a form or a datasheet when Access shut down unexpectedly, the last changes you made to the table will probably be lost, even after you repair the database. Return to the last records you were editing and verify whether your changes were saved.

❔ Why do I occasionally get the error message 'Database locked by user "Admin"' when I try to open a database?

When you see this message, it means someone else on your network has the file open in exclusive mode. When Access security has not been enabled on a database, anyone who opens the database is called "Admin." If you're unsure who has the database open for exclusive use, check with your network administrator—there are commands that she or he can use to determine who has the file open. Once you discover the culprit, tell that user to choose Options from the Tools menu, click the Advanced tab, and change the Default Open Mode option from Exclusive to Shared. When the user exits Access and goes back in, the database will no longer be locked, and you and the other user can use it simultaneously.

❔ I accidentally erased a database file. Is there a way to get it back?

Assuming the database was stored on your local hard drive, there is a chance that all is not lost. Files that you delete under Windows 95, Windows NT 3.51, or later are stored in the Recycle Bin. If you haven't emptied the Recycle Bin, you can get the file back by performing these steps:

1. Double-click the Recycle Bin icon on the Windows desktop.

2. Select the deleted file in the window that appears.

3. Choose Restore from the File menu.

If the file you erased was stored on a network drive, you should immediately contact your network administrator. Some network operating systems provide utilities that can recover recently deleted files. (On a Novell network, the network administrator can run a utility called Salvage to recover the deleted database.)

? I have two **file names** in my directory with the name I assigned to my database. Which one is my database?

The file with the .MDB extension is the database file. The file with the same name and the .LDB extension is a file that Access uses to store record-locking information for the tables in the database. When you are using a database on a network, Access uses the data in the .LDB file to determine which records are locked and which users have locked the records. This enables Access to prevent file contention errors or corruption of the database by multiple users. In a multiuser environment, each user who opens the database has an entry in the .LDB file.

The .LDB file gets created automatically when you open an Access database file. If you are working with Access on a stand-alone computer where no one else can open the database at the same time as you do, you can delete this file to free up disk space.

? Why does my **file size** increase so much when I embed or link graphics?

Access databases routinely increase by more than the size of the graphic alone when you embed or link a graphic. This happens because of the way Access displays images in forms and reports. Access can store graphics in many different formats, but it can display only bitmaps (which are graphic images stored in Windows .BMP format). When you paste a graphic into an OLE object field and the graphic is not originally stored in bitmap format, Access creates a bitmap of the graphic and stores that bitmap along with the actual image data.

If you embed a bitmap image, the database increases by the size of the bitmap image. If you embed an image that's not a bitmap, the database increases by the size of the image plus the size of the bitmap that Access creates. If you link an image, Access stores both the bitmap and the data needed to establish the link.

This increase in size can be significant. In our testing, embedding an image stored in a .JPG file of 63K resulted in an increase in database file size of 538K.

? Why do I get the error message "**Not enough memory on disk**" when I'm working with a database on a network drive that has plenty of free disk space?

It's possible that your temporary drive is not on the network drive. Access uses a temporary directory to store temporary files as you work with data. If this temporary directory is on a disk that's short of free space, such as your local hard drive, you may see this error even though your network drive has sufficient free space.

To check your temporary drive:

1. From within Access, choose About Microsoft Access from the Help menu.

2. In the dialog box that appears, click System Info. The Microsoft System Information window appears, like the example shown here.

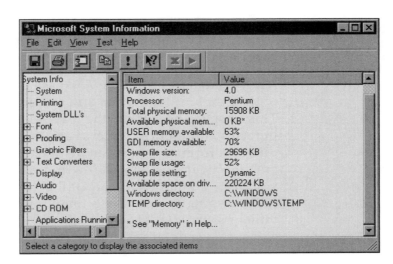

3. Look at the line that begins with TEMP Directory. This is your temporary directory. Check to see that this is a valid directory and that there is free space for it. You may need to make more space available on the drive that contains this directory in order to avoid getting these out-of-memory errors.

Tip: Many other applications use this temporary directory as well. Sometimes, not all of the temporary files are deleted when the applications are closed. Delete any .BAK or .TMP files in this directory to make space. Close all applications and restart the computer in MS-DOS mode before doing this, because you don't want to delete a temporary file that is still in use.

chapter

3 Answers!

Creating
Tables

Answer Topics!

Creating Tables
@ a Glance

Tables are the heart of your database—they are the Access objects that store all the data in your database. Before you can create and use forms, queries, or reports, you'll need to create tables and store data in them.

During the process of designing tables, there are a number of steps you can take to make the data entry process that follows a less tedious task. You can control the entry and the display of much of your data by means of settings that you establish while designing your tables. Also, effective database design requires the use of indexes and primary keys when necessary to speed searches and to make it possible to combine data from different tables in reports. These types of topics will be detailed throughout this chapter.

The questions you'll find in this chapter deal with the following areas:

➪ **Defining Fields** The questions in this part of the chapter deal with how you can work with the different field types available in Access, and with their specifications.

➪ **Working with Primary Keys** Here you'll find answers to questions about primary keys in Access tables.

> ☞ **Working with Indexes** The questions in this portion of the chapter help you decide when and how to use indexes as part of a table's design.
>
> ☞ **Controlling Data Entry and Data Display** In this part of the chapter, you'll find answers to questions about how you can design a table to control the ways in which your data is entered and displayed.

Designing Better Databases

If you're new to the intricacies of database design, you should spend some time learning about proper database design before you create your tables in Access. Any well-designed database involves careful planning of the necessary fields and the elimination of any unnecessary redundancies. This is an especially important process with relational databases, because it helps you to recognize when certain data should be stored in separate tables. Newcomers to database design often have a tendency to create single tables that contain all the data associated with a task. Such tables are hard to use and wasteful in regard to disk space. Careful planning of your tables helps avoid these kinds of problems.

When designing your tables, try to avoid duplicating information. For example, if you've already decided to store the names and addresses of customers in a table named Customers, don't include those names and addresses in another table called Orders. You can define a relationship between the tables to get customer addresses, rather than duplicate them in an Orders table.

You should also avoid duplicating information within the same table. For example, when you record the hours your employees worked for every week, you don't want to enter the complete employee name and address each week. That's a waste of time. Instead, create an employee ID number and enter the ID number for the weekly time records. This employee ID can link to your table of employee information so that the name and address are available without repeating them in each record.

After you arrange all of your tables and define any needed relationships, make sure that you check one last time with others who must use your database. You want to avoid editing the tables' design after you enter data.

DEFINING FIELDS

 How can I add new fields to an existing table?

You can add new fields to a table at any time you wish. You can add the new fields to the end of the table or put them at any desired location in the table. (Remember that the order of the fields in Design view initially determines the fields' order in the table's datasheet.) To add a field to a table, follow these steps:

1. Open the table in Design view.

2. To insert the field within the table, select the row below where you want to add the field by clicking the row selector button to the left of the field name, and press the INS key or choose Rows from the Insert menu. A new blank row appears, as shown here, and you can fill in the required information. Or, to add the field to the end of the table, move the insertion point to the first blank row.

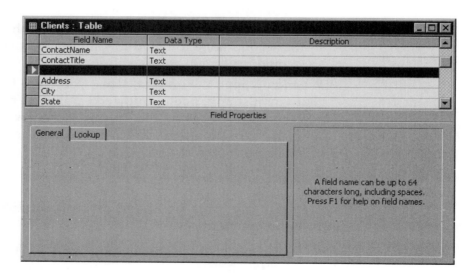

3. Define the field by entering a field name, a data type, and an optional description.

4. Make any desired changes to the field properties.

❓ How can I change the initial value of an **AutoNumber field** to something other than 1?

It's a little complicated to do, but you can change the starting value for an AutoNumber field. Use these steps to do so:

1. First, you need to create the table that contains the AutoNumber field that you want to start on another number. Do not enter any records.

2. Create a second, temporary table with just one field. Make the field type Number, with the Size property set to Long Integer. Name the field with the same name as the AutoNumber field in the table you wish to change.

3. Enter one record in the new table. In the number field, enter a number that is *one less than* the number you want the AutoNumber field in the first table to start at. For example, if you want to start the AutoNumber field with 100, then enter 99 in the Number field of the temporary table.

4. Create an append query to append the one record in the second table to the first table.

5. Run the append query. After appending the record from the second table to the first, you can delete the second (temporary) table and the query.

When you open the original table, you'll see the new record that you just appended, followed by a blank record. Enter any data in the existing record, and Access will continue numbering in the AutoNumber field with the next record. After you've entered a record, you can delete the first record you added with the append query.

❓ Can fields in my table be based on **calculations** involving other fields?

No, you cannot base fields in your table on the contents of other fields. In Access, tables hold raw data, not formulas or calculations. If you want to display the results of a formula using other fields in the record, you need to create a query with a calculated field or a form or report with a calculated control.

❓ If I **change a field type** in an existing table, will I lose all the data stored in that field?

Whenever you change a field type for a table that contains data, you risk losing data, depending on whether Access can handle the transfer of data or not. Access successfully keeps the data in an existing field if the change "makes sense"; for example, if you were to change a Text Field that contains entries composed completely of numbers to a Number field, Access would keep the data. If you were to change a Number field to a Yes/No field, any entries with a value of "1" would be converted to Yes values, and any entries of any other numeric amount would be converted to No values. If you were to change a memo field to an OLE Object field, all the data in the memo field would be lost. If you reduced the size of a Text field, Access would warn you that data may be truncated, and you would need to confirm the possible data loss before Access would proceed with the operation.

❓ How do I **create a table**?

You can create a table using these steps:

1. In the Database window, click the Tables tab.

2. Click New.

3. In the New Table dialog box that appears, click Design View, then click OK. A table window opens in Design view, as shown here. (If you select Table Wizard instead, Access starts a wizard that walks you through the process of creating a table. This wizard provides sample tables to use as the basis of your own.)

4. On each line in the top half of the table window, enter the name of a field, its data type, and a longer

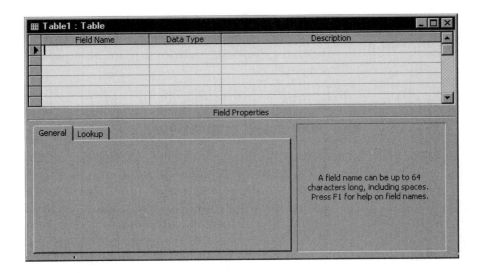

description to help you identify the field. It's a good idea to keep field names short to make them easier to work with in forms and reports.

5. As you define each field, the properties for that field appear in the bottom half of the Table window. (You can move between the top and bottom halves of the window by pressing F6 or by clicking in the desired portion of the window.) Move to the box for the property you want to change and enter the new setting.

6. If desired, create a *primary key*. (A primary key is a field or a combination of fields that is unique for each record in the table.) Click the *selector* (the small box at the beginning of the row) for that field, or click and drag through multiple row selectors to select more than one field. Then, click the Primary Key toolbar button or choose Primary Key from the Edit menu.

7. When you finish defining the fields for the table, choose Save from the File menu. Enter a name for the table, and click OK. If you didn't create a primary key before, Access prompts you about creating one now. Select Yes to have Access create an AutoNumber field and make it the primary key, or No to avoid creating a primary key.

What Is a Table?

Tables are the basis of your data, and when you define a table, you define the *fields* that will be used to store the data. Each field contains a single type of information, such as an address, a name, or a phone number. Tables contain records, which are complete sets of information about a single entity. As an example, you might have a complete record for each customer, including entries in the name, address, and phone number fields. When displayed in Datasheet view, tables have a column and row layout, as shown here. Each column is a field, and each row is a record.

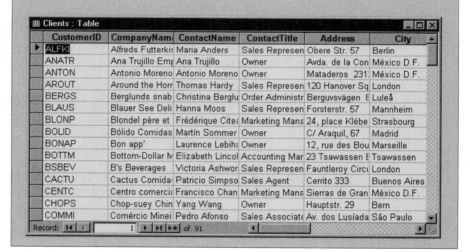

Clients : Table

CustomerID	CompanyNam	ContactName	ContactTitle	Address	City
ALFKI	Alfreds Futterkis	Maria Anders	Sales Represen	Obere Str. 57	Berlin
ANATR	Ana Trujillo Emp	Ana Trujillo	Owner	Avda. de la Con	México D.F.
ANTON	Antonio Moreno	Antonio Moreno	Owner	Mataderos 231	México D.F.
AROUT	Around the Horr	Thomas Hardy	Sales Represen	120 Hanover Sq	London
BERGS	Berglunds snab	Christina Berglu	Order Administr	Berguvsvägen 8	Luleå
BLAUS	Blauer See Deli	Hanna Moos	Sales Represen	Forsterstr. 57	Mannheim
BLONP	Blondel père et	Frédérique Cite:	Marketing Mana	24, place Klébe	Strasbourg
BOLID	Bólido Comidas	Martín Sommer	Owner	C/ Araquil, 67	Madrid
BONAP	Bon app'	Laurence Lebihi	Owner	12, rue des Bou	Marseille
BOTTM	Bottom-Dollar M	Elizabeth Lincol	Accounting Mar	23 Tsawassen E	Tsawassen
BSBEV	B's Beverages	Victoria Ashwor	Sales Represen	Fauntleroy Circl	London
CACTU	Cactus Comida:	Patricio Simpso	Sales Agent	Cerrito 333	Buenos Aires
CENTC	Centro comerci:	Francisco Chan	Marketing Mana	Sierras de Gran	México D.F.
CHOPS	Chop-suey Chin	Yang Wang	Owner	Hauptstr. 29	Bern
COMMI	Comércio Minei	Pedro Afonso	Sales Associat:	Av. dos Lusíada	São Paulo

Record: ◄◄ ◄ 1 ► ►◄ ►* of 91

I'm creating a new table and I have an existing table with a similar structure. Can I duplicate an existing table somehow and then just modify the structure?

You can do this with an "Edit/Copy" and "Edit/Paste" operation, even if the table is in another database. In the Database window, click the existing table whose structure you want to use, open the <u>E</u>dit menu, and choose <u>C</u>opy. (If you want to place the new table in a different database, close the current database and open the database where you want to place the new table.) Next, open the Edit menu, and choose Paste. In the Paste Table As dialog box that appears, enter a name for the new table, choose Structure Only, and click OK. The new table will appear in the Database window, and you can open it in Design view and make the desired changes to the table structure.

?   What are field properties and how can I set them?

In a table, each field has field properties that let you decide how data is stored and displayed. When you click in a field in Design view, its field properties are displayed in the lower pane of the window. Those properties differ depending on their data type.

➤ Use the Field Size property to define the maximum length for a text field or limit the number of values in a number field.

➤ Use the Format property to specify a format for showing and printing text, numbers, dates, and times.

➤ Use the Decimal Places property to specify how many decimal places appear to the right of the decimal point.

➤ Use the Input Mask property to specify the pattern to be used when entering data such as telephone numbers or Social Security numbers.

➤ Use the Caption property to change the default label for the field. The caption will appear instead of the field name in Datasheet view on forms and reports.

➤ Use the Default Value property to cause a default value to appear automatically in a field.

➤ Use the Validation Rule property to define rules for entering data.

➤ Use the Validation Text property to cause a dialog box with a customized message to appear if invalid data is entered.

➢ Use the Allow Zero Length property with a Text field to determine whether or not records are allowed to contain a zero-length, or empty, text string in this field.

➢ Use the Required property to specify whether an entry in the field is required for any new records.

➢ Use the Indexed property to indicate whether the field should be indexed.

If you wish to change the properties for the field, in Design view click on the field whose properties you wish to change. Then click the property you want to change, or press F6 and move the insertion point to the desired property. Then enter the setting you wish for the property. In some cases, you can click on the down arrow to see a list of available settings.

? What different field types are available when creating my tables?

Access has nine types of fields that can be used to store specific types of data. These include the following:

➢ **Text** Use these to store shorter text entries (up to 255 characters). The text can be any combination of letters, numbers, punctuation marks, blank spaces, and symbols.

➢ **Memo** Use these to store longer text entries (such as multiple paragraphs of text). Memo fields can store up to 64,000 characters. (Note that you cannot add indexes based on memo fields.)

➢ **Number** Use these to store numeric values that aren't currency. Depending on the format you apply, numbers can be whole or fractional values, and you can enter negative values by preceding the value with a minus sign.

➢ **Date/Time** Use these to store dates, times, or both.

➢ **Currency** Use these to store monetary values. (Access will use the unit of currency that is the Windows default.)

▷ **AutoNumber** This is a special type of numeric field that Access automatically increments for you each time a new record is added to the table. The first record added will be assigned a value of 1 in this field, the second record added will be assigned a value of 2, and so on. Once a record has been entered, the number in this field can't be changed. If a record is deleted, its value in the AutoNumber field will not be reassigned.

▷ **Yes/No** Use Yes/No fields to store logical (true or false, yes or no) values.

▷ **OLE Object** OLE Object fields are used to store objects from other Windows applications that support OLE (Object Linking and Embedding). You can store graphics, spreadsheets, word processing documents, sound, and other OLE objects in an OLE Object field. (You cannot index the contents of OLE Object fields.)

▷ **Hyperlink** Use Hyperlink fields to store a combination of text and numbers that are used as a *hyperlink address*, or a path to a web page or document file on your hard drive or on a local area network.

In addition to these field types, you can set the Field Size property to specify how many characters a Text field can contain or the range of numbers that a Number field can contain. As an example, if you know that a Text field is going to contain first names, you may want to set its Field Size property to 20, since you are unlikely to encounter a first name of more than 20 characters.

Tip: By default, the Field Size property for a Text field is 50. If you will have longer entries, you will want to change this property to allow additional characters during data entry.

❓ How do I decide whether to use a Text field or a **Memo field** for storing moderate amounts of text?

This question often arises when you must store amounts of text that may run the length of an average sentence or two. If you know you'll occasionally need to store more than 255 characters, the decision is automatic: You'll have to use memo fields, since text fields are limited to 255 characters. While memo fields can store up to 64,000 characters, they do have some limitations. You can't index a memo field, and you can't use a memo field to establish a relationship to records in another table. So if you need to use the field as part of a relationship, or if you want to index the field, you'll need to use a text field.

? I need to store large amounts of text from word processing documents. Should I use a Memo field or an OLE Object field?

If you're considering the use of memo fields to store very large amounts of text that are stored in documents of Windows word processors, you may want to think about using OLE Object fields. Memo fields are well suited for a number of sentences or a few paragraphs of text. If you have multiple-page documents stored in a Windows word processor, OLE Object fields will probably better serve your needs. Keep in mind that if you use OLE Object fields and you embed the data (as opposed to linking it), your database will quickly grow in terms of disk space consumed as you add documents, and you should exercise care not to delete documents that are linked to the database.

? How can I create a **relationship** to records in another table?

You can define a relationship between tables by doing the following:

1. Display the Database window, if it's not already visible.

2. Open the Tools menu and choose Relationships. Access displays the Relationships window, with the Show Table dialog box over it. If the Show Table dialog box doesn't appear, click the Show Table button on the toolbar.

3. At the Tables tab, double-click the names of the two tables you want to relate, then click Close. This causes the field list boxes for the tables to be added to the Relationships window.

4. In the Relationships window, drag the field that you want to relate from one table to the related field in the other table. When you do this, Access will display the Relationships dialog box.

5. Check the field names displayed in the two columns to make sure that they are correct. Change them if needed. The fields used to relate the two tables do not need to have the same names, but they have to be the same data type (there is one exception to this) and contain the same kind of information. The exception is that you can relate an AutoNumber field to a Number field whose FieldSize property is set to Long Integer.

6. Turn on the Enforce Referential Integrity option. (In most cases, you'll want to enforce referential integrity.)

7. Click the Create button to create the relationship. If you need to create any additional relationships, then repeat these steps. (You can define only one relationship between any two tables.)

When you close the Relationships window, Access will ask you if you wish to save the layout (or the arrangement of the window). The relationships are added to the database whether you save the layout or not.

? How can I establish a **relationship between two AutoNumber** fields?

You can't. Access will not let you draw a relationship between an AutoNumber field that is the primary key in one table and an AutoNumber field that serves as a foreign key in another table. But since AutoNumber fields store data as numbers in a long integer format, you can get around this obstacle by using a Number field, with the Size property set to Long Integer, as the foreign key field.

WORKING WITH PRIMARY KEYS

? **Access always asks me to define a primary key. Do I need one?**

When you do and don't need a primary key depends on the table itself. If the table won't be the basis for a relationship with any other table or you don't need to keep the records in the table in any specific order, then you don't need a primary key. If you do want to put the records in a specific order, however, you may want to use a primary key. A primary key is what gives Access a unique way to identify all the records in a table. Usually, primary keys are based on a single field, but you can base a primary key on more than one field. Automatically, the records in the table appear in ascending order based on the contents of the field or fields of the primary key, so the field of the primary key becomes the main index for the table. (You can change this by either sorting the table based on a specific field or creating a query that sorts on a different field.) Primary keys are used regularly in databases, even if you don't realize it. Some identifiers that are used as primary keys in many databases are patient ID numbers, employee numbers, and account numbers. Even though you don't have to use them, there are advantages to using primary keys. Primary keys let you create an index that will speed sorts, queries, and internal operations. They also let you establish relationships between tables. Finally, primary keys reduce the possibility of a duplicate record, because Access will not let you create two records with the same value in the primary key field. If you need a relationship between tables, or if you want to update two tables at the same time, you should use a primary key.

? **How do I delete a Primary Key designation?**

One process that is not so obvious is how to delete a Primary Key that's no longer needed. To delete a Primary Key, follow these steps:

1. In the table's Design view, click the Indexes button on the toolbar. Access will display the Indexes window.

2. Select the row or rows containing the primary key index, and then press the DEL key.

3. Close the Indexes window.

Tip: The Primary Key must not be a link relating this table to another table, or Access won't let you delete the Primary Key.

How can I create a primary key based on **multiple fields** that aren't adjacent in the table structure?

You can do this without moving fields around in the table structure. Open the table in Design view, and click the row selector button for the first field you want to use as part of the primary key. Then hold the CTRL key down as you click the row selector button for each additional field you want to use as part of the primary key. When the needed fields are selected, click the Primary Key button in the toolbar, or open the Edit menu and choose Primary Key.

WORKING WITH INDEXES

Can I **add an index** to a table?

You can add indexes to tables to make searches faster when your tables contain thousands of records. You can add indexes to Text, Number, Date/Time, Currency, AutoNumber, and Yes/No fields. Indexes are used to sort or search for data in a field quickly. You want to create indexes that order your records the way you need to access your data. For example, if you often sort your table by department number, then creating an index for the department number field will speed up those sorts. It is a good idea to avoid creating too many indexes for a single table. Indexes slow down editing or entering new records, so you don't want to have too many of them.

To create an index based on a single field:

1. Open the table in Design view, and select the field you want to index.

2. Press F6 to move to the field's properties.

3. Set the Indexed property to Yes (Duplicates OK) if you want to allow duplicate entries in this field, or Yes (No Duplicates) if you want to keep this field unique for each record.

To create a multiple-field index:

1. Choose Indexes from the View menu, or click the Indexes toolbar button.

2. Enter the name for the index in the Index Name column.

3. Enter the name of the first field in the Field Name column next to the name of the index.

4. In the Field Name column below the first field, enter the name of the second field in the index. Continue this until you've added all of the fields you want to index by.

5. Close the Indexes Window.

? How can I avoid **duplicate values** in a field that's not used for a Primary Key?

You can ensure that you never have two records in a table with the same value in a field by adding an Index with the No Duplicates property turned on to that field. (Primary keys use this type of index by nature, since they do not allow duplicate values in the field.) As an example, a table of insured cars at an automobile insurance agency might have a primary key field based on automobile ID numbers, and another field containing the license plate numbers of the automobiles. It would make sense to allow only unique entries in the license plate field, since no two automobiles would have the same license plate number. To add an index to a field and specify no duplicates, open the table in Design view and click anywhere within the field. Then, in the Indexed property for the field, choose Yes (No Duplicates).

CONTROLLING DATA ENTRY AND DATA DISPLAY

❓ Is there any way to specify a **default value** for a field?

Open the table in Design view, click in the desired field, then use the Default Value property to specify a default value for a field. The default value is added automatically when you add a new record. For example, in a table of names and addresses you might set the default value of a City field to **Pasadena**. Pasadena would then automatically appear in the City field when new records are entered. The user can leave that value unchanged or enter the name of a different city. All field types can have default values except for AutoNumber and OLE Object fields. For text, number, and Currency fields, default values will be an arbitrary value that you choose, depending on the application. The default value for Yes/No fields are usually No, but you can change that to Yes if most of your records will probably have a Yes value in a Yes/No field. You can also use expressions beginning with an equal sign as default values. Two common ones are =date, which provides the current date according to your PC's clock, and =now, which provides both the date and the time. You can use math calculations as well. For example, the expression **=date()** **+ 30** produces a default value 30 days ahead of the current date.

❓ What's the difference between an **Input Mask** and a Format?

Both input masks and formats affect the way data appears in a table in Datasheet view. However, they serve very different purposes. The Format property setting affects the data in the field once it is entered. It changes how the data is displayed and can make it easier to read. For example, if you apply the Long Date format to a Date/Time field, a date of 11/24/98 appears as "Tuesday, November 24, 1998."

An Input Mask property actually restricts the type of entry you can make in the field. As you begin to make an entry, a template appears indicating the entry needed. This template can also format the entry to make it easier to interpret. For example, if you start to make an entry in a phone number field with an input mask, it might look like this:

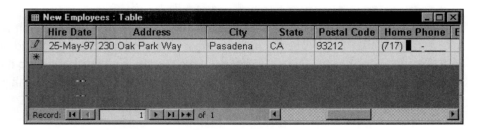

The underscores (_) are placeholders for entries. The hyphen and the parentheses make the phone number entries easier to read.

In creating an input mask, you use placeholder characters for entries. Some placeholder characters allow users to enter a character, digit, or text; other placeholder characters require an entry. For example, you might use a placeholder character that requires an entry for each of the ten positions in the phone number.

? Can I display negative **numbers** enclosed in parentheses, while positive numbers are displayed normally?

The way to accomplish this is to design a *custom format* that displays negative numbers in parentheses. Custom formats are created with special symbols that indicate what can appear in the field. You can enter this custom format as the setting for the Format property for the field. Table 3-1 shows the symbols you use to create a custom format.

A custom format can have up to four parts, with each part separated by a semicolon. The first part of the format controls how positive numbers display, the second controls how negative numbers display, the third controls how zeros display, and the fourth determines the appearance of a null field. You do not have to enter all four parts. If you enter only one part, all numbers use that format; if you enter two parts, zeros and nulls display using the setting for positive numbers.

Table 3-1:   Symbols Used to Create Custom Formats

Symbol	Effect
"*xxx*"	Displays the characters between the quotation marks without interpreting them as symbols, as in **"N/A"** to display N/A
\	Displays the character after the backslash without interpreting it as a symbol, as in \ **N**/\ **A** to display N/A
0	Displays a digit if one is entered or a zero if one isn't
#	Displays a digit if one is entered or a blank if one isn't
@	Marks a required character
&	Marks an optional character
.	Marks the location of the decimal point
%	Multiplies the entry by 100 and displays a % after it
,	Inserts a thousands separator
E− or e−	Shows the number using scientific notation with a − for negative exponents and nothing in front of positive ones
E+ or e+	Shows the number using scientific format with a − for negative exponents and a + for positive ones
-	Displays the hyphen as a hyphen
+	Displays the plus sign as a plus sign
$	Displays the dollar sign as a dollar sign
()	Displays the parentheses as parentheses
[*color*]	Displays the number using the color given. You can use Black, Blue, Green, Cyan, Red, Magenta, Yellow, and White
*	Fills the field with the following characters
!	Forces left alignment instead of right alignment

For example, to display negative numbers in parentheses, you can enter *#,###;(#,###)* as the setting of the Format property of a Number field. This format displays numbers as shown here.

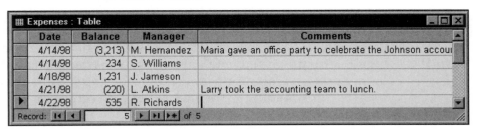

How can I cause a phone number field to display parentheses and a dash?

You can manage this task by changing the format specified in the Format Property to add the parentheses and the dash. To create this format, you use a series of symbols that indicate how to display such data, as shown in Table 3-2. Text fields, such as your Phone Number field, have several unique symbols that are available to all types of fields.

For example, to force a Phone Number field to display the phone numbers entered in a field of a table along with parentheses and a dash, you would use these steps:

1. Open the table in Design View and choose your Phone Number field.

2. Move to the Format property in the lower half of the window.

3. Enter **(&&&)&&&-&&&&**.

You could also use this format to enter social security numbers. For example, you could enter **&&&-&&-&&&&** in the property field.

Table 3-2:   Symbols Used by the Format Property

Use	To
<	Display all characters as lowercase
>	Display all characters as uppercase
!	Fill the field from left to right rather than right to left
@	Display an entered character or space
&	Display an entered character or leave the position empty
[*color*]	Display the text in a specific color
\	Display the following character literally rather than interpreting as a symbol
*	Fill the field with the following character
a space	Insert a space in the field
" "	Enclose text to display literally instead of interpreting as symbols

？ How can I enforce **referential integrity?**

With relationships, Access can enforce referential integrity to protect users from adding or deleting data that could break the relationship. For example, you might have a table of customers related to a table of orders they placed. In the Orders table, there would most likely be a number of records associated with each customer. You wouldn't want to delete a customer record without deleting the records of the purchases they made, or you would have a number of order records with no matching customers. When referential integrity is enforced, these kinds of accidental deletions aren't allowed to happen. Access can enforce referential integrity when these conditions are met:

▷ The matching field of the primary table is a primary key, or is indexed with no duplicates.

▷ The related fields have the same data types.

▷ Both tables are in the same database.

If you wish to enforce referential integrity, turn on the Enforce Referential Integrity option that appears in the Relationships window when you are establishing the relationship. After referential integrity has been enforced, Access displays a dialog box that does not permit the change if it threatens to destroy the referential integrity of the database. For details on creating a relationship, see the question "How can I create a relationship to records in another table?" under the heading "Defining Fields."

？ Can I display **Text field** entries in all uppercase letters, no matter how they were entered?

You can control the case in which table entries display by setting the Format property for that field. In Design view, you need to select the field, and then move to its Format property, displayed in the lower half of the window. Enter > for this property to force all entries to display in all uppercase, or < to have all entries display in all lowercase. If you use the > setting, the field might resemble the customer ID field shown here.

CustomerID	CompanyName	ContactName	ContactT
ALFKI	Alfreds Futterkiste	Maria Anders	Sales Repr
ANATR	Ana Trujillo Emparedados y helados	Ana Trujillo	Owner
ANTON	Antonio Moreno Taquería	Antonio Moreno	Owner
AROUT	Around the Horn	Thomas Hardy	Sales Repr
BERGS	Berglunds snabbköp	Christina Berglund	Order Adm
BLAUS	Blauer See Delikatessen	Hanna Moos	Sales Repr
BLONP	Blondel père et fils	Frédérique Citeaux	Marketing

Record: 1 of 91

❓ Can I display **Yes/No fields** as "Affirmative" and "Negative," using different colors for each?

You can change how the values in the Yes/No field display by changing the Format property setting for the field. For example, you can enter **"Affirmative"[Black]; "Negative"[Red]** to display a black Affirmative for Yes and a red Negative for no. You enclose the text you want to display in place of Yes and No in quotation marks. The colors appear in brackets to indicate that they are the colors rather than text to display. (You must also change the Display Control value in the Lookup tab of the Properties window to "Text Box.")

❓ How can I format a field to display a **ZIP+4 code**?

For this task, you can use either an input mask or a format. With an input mask, Access prompts you for the correct data by showing a template in Datasheet view. Whichever method you choose, you must make sure that the field to contain this extended ZIP code is a Text type field. Select either method by switching to Design view, moving to the field, and changing one of the properties.

To add an input mask for the field, move to the Input Mask property. Then click the Build button at the end of the line. Select the standard ZIP code input mask and Next twice. Select whether you want the data stored with the hyphen or not, and then select Next. Select Finish to add the input mask to the Input Mask property.

If you choose to use a format for the field, click on the desired field while in Design view, then move to the Format property and enter @@@@@-@@@@.

Working with Access Data

Answer Topics!

Working with Access Data @ a Glance

As the database objects used to store your data, tables lie at the heart of your database. In the last chapter, you learned about solutions for creating tables. In this chapter, your questions about working with tables are answered. When you have problems with entering, editing, or sorting data, this is where you can find the answers.

The questions you'll find answers to in this chapter deal with the following areas:

☞ **Displaying Your Data**   In this portion of the chapter, you'll find the answers to questions about how you can change the ways in which datasheets display the data in your tables.

☞ **Entering and Editing Data**   This portion of the chapter provides answers that will help you enter data faster and make changes to your data without problems.

☞ **Sorting and Filtering Data**   The answers detailed in this portion of the chapter help you best arrange your data, in terms of sort order and what records are selected.

> ➤ **Working with Relationships**   Here you'll find answers to questions about relationships between tables; how you can best define them, as well as when and why you would want to.
>
> ➤ **Troubleshooting**   The answers in this part of the chapter help you deal with unexpected error messages and other general problems when running Access.

DISPLAYING YOUR DATA

❓ Can I change the **column widths** of a number of columns as a group?

You can change the width of any column by dragging its border in the column header area as desired. You can also do so for a group of columns. First, drag across the field selector buttons of the desired columns to select them as a group. Then double-click the right border of the field selector button for any one of the selected columns. As you do this, all the selected columns will resize as a group.

❓ Can I **divide a name field** into separate last name and first name fields?

One way you can split a full name field into its components is with a query. For example purposes, assume that the field name that you want to split is called Full Name and that each entry in the Full Name field comprises a courtesy title (such as Mr. or Ms.), a first name, and a last name. Create a query to split it into three calculated fields. The following entries should appear in the Field row of the QBE grid:

```
Title: Left([Full Name], InStr([Full Name]," "))

First Name: Mid([Full Name], InStr([Full Name]," ")+1,
InStr(InStr([Full Name]," ")+1,[Full Name]," ")
-InStr([Full Name]," "))

Last Name: Trim(Right([Full Name],Len([Full
Name])-InStr(InStr([Full Name]," ")+1, [Full Name]," ")))
```

Next, run the query to see that the formulas are entered correctly. You can then change the query to a make-table query or an append query, depending on your specific situation. You can also change the query to an update query. Before you change the query, you need to add the fields to the table that will hold the parts of the name. Then change the query from a select query to an update query. Under the field names that hold the parts of the name, enter the same formulas that the calculated fields use. You can even copy the formulas from the calculated fields in the Field row to the Update To row. You can see how these formulas are placed under the field names in this QBE query:

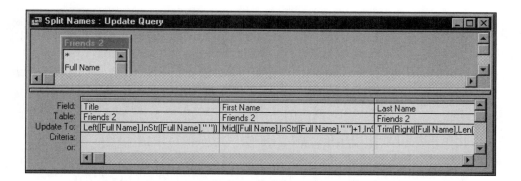

Once you have the query designed, run it. The formulas divide the full name into its parts and use the parts as the updated values for the fields. After the query runs, the Title field contains entries like Mr., Mrs., and Miss, while the First Name and Last Name fields contain the first and last names. This example focuses on names, but you use similar calculated fields in a query for other fields that you want to divide.

? How can I **find specific data** in a large table?

A natural part of the editing process is finding what you want to edit. You can use the Find button on the toolbar or its equivalent, the Find command on the Edit menu, to search for data. You use these steps:

1. Open the desired table in Datasheet view.

2. Click anywhere within the field you want to search, unless you want to search all the fields. (In a large table, searching a single field is faster than searching all the fields.)

3. Open the Edit menu and choose Find. When you do this, Access displays the Find dialog box, as shown here.

4. Enter the text that you want to find in the Find What: text box.

5. If you want to search all the fields, turn off the Search Only Current Field option.

6. Change the Match entry to Any Part of Field, unless you've entered the complete field contents as a search term.

7. Click Find Next. To search for additional entries with the same search instructions, click the Find Next button again.

? Can I change the **fonts** used to display my data in Datasheet view?

Yes, you can easily change the font and its size used to display your table in Datasheet view. You can make the change for a single table or change the default font used by all datasheets that do not have their own font setting. Open the table and choose Font from the Format menu. In the Font dialog box that appears (shown here), select the font, font size, and font style you want used to display your table.

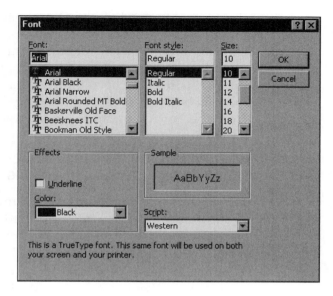

After making your selections, choose OK to close the Font dialog box. If you enlarge your font to make your table easier to read, the table might look like Figure 4-1.

You can also set the default font used by all tables and queries in Datasheet view. To do so, choose Options from

Customer	CompanyName	ContactName	ContactTitle
ALFKI	Alfreds Futterkiste	Maria Anders	Sales Repres
ANATR	Ana Trujillo Emparedad	Ana Trujillo	Owner
ANTON	Antonio Moreno Taquer	Antonio Morer	Owner
AROUT	Around the Horn	Thomas Hardy	Sales Repres
BERGS	Berglunds snabbköp	Christina Berg	Order Adminis
BLAUS	Blauer See Delikatesse	Hanna Moos	Sales Repres
BLONP	Blondel père et fils	Frédérique Cit	Marketing Ma
BOLID	Bólido Comidas prepara	Martín Somme	Owner
BONAP	Bon app'	Laurence Leb	Owner
BOTTM	Bottom-Dollar Markets	Elizabeth Linc	Accounting M
BSBEV	B's Beverages	Victoria Ashw	Sales Repres

Record: 7 of 91

Figure 4-1:   A table with enlarged fonts

the Tools menu. Click the Datasheet tab in the dialog box that appears. In the Default Font portion of the dialog box, choose the font name, font size, and various font attributes, including italics. After setting the options, select OK. The options you select become the defaults for all tables and queries in Datasheet view unless you use the Font command from the Format menu to change the settings for a specific datasheet.

? How can I **hide columns** in a datasheet?

When you wish to remove one or more columns from view, you can do so with the Hide Columns command on the Format menu. You hide columns with the following steps:

1. Select the field you want to hide, by clicking its field selector. (You can select multiple adjacent columns by holding the SHIFT key and clicking each field.)

2. Open the Format menu and choose Hide Columns.

To reveal columns you've hidden previously, open the Format menu and choose Unhide Columns. The Unhide Columns dialog box, shown here, appears. Click the hidden columns that you wish to be redisplayed, then click Close.

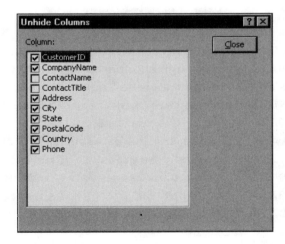

•••••• *Tip:* The ability of Access to hide one or more columns can be a valuable aid in getting a quick report of the precise data you want. You can hide unwanted columns to omit fields you don't want to see, use the filter techniques to omit records you don't want included, then print a report by choosing Print from the File menu.

? How can I view long entries I make in **Memo fields** while working on a datasheet?

Data entry into memo fields is usually done through a form, but there is an easy way to add data to Memo fields without opening the form. You can use the zoom box to open a window into the Memo field. To enter the data using the Zoom box, move to the Memo field in which you wish to enter the data and press SHIFT-F2. When you do this, a Zoom dialog box opens, as shown here. Type the desired data of the memo and then click OK to store the data.

•••••• *Tip:* The Zoom box can be used in any location designed to accept text (not just Memo fields), such as criteria cells, field property cells, and the like.

? How can I **open tables** I work with automatically?

If you use the same tables every day, you might prefer to open them automatically when you open a database. You can accomplish this task by means of a macro. To create a

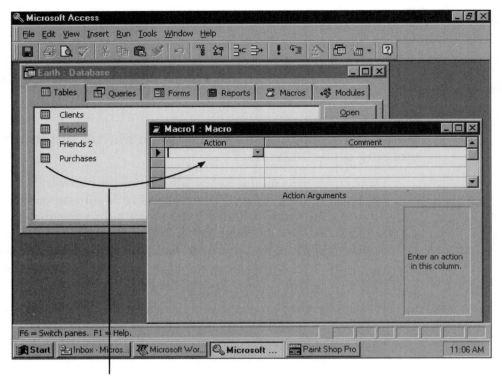

Drag the desired tables to the
Action column of the Macro window

Figure 4-2: The Macro window

macro that opens a table automatically at the same time you
open a database, follow these steps:

1. In the Database window, click the Macros tab, then
   click New.

2. Move and size the Macro window that appears (see
   Figure 4-2) so that you can see both it and the Database
   window at the same time.

3. In the Database window, click the Tables tab.

4. From the list of tables, click and drag the first table that
   you want to open automatically to the first row of the
   Action column in the Macro window.

5. Click and drag the next table that you want to open
   automatically to the next row of the Action column in the
   Macro window.

6. Repeat Step 5 for all remaining tables that you want to open automatically.

7. With the Macro window still active (click anywhere within it if it is not active), open the File menu and choose Close. Click Yes in the Save Changes dialog box that appears. When prompted for a name, enter **Autoexec**, then click OK.

After performing these steps, you can close the database (while the Database window is still active, open the File menu and choose Close). Afterward, whenever you open the database, the tables you added to the macro will open automatically. In Access, any macro saved under the name Autoexec runs whenever the database containing the macro is opened. (You can prevent the macro from running by holding the SHIFT key down as you open the database.)

? How do I change the **order of fields** in a datasheet?

The original display of fields will match the order in which the fields were laid out in the table's design. Your preferred method of data entry may involve a different arrangement of fields, or you may want to move them around so that you can sort them easier. In Access, rearranging fields is done by a drag-and-drop operation with the mouse. To rearrange a table's fields, perform these steps:

1. Open the desired table in Datasheet view, if it is not already open.

2. Click the field selector for the field you want to move. When you do so, the field becomes selected, as shown in Figure 4-3.

3. Place the mouse pointer over the field selector, and click and hold the left mouse button. (The rectangular drag-and-drop symbol will be added to the mouse pointer.) As you drag the mouse pointer to the left or right of the selected field, a heavy vertical bar appears, indicating the new position of the field.

4. Drag the mouse pointer (and the vertical bar along with it) to the desired location for the column, then release the mouse button. In the example shown in Figure 4-4, the First Name field has been placed in front of the Last Name field.

Selected field is shown
in reverse video.

Figure 4-3:   Selected field within a datasheet

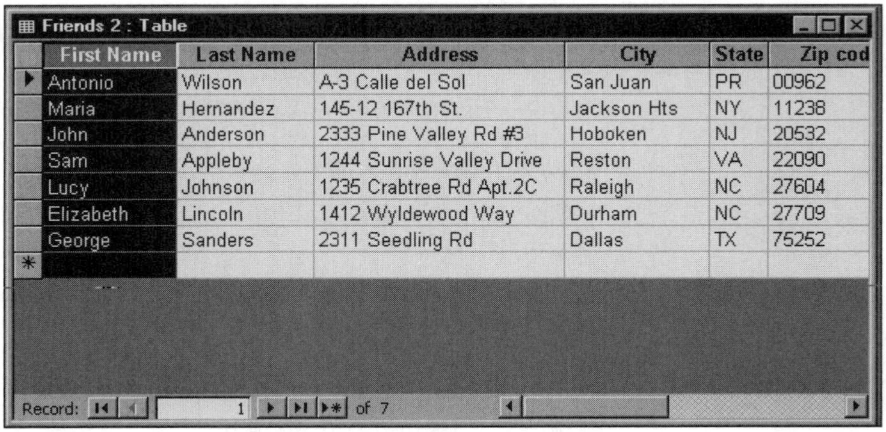

Figure 4-4:   First Name field relocated ahead of Last Name field

••••••   *Tip:*   You can move more than one column at a time if the
columns are adjacent to each other; just hold SHIFT while
clicking additional columns. Then, with all the columns
selected, click in the field selector of any of the desired
columns and drag the columns to a new location.

? How can I find all my **overdue accounts?**

To find all of your overdue accounts, add a filter that compares the due date in the table with today's date. The filter's criterion is <**Date( )**, entered under the date field used to indicate your due date. You can use the following steps:

1. Open the Records menu and choose Filter, then choose Advanced Filter/Sort from the next menu that appears.
2. Drag the date field used as your due date from the Field List to the Field row of the first column.
3. In the Criteria row for that column, enter <**Date( )** as the desired expression.
4. Open the Records menu, and choose Apply Filter/Sort.

? How can I **right-align entries** in a text field?

Right-aligning text and Memo fields is as simple as changing the field's Format property. Display the table's design and move to the field you want to right-align. Switch to the bottom half of the window and type * for the Format property. This change fills the entry's display with spaces. It also right-aligns the entry. When you save the table's design changes, you will see that your modified fields are right-aligned.

? How do I change the **row heights** in a datasheet?

You can change the height of a datasheet's rows by dragging the bottom edge of any record selector button. At the far left side of the datasheet, move the mouse pointer near the bottom of any record selector button until the pointer changes shape to a double-headed arrow. Then drag to the desired new row height. As an alternative, you can open the Format menu, choose Row Height, and enter a desired value for the row height.

ENTERING AND EDITING DATA

? **I'm attached to tables outside of Access. I can open and view the data, but why can't I make changes to attached tables?**

When you're working with tables attached from SQL servers, you can't normally edit the data in a table unless that table has a unique index on the server. If you want to edit a table that does not have a unique index, you can create an index in Access by means of a data definition query using the CREATE INDEX statement in SQL. The index must be based on a field containing unique values. If any of the field's values in the table are duplicates, all attempts to update the table are unsuccessful.

? **How can I carry data forward from one record to the next?**

You may find that you use the same entry over and over again in one field of your table. For example, if your employees live in one state, you don't want to enter the state in each record of the Employee table. To copy the entry made for the same field in the previous record, just press CTRL-' (apostrophe). Access copies the same field's entry from the previous record to the new record.

? **I enter 01/01/32 in a date field and Access assumes the date to be in the 1900s, while I want it to be in the 21st century. When I enter a date of 01/01/28, I get the desired results. What's going on?**

Access assumes that any two-digit year between 30 and 99 belongs to the 1900s but that any two-digit year between 00 and 29 comes after 1999. The easiest way to get around this problem is to provide room for the user to enter the full year when entering dates. You could choose the Long Date Format in the field's design, but that makes dates take up a lot of space on the screen. A better solution is to use a custom format that uses the full year in the table's design. Open the table in Design view. In the Format property for the date field, enter **mm/dd/yyyy** as the desired format. This displays the date in the short date format, but with all four digits shown for the year. The user must do a little more typing when entering dates, but at least you're sure you'll get the correct year.

? How can I **delete all records** in a table?

Before proceeding, remember that deletions are *not* undoable; once you delete all the records in a table, there's no way to get them back (short of restoring from a backup disk or re-entering them). With this in mind, you can use the following steps to delete all the records in a table:

1. Open the table in Datasheet view.
2. At the upper-left corner of the Datasheet, click the table selector button (the unmarked button located at the intersection of the row of field selector buttons and the column of record selector buttons). When you do this, the entire table will be selected.
3. Press DEL.
4. Answer **Yes** in the confirmation dialog box that appears.

If you are relatively sure you want to delete all the records but you'd like to keep a copy of the data as a backup, an alternative method of accomplishing the same task is to create a new copy of your table without any data in it. You can use these steps to do this:

1. Select the table you want to copy in the Database window.
2. Choose Copy from the Edit menu.
3. Choose Paste from the Edit menu.
4. Enter the name for the new table in the Table Name text box.
5. Select the Structure Option button and click OK.

The table you create has all the same attributes and settings as the original table but contains none of the data.

? How can I delete **duplicate records?**

You can create a query that lists duplicate records with the Find Duplicates Query Wizard. However, the dynaset that results from this query is read-only, so you won't be able to delete the entries directly; you're left to examine or print the list and go back into the original table to find and delete the duplicates. An alternative method to using the wizard is to create a new table without the duplicate records, and then delete the old table and give the new table its name. You can use these steps to do this:

1. Create a make-table query based on only the table containing the duplicate records. Make sure that all the fields in the table are included in the QBE grid.

2. Click in any blank area of the query, and open the query's property sheet by choosing <u>P</u>roperties from the <u>V</u>iew Menu.

3. Set the Unique Values property to Yes.

4. Run the make-table query. The query selects all the records that have unique values and creates a new table. There are no duplicate records in the new table. You can now delete the old table and give the new table its name.

Tip: Make sure you include all the fields from the table in the QBE grid and display them. Otherwise, your new table might not have all the same fields as your original table.

? Why can't I **edit** certain fields in my table?

There are certain types of fields that can't be edited in Access. These fields look like other fields in a datasheet, but Access won't allow you to edit them when you try. Possible reasons for this inability are listed below:

▷ **Calculated fields** These fields are a result of calculations based on one or more other fields. Because they do not contain actual table data, they can't be edited.

➤ **AutoNumber fields** You can't edit AutoNumber fields, because Access automatically maintains the entries in these fields, even after they have been added to the table.

➤ **Fields in a locked record** Access will not let you make any changes to data in records on a network that have been locked by others. If the record you are trying to edit displays a circle with a diagonal slash in the record selector area, that means the record is being changed by another user on the network. You must wait until the other user is done before you can make any changes.

➤ **Fields in a locked database** If the database was opened in read-only mode, or if it was locked by the network operating system software, you can't make any changes to its records or any other objects in the database.

Also, if you have set validation rules and the data you wish to enter doesn't meet the validation criteria, Access rejects the data you entered.

Why can't I **insert records** between rows, as I could with dBASE or FoxPro?

Unlike dBASE and FoxPro, Access has no insertion capability. In other words, there is no simple way to insert a new record between existing records. The new records must be added to the end of the table. But this capability is not really needed if you think about it. In older products, insertions were used mostly to keep databases in order, but with Access, you can maintain order in a table at any time by sorting the table. Also, Access queries, forms, and reports can easily be designed so that they automatically sort the data before producing a result.

How can I enter data into an **OLE Object field**?

You use Windows cut-and-paste techniques to enter OLE data into OLE Object fields of an Access table. You can do this with the following steps:

1. Use normal Windows techniques (such as pressing ALT-TAB or clicking on the appropriate Windows Taskbar icon) to switch to the application that contains the OLE data you want to place in the Access table.

2. Using normal Windows selection techniques, select the desired data.

3. Open the Edit menu in the other Windows application and choose Copy.

4. Switch back to Access, and locate the record in the datasheet where you want to place the OLE data.

5. Click in the OLE Object field.

6. If you want to embed the OLE data, open the Edit menu and choose Paste. If you want to link to the data, open the Edit menu and choose Paste Special, then turn on the Link option in the dialog box that appears and click OK.

How can I **update records** in my table with the values from another table?

If the updated table is simply an updated version of the table in your database, you might delete the old table and give the imported table its name. However, you may find that the imported table contains data for only some of your fields and that you need to use an update query.

For example, suppose your company just installed a new phone system, so that all your employees have new phone numbers. The department in charge of installing the phone system just sent you an Access table containing Employee IDs and the new phone numbers assigned to each employee. You don't want to delete your old employee table, which contains additional data such as benefits, home address and phone numbers, and payroll data. To update only the field containing the employees' work phone numbers, do the following:

1. Create a new query, adding both the original table and the table with the new phone numbers.

2. Create a join between the tables using the primary key, which should be the Employee ID field.

3. Add the fields you want to update from the original table, in this case the Work Number fields from the Employee table, to the QBE grid.

4. Make this query an update query by choosing Update from the Query menu, or by clicking the down arrow beside the Query Type toolbar button, and choosing Update Query from the pulldown menu.

5. In the Update To row of the QBE grid under each field you want to update, enter the name of the table, a period, and the field from the table with the new data you want to use to update the original table. For example, to update the work phone numbers of your employees, you would enter the expression **[New Numbers].[Numbers]** in the Update To row in the column below the field from the original table that the query will update.

6. Run your update query.

SORTING AND FILTERING DATA

? Is there a way to filter data shown in a datasheet?

You can filter a datasheet so that only certain records appear. You do so through the following steps:

1. Open the table in Datasheet view.

2. Find a record that contains data like the one you want to filter. (Figure 4-5 shows an example; in the figure, Spain is shown in the Country field.)

3. Click in the field you want to use as a filter.

4. In the toolbar, click the Filter By Selection button, shown here.

When you do this, a filtered datasheet appears, like the one shown in Figure 4-6. To cancel the effects of the filter when you are done using it, open the Records menu and choose Remove Filter/Sort, or click the Remove Filter button.

If you want to filter the datasheet on more than one field or add sorting criteria, you can create an *advanced filter* for

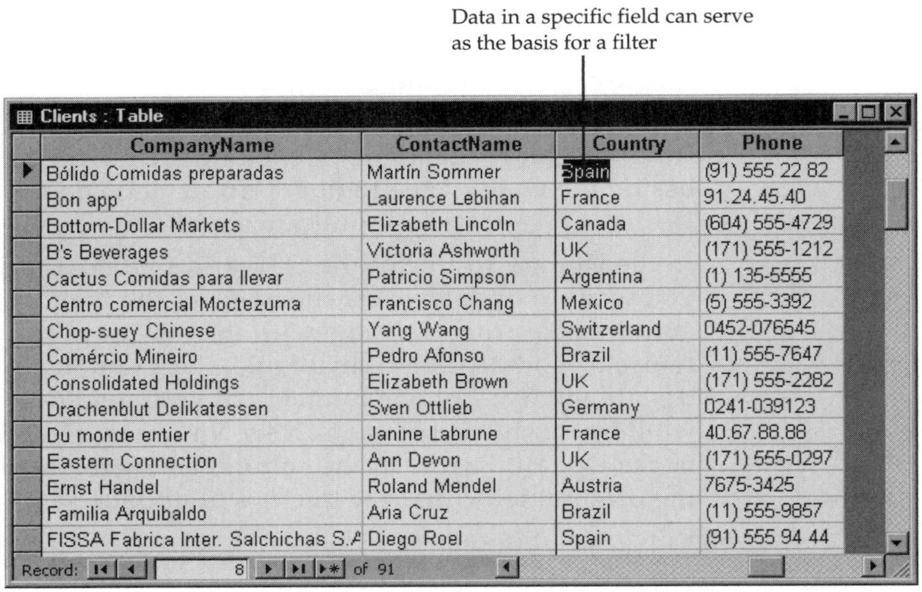

Data in a specific field can serve
as the basis for a filter

Figure 4-5:   Data in a particular field of a record serves as the basis for a filter

Filtered datasheet shows only those records
with "Spain" in the country field.

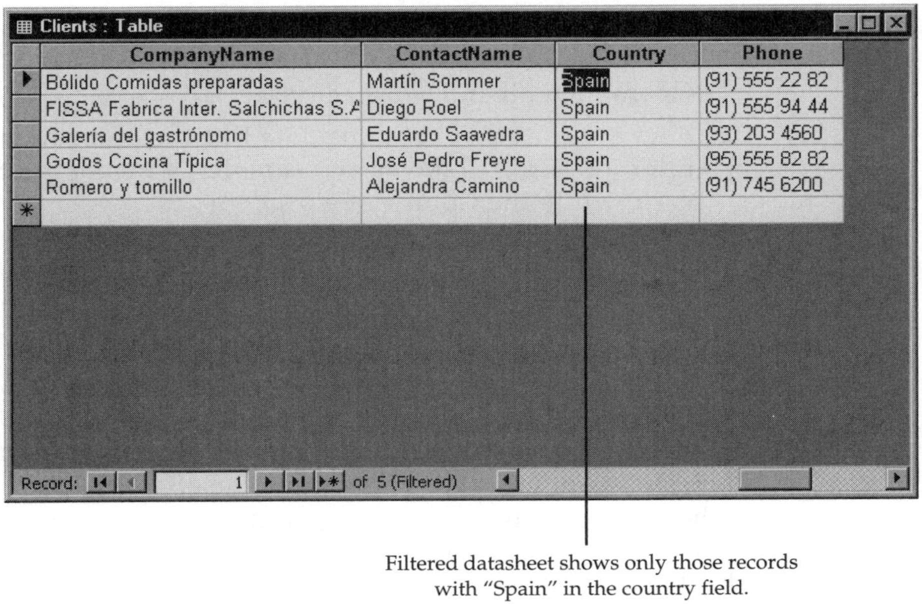

Figure 4-6:   Filtered datasheet after use of Filter By Selection button

the datasheet. This process is similar to designing a query—
you fill in a filter form that resembles the QBE grid used
in queries, and you add the desired sorting and selection
criteria. You use these steps to create an advanced filter:

1. Open the table in Datasheet view.

2. Open the Records menu and choose Filter, then choose
   Advanced Filter/Sort from the next menu that appears.

3. In the Filter Design View window that opens, choose a
   desired sort order and enter criteria to limit the records
   that appear.

To use an advanced filter once you've created it, open
the Records menu and choose Apply Filter/Sort or click
the Apply Filter button in the toolbar. To cancel the effects
of the filter, open the Records menu and choose Remove
Filter/Sort.

Caution: Be aware that filters exist on a temporary basis.
Once you close a table, or exit Access, the filter is lost. If you
plan to use the same filter conditions repeatedly, you should
create and save a query that provides the same results, or save
the filter as a query.

Can I **sort data** that's in a datasheet without creating a query?

Access provides two ways to sort the records in your table
without using a query. You can either use the sorting
toolbar buttons or create an advanced filter that sorts the
records in a datasheet (see the previous question).

When you sort using the toolbar buttons, you have to
select the fields you want to use in sorting the records. In
Datasheet view, you can select multiple fields for sorting.
The first selected field sorts all records. The second field
selected sorts only the records with the same first field
value. In a form, you can only sort on a single field. Select
the field or fields you want to sort by, and then click the
Sort Ascending or Sort Descending button.

Note: The Sort Ascending and Sort Descending buttons are
equivalent to choosing Sort from the Records menu and then
selecting Sort Ascending or Sort Descending.

≡   *Note:*   Because Access sorts the fields from left to right, it may be necessary to change the order of the fields to obtain the desired sort order.

WORKING WITH RELATIONSHIPS

 How can I create a relationship when one field is an AutoNumber field?

As a rule, the fields you use to create a relationship must be the same type. However, if you are trying to create a relationship using an AutoNumber field, the second field must be a Number type field with the FieldSize property set to Long Integer.

 What are cascading updates and deletes?

Cascading updates and deletes affect what Access does with data when you update or delete a record in one table that relates to records in other tables. If you have a cascading update, all records in related tables are updated when you change data in a primary table. For example, if you change a customer number in the Customer table, all related tables that contain the customer number update their records to use the new customer number. With a cascading delete, when you delete a record in a primary table, all related data is deleted. This means that when you delete a customer in your Customer table, Access deletes all records for that customer in related tables.

Cascading updates and deletes can be useful, because they can speed data entry and make sure that all related records are updated at the same time. On the other hand, they can also change or delete data without your realizing it. Cascading updates and deletes are not set automatically. You have the opportunity to create them as you create the relationships. In the Relationships dialog box, after you select the Enforce Referential Integrity check box, the additional options in the dialog box are enabled. You can then select the Cascade Update Related Fields and Cascade Delete Related Records check boxes before clicking Create to create the relationship. Unless you select one of these check boxes, you don't have cascading updates or deletes.

❓ How do I **create a relationship?**

You can create a relationship between two tables using the following steps:

1. Click the Tables tab in the Database window.

2. Open the <u>T</u>ools menu and choose <u>R</u>elationships, to display the Relationships window. If this is the first time you're establishing this relationship, the Show Table dialog box shown here appears in front of the Relationships window.

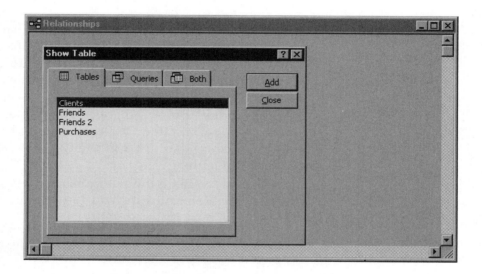

3. Choose the table or query you want to use as part of the relationship, then click <u>A</u>dd to add it to the Database window.

4. Repeat step 3 for each additional table or query needed as part of the relationship.

5. Establish the desired relationships by dragging the field or fields you want to use for the link from one table to the related field or fields in the other table. (Usually, the primary key in one table is related to a field containing similar data in another table.) When you drag and drop the field, the Relationships dialog box appears as shown next.

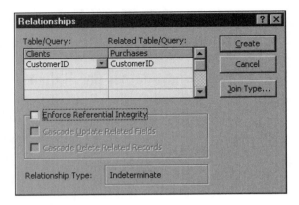

6. Check that the fields being used are the correct fields for a relationship. (Access makes a fairly accurate guess as to which fields it should use, but you may prefer a different set of fields than Access chooses by default.)

7. Select the Enforce Referential Integrity check box to maintain the relationship between the tables. When you enforce referential integrity, Access keeps you from entering records that don't fit the type of relationship between the tables.

8. Click Create to create the relationship. Relationships are shown in the Relationships window using lines, as you can see here.

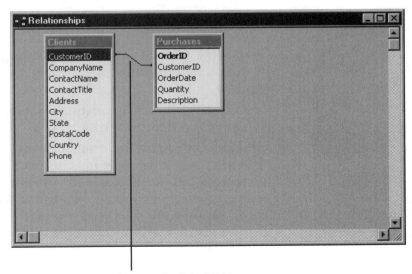

Join line appears between the linked fields
in the related tables.

Note: When you create a relationship between two tables using an AutoNumber field, the other field must be a Long Integer Number field.

How do I **delete a relationship?**

You can delete a relationship in Access by opening the Relationships window, and removing the join line between the tables. Use these steps:

1. Open the Tools menu and choose Relationships to open the Relationships window.
2. Select the line between the tables that indicates the relationships.
3. Press DEL.
4. Select OK when Access prompts you to confirm that you want to delete the relationship.

Can I **remove tables** from my Relationships window?

Yes, you can remove the tables from your Relationships window without deleting the tables themselves from your database. Just select the table in the Relationships window, and choose Hide Table from the Relationships menu. You can also right-click the table's title bar and select Hide Table. Access removes the table from the Relationships window. Removing the table does not change the relationships the table has. You can always put the table back later by choosing Show Table in the Relationships menu, or by clicking the Show Table button.

What is a relationship?

In Access, a relationship is a link between two tables that indicates how the data in those two tables is related. When you create a relationship, you tell Access which fields in the two tables contain the same data. For example, you might create a relationship between your employee table and your Payroll table using the Employee ID field in each table. Usually, one of the fields used to create the relationship is the primary key for its table. Both fields must have the

● ● ● ● ● ● ● ● ● ● ●

The ABCs of Relationships

With relational databases, there are three ways in which you can establish relationships between tables. Tables can have a one-to-one, one-to-many, or many-to-many relationship. Access directly supports the first two, and you can indirectly accomplish the third by redesigning many-to-many relationships into multiple one-to-many relationships.

The first step is understanding which table is primary and which tables are related to it. As an example, you could create a relationship between a Customers table and an Orders table. The relationship would indicate which items have been ordered by a specific customer. In this case, the Customers table is the primary table, and the Orders table is the related table (also known as the *foreign* table). By relating the two tables, you eliminate any need to store a customer name and address in the Orders table. Instead, you store just the Customer ID for each order that's stored in the Orders table. Other data needed on invoices or sales reports, such as the customer name and address, can be obtained from the Customer table.

A *one-to-one* relationship exists when each record in the related table corresponds to only one record in the primary table. One-to-one relationships are usually a bad idea, because the duplicated fields in the two tables waste disk space. In most cases, you could add the fields in the related table to the primary table and make one larger table. However, situations do arise when one-to-one relationships are needed. As an example, an employee database might use separate tables with employee home addresses and employee medical data. If different security levels were desired for the different tables, it would make sense to store them separately and establish a one-to-one relationship between the two.

A *one-to-many* relationship is the most common type of relationship used in a database. In a one-to-many relationship, each record in the primary table corresponds to one or more records in the related table. The relationship described in the above example of customers and their orders is a one-to-many relationship. Any one customer may have placed several orders, but each order belongs to only one customer. One-to-many relationships like this one avoid unnecessary and repetitive data entry.

A *many-to-many* relationship exists when many records in one table are related to many records in another table. Access (along with most PC-based database managers) does not directly support many-to-many relationships. However, you can indirectly support this type of relationship, by joining together two one-to-many relationships by means of a query. A common example of a many-to-many relationship involves an inventory of parts and the suppliers of those parts. The Inventory table contains a number of parts that have come from one or more suppliers, and each supplier in the Suppliers table provides one or more parts. The Inventory table might contain the description, cost, and quantity for each item in the inventory, along with a unique item number for the item. The Suppliers table might contain the name and address of each supplier, along with a unique Supplier ID number. To relate the tables and provide data on the many-to-many relationship, you would need another table containing just two fields: Item Number and Supplier ID. The third table would serve as an intermediate table linking the other two tables, which contain the "many" data.

Regardless of the types of relationships you use, you will need key fields containing unique data so that the relationships can be easily established. This is why Access is so insistent about suggesting your use of primary keys when you create new tables.

same data type. You could not create a relationship using a Number field in one table and a Text field in the second table, because they contain different types of data.

The tables can have a one-to-one relationship or a one-to-many relationship. In a one-to-one relationship, each record in table A (the primary table) matches exactly one record in table B (the related table) and vice versa. Therefore, you cannot enter a record in table B unless the related record is already entered in table A and unless no other record in table B is related to the record in table A. In most such cases, you want to redesign your tables to combine the information in the two tables. However, sometimes the one-to-one relationship is intentional.

In a one-to-many relationship, each record in table A (the primary table) matches many records in table B (the related table), but each record in table B relates to only one record in table A. Therefore, you can enter records in table B, the related table, only when the related record is already in table A. Unlike a one-to-one relationship, you can add records in table B when table B already has records that are related to the same record in table A. For example, you might have one record in your Employees table with many related records in your Projects table.

TROUBLESHOOTING

?   **I get a "duplicate key" error when I try to enter a record. What does this mean?**

Whenever you get an error that says "Can't have a duplicate key", that means that the record you entered is the same as another record in the table. When the Indexed property of a field is set to Yes (No Duplicates), you cannot have two values in that field that are the same. One of the values must be changed.

?   **Why do I see tables starting with "Msys" in the Database window?**

The tables you see with the strange names are system tables, and they are used by Access to keep track of its internal operation. Attributes for various objects, file locking information, and custom toolbar designs are just a few of the types of information stored within the system tables. You should *not* modify or delete data in any of these tables. If you change these tables, you can cause major problems with the operation of Access. By default, the tables are hidden. You can hide them again by performing the following steps:

1. Open the Tools menu and choose Options.
2. In the dialog box that appears, click the View tab if it isn't already selected.
3. Turn off the Show System Objects option.
4. Click OK.

chapter

5 Answers!

Basic
Queries

Answer Topics!

Basic Queries @ a Glance

In Access, a *query* is basically a question you ask about the data that's stored in your tables. You ask the question, Access processes the data, and it displays the records that answer your question in the form of a temporary table called a *dynaset*. This chapter answers questions about queries in general; the basic select query, which responds to your questions; and action queries, which update or delete existing data. Chapter 6, "Advanced Queries," answers your questions about the more advanced query types in Access, such as relational queries and queries that produce crosstabs of your data.

The questions you'll find answers to in this chapter deal with the following areas:

➡ **Query Basics** Here you'll find information on the terms behind queries, the types of queries you can work with, and the specifications and limitations of queries.

➭ **Managing Fields** The questions in this portion of the chapter will help you ensure that your queries' fields appear where and when you want them to.

➭ **Using Criteria** In this part of the chapter, you'll find answers that help you structure criteria in your queries to get at the data you need.

➭ **Action Queries** This portion of the chapter provides answers to questions about action queries, which let you update or delete tables based on the design of the query.

➭ **Sorting Data** The answers detailed in this part of the chapter help you control the order of the data that's retrieved by your queries.

➭ **Performing Calculations** These answers tell you how to obtain the kinds of calculations you want and what to do when a type of calculation doesn't give you the results you expected.

➭ **Troubleshooting** The answers in this part of the chapter help you deal with unexpected error messages and other general problems when running Access.

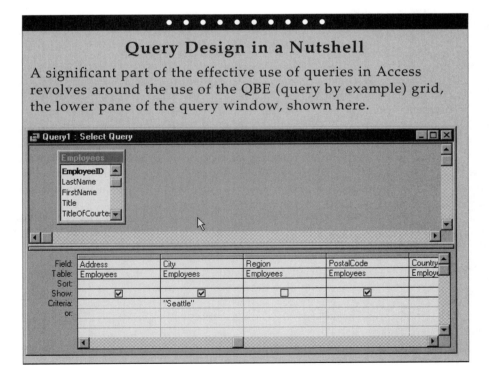

Query Design in a Nutshell

A significant part of the effective use of queries in Access revolves around the use of the QBE (query by example) grid, the lower pane of the query window, shown here.

You fill in the various rows of the QBE grid to tell Access what conditions to use in retrieving your data. The various rows of the QBE grid allow you to select desired fields to include in the query results, choose a sort order, show or hide fields from the results, and specify criteria that determine which records appear in the results. The rows of the QBE grid include these:

- The *Field row* contains the names of the fields. You can add field names by dragging fields from field lists above the QBE grid, or by choosing field names from a drop-down list box that appears when you click in the row. The Field row can also contain *calculated fields*, which are expressions that provide values based on a calculation involving one or more fields.

- The *Sort row* determines whether the field sorts the records in the dynaset.

- The *Show row* determines whether the field appears in the resulting dynaset or is hidden.

- *Criteria rows* contain the criteria that select which records appear in the dynaset.

There are three basic steps in designing a query. First, you tell Access which tables or other queries the data should be retrieved from. (In Access, a query can be based on tables, on other queries, or on a combination of both.) Next, you tell Access which fields you want included in the results of the query. Finally, you describe any sorting and selection criteria that should apply to the results. Here are the steps you'll need to perform to create a basic query in Access:

Identifying the Source of the Data

1. In the Database window, click the Queries tab.
2. Click New. Access displays the New Query dialog box.

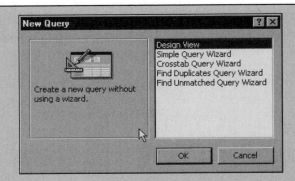

3. Click Design View, then click OK. (The remaining choices are used for the special-purpose queries listed.) In a moment, Access opens a new Query Design View window and displays a Show Table dialog box above it.

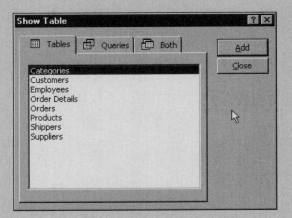

4. Choose the table you want to ask about by clicking it and then clicking Add.

5. Repeat step 4 for each additional table you want to add to the query. (You can also query queries, by clicking the Queries tab and choosing an existing query as a data source for the new query.)

6. Click Close to close the Show Table dialog box. The Query Design View window underneath shows a grid for the query itself (in the lower half of the window)

and field lists for the tables or existing queries that are
supplying the data (in the upper half).

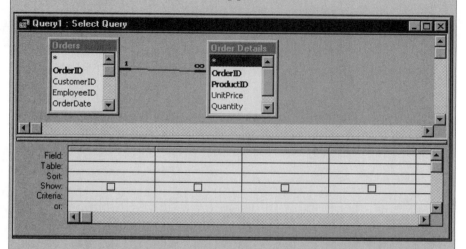

Choosing the Fields Returned by the Query

Once you've identified the source of the data for the query,
you'll need to tell Access which fields should be included in
the query results. Follow these steps to do this:

1. In the Field List in the upper half of the window, choose
   the first field that you want to see in the query results. Click
   that field, and drag it down to the first empty column in the
   Field row.

2. Repeat Step 1 for each field that you want to add to the
   query results.

Specifying Sorting and Selection Criteria

The final step in designing a query is to tell Access how you
want the data sorted, and what *criteria*, or selection rules,
should apply to the data. You can use these steps to choose a
sort order for the data retrieved by the query:

1. Choose the field that you want Access to use first in
   placing the records in order. As an example, if you

are querying a table of customers, you might want to retrieve the records in alphabetical order of last names.

2. Click in the Sort row for that field, and from the drop-down list choose the desired sort order (Ascending or Descending).

3. To sort on multiple columns, repeat steps 1 and 2 for each additional column to be sorted. Note that when you are sorting on more than one column, the column of most importance in the sort order must be the leftmost column. (You can click and drag columns around in the query grid as needed.)

You can specify your selection criteria by performing these steps:

1. Click in the Criteria row within the field that Access should use to retrieve the desired information.

2. Enter the selection criteria in the column. If you're searching for records where a field contains a specific value (like a numeric amount or a date), enter that value. If you want to retrieve records with a specific text entry—such as a City equal to San José—enter that text. As an example, entering **CA** in a Criteria row under a State column as shown here would retrieve all records where the letters "CA" appear in the State field of a table.

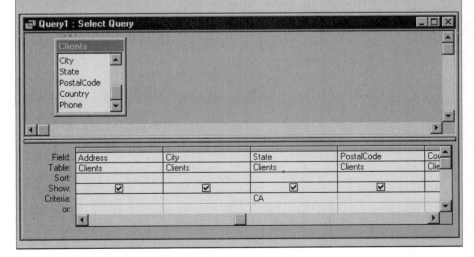

3. Repeat step 2 for additional fields where you want to specify selection criteria.

After performing these steps, you can run the query to retrieve the desired data by clicking the Run button on the toolbar or by choosing <u>R</u>un from the Query menu. The results of the query are displayed in a dynaset like that shown here.

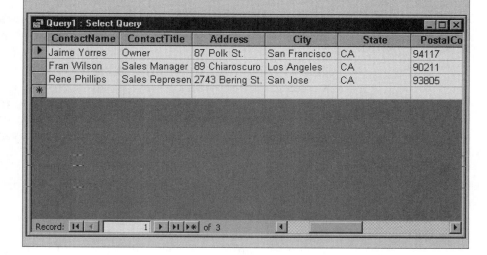

QUERY BASICS

What is an **action query**?

An *action query* is a query that performs an action, such as deleting records or changing your data. As opposed to select queries, which just let you view your data, action queries actually do something to the data in your tables. You typically use action queries to handle mass updates to your data. For example, you could use an action query to increase every value in a Cost field of an Inventory table by 4 percent. Access provides four types of action queries:

➤ *Append* queries add data to an existing table.

➤ *Delete* queries delete records that meet certain criteria specified by the query.

> ☞ *Update* queries change the data in existing tables for all records that meet certain criteria specified by the query.

> ☞ *Make-table* queries create new tables using the data extracted from existing tables.

❓ What is a **dynaset**?

A *dynaset* is a temporary table that Access creates when a query runs. The term *dynaset* is an abbreviation for *dynamic set of records*. The word *dynamic* refers to the fact that when Access displays a dynaset, it is displaying live data from the tables included in the query. In other words, what you see in a dynaset is the real data, and not some static representation of it. You can make changes to the data in a dynaset, and when you do so, you are changing the underlying data in the table. You can even add new records to a table by entering new records into a dynaset. Likewise, if you change the data in the tables that are used as a data source for the dynaset, the data in the dynaset changes accordingly.

Tip: Because Access uses the same view for a dynaset as it does for a table's datasheet, you can apply the same changes to properties as you would for a datasheet. You can increase or decrease the width of columns, change row heights, move columns around, and hide columns, just as you might do with a datasheet.

❓ How large can a query's resulting dynaset be?

The maximum size of a resulting dynaset is actually a limitation of disk space. Dynasets created by your queries are limited to one gigabyte in size.

❓ How many characters can I have in a cell of the QBE grid?

You can have up to 1,024 characters in any single cell of the QBE grid. (You may need a large number of characters when entering complex expressions for criteria or for calculated fields.)

? How many fields can I sort by in my query?

You can sort by up to 255 characters total, which can be contained in one or more fields. To sort by a field in your query, you choose Ascending or Descending from the Sort row underneath the field's name. Access starts sorting by the leftmost field and works its way right. Note that the maximum differs from earlier versions of Access, which limited you to ten fields. You can now sort on more than ten fields as long as the total number of characters involved in the sort doesn't exceed 255 characters.

? How many tables can I include in a query?

You can use up to 32 tables in a query. The fields can either appear in the query's dynaset or select which records from another table will appear in the dynaset.

? Why can't I name a query with the same name as an existing table?

For the purposes of holding data, Access considers tables and queries to be the same type of objects. This enables Access to display both tables and queries as data sources for other objects, like forms and reports. If you try to give a query the same name as an existing table, Access will display a dialog box asking you if you want to replace the existing table with the query. If you click Yes, the existing table will be overwritten by the query.

Tip: Many professional Access developers use three-character identifiers in object names to specify the object type. Thus, if you had an Employees table and an Employees query, their names would not conflict, because they'd be something like "tbl Employees" and "qry Employees".

? What does QBE stand for?

QBE stands for Query By Example. Query By Example is a term for a method of obtaining data that was pioneered by IBM in the 1970s. Access makes use of *graphical QBE,* or *graphical query by example,* to describe the data you're looking for and to obtain results quickly. With graphical QBE, you can perform most of the aspects of designing the query by dragging objects around on a query form. Using QBE lets you retrieve the information you want without programming.

Access converts the query design in the QBE grid into a SQL (Structured Query Language) statement. SQL (pronounced "sequel") is a standard language used by many database management applications. You can create a SQL statement directly without using the QBE grid. However, unless you are already comfortable using SQL, there's really no good reason to do so.

? What is a **select query**?

In Access, *select* queries are the most commonly used type of query. These are queries that ask a question and select desired information in response, based on how you structure the query. As an example, you might create a query to find out which employees worked over 50 hours last week or which clients had overdue invoices.

When your tables become large, you need to find the data you want quickly. That's what select queries do. Without select queries, your tables are nothing more than long lists of data. When run, select queries display *dynasets,* showing temporary tables that display exactly the information you need.

Figure 5-1 shows a select query, both in its Design view and as a dynaset (after the query has been run). The upper portion of the window shows the query's design. You can see that the QBE grid selects the fields that will appear in the resulting dynaset. The query also selects which records will appear by including only records whose Unit Price is greater than $30.00. The query's dynaset, which you can see in the lower half of the window, shows these records.

Tip: Switch to the dynaset from a Query window by clicking the View toolbar button, shown here, or by choosing Data<u>s</u>heet View from the <u>V</u>iew menu. This button, which alternates

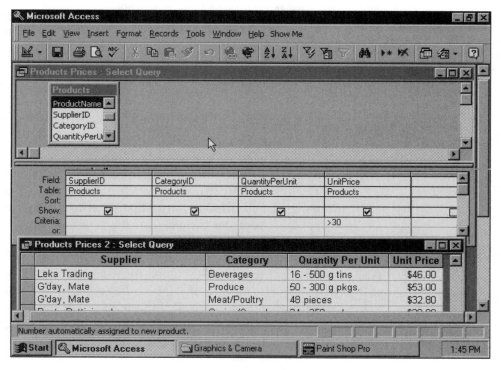

Figure 5-1: A select query and its resulting dynaset

between Datasheet and Design views, is just like the one you use to switch between Datasheet and Design views for a table.

❓ What is a **SQL-specific query**?

A SQL-specific query is any query that you can't create by using the QBE grid alone. Instead, you create the query by typing an appropriate SQL statement directly into the SQL view window. The following types of SQL-specific queries are common to Access:

▷ *Union queries* combine data from multiple tables into a single table. The resultant table is called a *snapshot* because, unlike a dynaset, it is *not* updatable.

▷ *Pass-through queries* let you send SQL statements ("pass them through") directly to a database server on a network, using the syntax of SQL that's appropriate to your database server. You use pass-through queries to work with tables stored on a database server without actually attaching to them.

▷ *Data-definition queries* can create or modify tables and their indexes. You can use these to create tables, delete tables, add new fields to the design of existing tables, or create or remove indexes for a table.

▰▰▰▰ *Tip:* If you want to use a SQL-specific query, search Access' online help for information on SQL and SQL-reserved words to get more information. Also, if you are creating pass-through queries, be sure to check the documentation for your database server for the proper SQL syntax.

❔ Why can't I **update the data** in my query?

In Access, some types of queries and certain fields in queries can't be updated. An easy way to tell whether a query is updatable is to look at the last record in the resulting query's dynaset. If the last record is a blank record with an asterisk on the selector, then the query is updatable (although it is still possible that some of the individual fields are not). The following types of queries aren't updatable in Access:

▷ Crosstab, pass-through, or union queries

▷ Queries that calculate a sum, average, count, or other type of total on the values in a field

▷ Queries that include attached tables lacking indexes or primary keys

▷ Queries for which permission to update or delete records is not available

➤ Queries with the Unique Values property set to Yes

➤ Query based on three or more tables in which there is a many-to-one-to-many relationship

➤ Queries that include more than one table or query, and the tables or queries aren't joined by a join line in Design view

Some queries let you update some fields in the queries but not others. Fields that cannot be updated include

➤ Some fields in a query based on tables with a one-to-many relationship

➤ Calculated fields

➤ Fields from databases that were opened as read-only

➤ Fields deleted or locked by another user

➤ A memo or OLE Object field in a *snapshot*, which is an unchanging dynaset created by SQL-specific queries

⬤⬤⬤⬤⬤ *Tip:* Another way to check whether a query is updatable is to see whether the Data Entry command on the Records menu is dimmed or not. If it is dimmed, you can't update the records in the query.

❓ What's the difference between **View/Datasheet** and **Query/Run**?

When you are in Design view for a query and you choose Datasheet View from the View menu or click on the toolbar's View button, you see the dynaset containing the results of the query. You also see a dynaset with the query results if you choose Run from the Query menu or click the Run button in the toolbar. So the obvious question arises: What's the difference between the two?

For select queries it turns out that there is no difference. Running a query or changing from Design view to Datasheet view provides the same results. The difference is important with action queries, which change existing data or create new tables. When you have an action query open in Design view, switching to Datasheet view displays a dynaset that shows how the data will be affected, but the changes specified by the action query aren't performed. On the other hand, if you run the action query, the changes specified by the design of the action query (adding or updating records, deleting records, or creating new tables) are carried out.

MANAGING FIELDS

? How can I **hide fields** in the resulting dynaset?

You can hide fields from the dynaset that results from your queries. As an example, you might want to display only those customers based in Canada, but you do not want the data from the Country field of the table included in the results of the query. To omit a field from the results, click the Show check box to remove the check mark in the box. (By default, a check mark appears in the Show check box for any field included in the query, indicating that the field will be shown in the results.) As an example, in the query shown here the Country field contains a criteria limiting the records to Canada, but the check mark has been removed from the Show box in the field column; hence, the dynaset that results from the query will not include the data from the Country field.

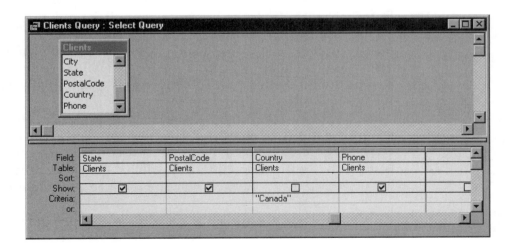

■■■ *Caution:*   You can't omit any fields that you plan to use in forms or reports based on the query.

❓ How can I change the **order of the fields** in a query's dynaset?

You can rearrange the fields in a dynaset with the same methods used to move fields in a datasheet. Use these steps to move the fields in a query dynaset:

1. Select the field you wish to move by clicking the Field Selector at the top of the column.

2. Click and hold down the left mouse button as you point to the Field Selector. The mouse pointer changes shape to a small square.

3. While keeping the mouse button depressed, drag the field to the desired location. As you drag the field, a solid bar appears, showing where the relocated field will appear when you release the mouse button, as shown here.

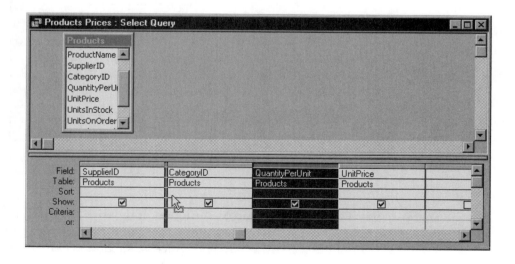

?   **Can I rename a column to make its title different from the field name?**

You can change the column titles in a dynaset by specifying a different name as part of the query's design. In the Field Row for the desired field, click at the start of the field name, and type the new name, followed by a colon. As an example, if a field were named 97 Sales and you wanted the column in the resulting dynaset to be titled "Sales for 1997," your entry in the Field Row would look like this:

Sales for 1997:[97 Sales]

?   **How can I easily view a long expression in the QBE grid?**

Access offers a way to easily see lengthy entries in the QBE grid. Click in the desired cell of the grid, and press SHIFT-F2. Access opens the Zoom box displaying the entry, as shown here:

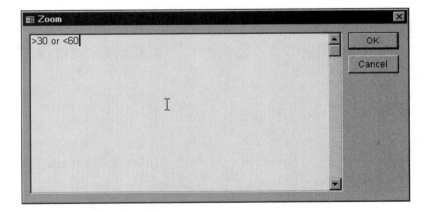

⸭⸭⸭⸭⸭⸭   *Tip:*   The Zoom box can also display long entries in other parts of a query, such as an entry in a Field row. You can use this Zoom box in other areas of Access, such as when entering data in memo fields of a table or when entering expressions into controls used in forms and reports.

QUERY CRITERIA

? **I want to search for text that includes the word "and" within the text, but Access thinks I'm trying to use the And operator. How can I change this?**

Access considers the words **and, or,** and **not** to be operators. So if you use them as part of a query string, Access assumes the words are to be used as operators and not as literal text. The way around this problem is to enclose the entire text string containing the word "and" (or any other operator) within quotes when entering the criteria, so Access knows that the entire term is a text string. For example, if you enter **scotch and soda** in the Criteria row of a query, Access interprets this to be an **And** statement meaning "scotch" And "soda". But if you instead enter the criteria as **"scotch and soda"** with the quotation marks included in the entry, Access will interpret the entry as a single string of text.

? **How can I structure my query criteria to search for dates based on today's date?**

You can include the Date() function to create queries that retrieve data based on the current date, according to your PC's clock. As an example, you could enter a criterion $<=$**Date()**-30 in a query field called Hire Date to tell Access to retrieve any employees hired 30 or more days ago. An expression like $=$**Date()** would retrieve records with today's date in the date field.

? **How can I search for records that don't match a value?**

You can use the **NOT** operator to select records that don't meet a specific condition. As an example, you could enter an expression like **Not Atlanta** in the City field of a query to retrieve records with any entry in the City field except "Atlanta." You could enter an expression like **Not 4/15/98** in a Date Sold field to find all records with a date sold other than 4/15/98.

? Can I design my query criteria to select records based on one word in a Memo or Text field?

Yes, you can have your query search for a single word in a longer entry. For example, to search for the word "Blue" in a field, open the query in Design view. Move to the Criteria row beneath the field and enter **Like "*Blue*"**. Run the query by clicking the Datasheet View button, or by choosing Datasheet View from the View menu.

? How can I structure my query criteria to find all records in a table that were entered this month?

Assuming that the table has a field containing the date that records have been entered, you can create a query that chooses only the records you entered this month. To do this, create your query as normal. Then, assuming the field that contains the date of entry is named Entry Date, add the Entry Date field to the QBE grid. Move to the Criteria row for this column and enter **Year([OrderDate])=Year(Now()) And Month([OrderDate])=Month(Now())**. When you run this query, the dynaset shows only the records entered during the current month.

? How can I search for records that contain no value?

You can use the Is Null operator to retrieve records that are missing data in a particular field. As an example, you might want to see a list of all clients who have no fax numbers. You could do this by entering the criterion **Is Null** in the Criteria cell underneath the Fax Number field of the query. The opposite of this expression is Is Not Null; you could enter **Is Not Null** in a Criteria cell to find all records that contain a value of any kind in the field.

? How can I query a table for a large range of values, like all sales between January 1 and June 31?

The *comparison operators*, > for greater than, < for less than, and = for equal to, can be used to select records that fall within a certain range of values. Database users often think of numeric and currency values as falling within certain ranges, but you can use the comparison operators with text and date values also. The comparison operators can be used to construct these types of queries. With a date field, for example, you could use **>= 1/1/99 and <=6/30/99** to retrieve records with entries in the date field that fall between January and June of 1999. With a Cost field containing currency amounts, you could enter the criterion **>10 and < 50** to specify a range between 10.00 and 50.00. In a query field containing last names, you could enter **> "M" and < "Zz"** in the QBE grid to retrieve all last names beginning with the letters *M* through *Z*. In this example, note the addition of the second letter *z*. It is important in this case, because if it were omitted, Access would retrieve all names up to Z, but none following the letter Z alone. This would have the effect of omitting all last names containing more than one character and beginning with the letter Z.

▪▪▪▪▪▪   *Tip:*   You can also use the **Between...And** operator to specify ranges. For example, you could enter **Between 10 And 50** as a criterion value in a query.

❔ How can I **specify my criteria when the query runs?**

You can provide different criteria each time a query runs by creating a *parameter query*. A parameter query is simply a query that automatically asks for the needed criteria each time the query runs. You can use the same select queries that you have already created as the basis for parameter queries. Instead of having to open the query window and type the new criteria into the query grid, Access will display dialog boxes with prompts, asking you for the criteria. You can create a parameter query with the following steps:

1. Create a query with the tables and the fields that you want.

2. In the Criteria cells underneath the fields that you want to use as parameters, enter your parameter text, enclosed in square brackets. (This text will be used as a prompt in the dialog box that Access displays when the query runs.) As an example, if you wanted a parameter in a **Country** field to ask for the name of the desired country when

the query runs, you could enter an expression like
[Enter the desired country name:] in the **Country** field
as shown here.

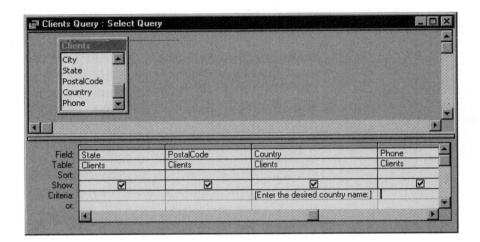

3. Save the query (choose <u>S</u>ave from the <u>F</u>ile menu, or press
CTRL-F4 and answer **Yes** to the prompt that appears.)

When you run the query, Access displays a dialog box like
that shown here, asking for the parameter value.

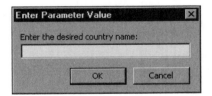

When you type in the data and click OK, the query runs and
provides the data according to your criteria.

Tip: While this example makes use of a parameter with a
single value, note that you're not limited to a single value in
a parameter. One common use of multiple values in the same

parameter is to prompt for a range of values, usually done with numbers or dates. For example, consider a query based on a table that contains a Date field for the date of hire of employees. If you want a parameter query that prompts for all employees hired between two dates, you could enter an expression like **Between [Enter the starting date:] And [Enter the ending date:]** in the criteria cell for the **Date** field. When you run the query, Access would first ask for the starting date, then for the ending date. The resulting records shown in the query would contain only those records falling between the two dates.

Tip: Parameter queries are useful as a data source for forms and reports, as they provide an easy way to ask users of the database for needed information to obtain selective data. You can create parameter queries and then change the RecordSource properties of your forms and reports to draw data from the parameter queries. As an example, if your application has a sales report and that report needs to be run on a weekly basis, you can base the report on a parameter query that asks for the starting date and the ending date of sales. That way, each time the report runs, the user enters the appropriate dates for that week, and the resulting report contains records from the desired week's sales.

How can I use **wildcards** in my query criteria?

You can use the wildcard characters to find groups of records where the entries match a specific pattern. The valid wildcards are the question mark (?), which represents any single character in the same position as the question mark, and the asterisk (*), which represents any number of characters in the same position as the asterisk. You can use these wildcard characters in text-based or date-based expressions. For example, the expression **"M*s"** could be used in a Criteria cell underneath a Last name field to find names that would include Morris, Masters, and Miller-Peters. The expression **Like "6/*/98"** in the Criteria cell for a date field could be used to retrieve all records where that date falls in June 1998.

ACTION QUERIES

? How can I **add records** from one table to another?

For this task, you'll want to create an *append query*. Append queries are action queries that add the results of the query to other tables. Use the following steps to create an append query:

1. Design a select query that produces a dynaset containing the records you want to add to the other table.

2. Run the query to make sure the results provide the data that you want to add to the other table.

3. Click the View button on the toolbar, or choose <u>D</u>esign View from the <u>V</u>iew menu to switch to Design view.

4. Choose Append Query from the <u>Q</u>uery menu. When you do so, Access displays the Append dialog box, shown here.

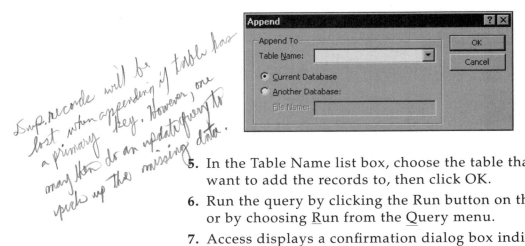

Dup. records will be lost when appending if table has a primary key. However, one may then do an update query to pick up the missing data.

5. In the Table Name list box, choose the table that you want to add the records to, then click OK.

6. Run the query by clicking the Run button on the toolbar, or by choosing <u>R</u>un from the Query menu.

7. Access displays a confirmation dialog box indicating how many records will be appended to the destination table. Click the Yes button.

? How can I use a query to **delete a batch of records**?

You can do this with a *delete query*, which is a type of action query that deletes all records found by the query's criteria. Use these steps to create a delete query:

1. Design a select query that produces a dynaset containing the records you want to delete from the table.

2. Run the query to make sure the results provide the data that you want to delete from the table.

3. Click the View button on the toolbar, or choose Design View from the View menu to switch to Design view.

4. Choose Delete Query from the Query menu. The title of the Query window will change to "Delete Query," indicating that when run, the query will delete all the specified records.

5. Run the query by clicking the Run button on the toolbar, or by choosing Run from the Query menu. Access will display a confirmation dialog, telling you how many records will be deleted from the table.

6. If you do not want to delete the records, click No. Otherwise, click Yes to run the query and delete the records.

How can I be sure an action query will have the **desired results** before I run it?

You can check which records your action query will affect before you run it. It's a good idea to do so, to avoid accidental and unwanted modifications or deletions of data. To check an action query's results before running it, after designing the query choose Datasheet View from the View menu. The dynaset that appears displays the records that will be affected by your action query.

If the query selects the correct records, you can switch back to the query's Design view and run the query. (Click the Design View toolbar button, or choose Design View from the View menu.) Run the action query by clicking the Run button on the toolbar, or by choosing Run from the Query menu.

Can I use a query to find **duplicate values** in a table?

The easiest way to locate duplicate values in a table is to use the Find Duplicates Query Wizard. This wizard prompts you for information about how you want to search for duplicates and then creates the query based on your answers. In the Database window, click the Queries tab, then click New. In the New Query dialog box that appears, click Find Duplicates Query Wizard, then click Next to start the wizard. The wizard has four steps:

1. Select the table in which you want to find duplicate records.

2. Select the fields you want to search for duplicates. The query will count as duplicates any records that are the same in all of the fields you select here, even if they are different in other fields.

3. Select any other fields you want displayed in the query's dynaset. These fields won't be checked for duplicates.

4. Enter a name for the query, and choose whether you want to open it in Datasheet view or Design view.

❓ I get a "**key violations**" error message when I try to run an append query. What does this mean?

This message appears when your append query is attempting to add records to an existing table, and the new records have values in key fields that are the same as values that already exist in the key fields of the table. Access will not allow an append query to cause changes that would create duplicate values in the key fields of records. Nor will Access permit any changes that attempt to create null (or empty) values in key fields. When update or append queries attempt to create records that violate these guidelines, the results are *key violations*. You must change the values in the incoming records or in some other manner omit the new records or the changes that are causing the problem.

❓ How can I **update the values** in a table based on the results of a query?

For this task, you want to use update queries, which are action queries that update (or make specific changes to) all records meeting certain criteria. Update queries are a very handy tool to have when you need to change data in a global fashion. For example, you might need to give a new telephone area code to all residents living in a particular city. In an employee table, you might want to increase all salaries of a given type of worker by $.50 an hour. You can use the following steps to create an update query:

1. Design and test a select query that retrieves the records that you want to update.

2. Choose Update Query from the Query menu, or click the Update Query button in the toolbar. Access adds the Update To row to the query grid, as shown here.

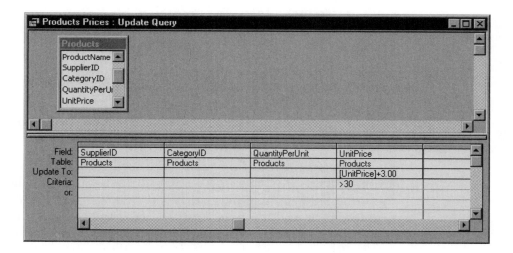

3. In the Update To cell for the field that you want to update, enter a desired expression or a value that will change the data. As an example, you could increase salaries by $.50 in a Salary field by entering **[Salary]** + **.50**. If you wanted to change all area codes for residents of Stafford, Virginia, from **703** to **540**, you would enter **Stafford** in the Criteria cell of the City field, **VA** in the Criteria cell of the State field, and **540** in the Update To cell for the Area Code field.

4. Run the query by choosing Run from the Query menu or by clicking the Run button on the toolbar. Access displays a confirmation dialog, telling you how many records will be updated. Click Yes to run the query and update the records.

SORTING DATA

? **How can I sort records if I used the asterisk to drag all the fields to the query?**

To sort on a field, that field must be included individually in the QBE grid. However, you can avoid dragging all the fields individually. Just drag the field you want to sort on into the QBE grid, in the column beside the one containing the asterisk. This means the field is in the query twice: once as part of the asterisk selection of all fields, and once in the column you just added. Turn off the Show box for the field (so that it doesn't appear in the resulting dynaset twice), and choose the desired sort order from the Sort row.

? **I'm sorting on a combination of fields and I want the first field used for the sort to appear in a different column of the query's dynaset instead of at the left of the other fields used for the sort. How can I do this?**

Fields that you use for a primary sort order must be the leftmost fields, but there's no law that says you can't place the same field in the QBE grid twice. So a way around this problem is to add the field for the sort at the left side of the QBE grid, and turn off the Show check box for that field. Then add the same field again at the desired position in the QBE grid, and leave the Show check box turned on in that column.

? **The records in my dynaset aren't being sorted properly. What's wrong?**

Incorrect sorts in queries are virtually always caused by an improper arrangement of the fields used for the sort within the QBE grid. When you are sorting on more than one field, the fields must be arranged from left to right in *order of precedence*, because Access sorts multiple columns according to this left-to-right order of precedence. Among a group of sorted fields, the leftmost field gets the highest priority in a sort, followed by the field to its right, followed by the next field to the right, and so on. Suppose you wanted to sort a group of records in a mailing list by state; where states are the same, by city; and where cities are the same, by last name. In such a case, the State field would need to be to the left of the City field, and the City field would need to be to the left of the Last name field, as shown here.

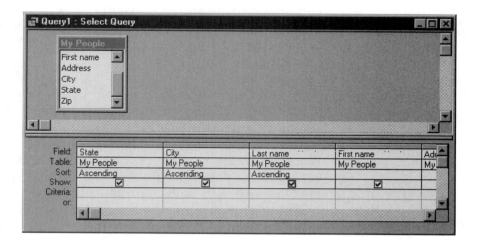

You can drag fields around within the QBE grid to achieve the desired order of precedence when sorting on multiple fields.

 Note: Another common sorting problem is caused by poor data entry training. If the person who entered the data learned to type on a typewriter, the record may contain the letter "l" (ell) instead of the number "1" (one), or the letter "O" (oh) instead of the number "0" (zero).

CALCULATIONS

What are calculated fields, and how can I add one to a query?

Besides having fields that are a normal part of a table's design, you can also include *calculated fields* in an Access query. Calculated fields are fields containing data that is the result of calculations involving other fields. Calculated fields are usually based on numeric or date fields that are in the same table. You can create a calculated field in a query by entering an expression in an empty cell in the Field row of the QBE grid. The expression that you enter is what performs the calculation. You can precede the expression with a name and a colon: if you do so, that name will be used for the field name in the resulting dynaset. If you omit a name and a colon, Access will name the field **ExprN**, where **N** is a numeric value starting with 1 for the first calculated field used and incrementing by 1 for each calculated field in the query.

As an example, if the query contained fields for Sale Price and Quantity Sold, you could create a calculated field named Total Cost by entering an expression like this one in an empty cell of the Field row:

Total Cost:[Sale Price] * [Quantity Sold]

When the query runs, Access would multiply each of the values in the Sale Price field by the corresponding values in the Quantity Sold field to produce the new values, which would be stored in the field named Total Cost. Table 5-1 shows examples of expressions that could be used to create calculations.

Tip: Calculated fields can also be used to concatenate, or combine, text strings. To do so, use the concatenation operator (&) as part of the expression. As an example, you could create a calculated field in a query that would combine the Last name and First name fields into a single name using an expression such as **[First name] & " " & [Last name]**. When you enter

Table 5-1

Calculation type	Result
Sum	Total of values in a field
Avg	Average of values in a field
Min	Lowest value in a field
Max	Highest value in a field
Count	Number of values in a field (null values are not counted)
StDev	Standard deviation of values in a field
Var	Statistical variance of values in a field
First	Value from the first record in the underlying table or query
Last	Value from the last record in the underlying table or query

long expressions to perform calculations, you can see the entire expression without scrolling, by pressing SHIFT-F2 to show the expression within the Zoom box.

? How can I include **calculations** in my queries?

Often you may want to perform calculations on groups of records. While you can obtain totals in reports, you can also do this in your queries. You can obtain the following types of calculations in your queries:

- Totals
- Averages
- Maximum or minimum values
- A count of the numbers of values
- Standard deviation
- Variance (which is the square of standard deviation)
- First value in a field
- Last value in a field

Because you obtain calculations based on groups of records, you need to decide how you want to group the records in your query and include those fields that will be necessary to group the records in the query. To perform calculations in the query, open the query in Design view and choose Totals from the View menu (or click the Totals button on the toolbar). When you do this, the Totals row appears in the QBE grid, and the designation "Group By" appears in every field of the query. Click within the Group By row in any desired field to open a list box of available calculation types, and choose the desired type, as shown in Figure 5-2. Once you've chosen the desired type of calculation, you can run the query, and the calculation will appear as a result.

? Can I use a calculation to **convert text** in a text field to all uppercase, or to all lowercase?

You can convert the case of text in a query's resulting dynaset by using the Ucase() and Lcase() functions within the query criteria. The Ucase() function converts text to all uppercase, while the Lcase() function converts text to all lowercase. You

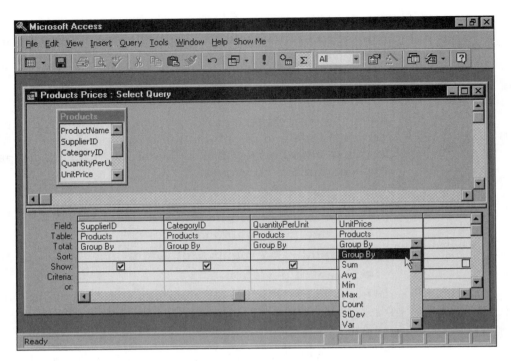

Figure 5-2: A QBE grid containing calculations

enter Ucase(*fieldname*) or Lcase(*fieldname*), where fieldname is the name of the existing field. Since this use of an expression will result in the column of the dynaset being named Expr: followed by your expression, you may want to give the column a new name by adding that name, followed by a colon, and then the function. As an example, if you wanted to capitalize all the text in a field named First name, you could enter an expression like this in the Criteria row of the QBE grid:

Firstname:Ucase([First name])

Note that if you use the trick shown here of providing an alternative name followed by a colon, you can't use a name that's the same as the existing field. If you do so, Access will display an error message warning you of a circular reference in the expression.

? **My query includes a calculated field that subtracts two Date/Time fields.** **However, the calculated field displays fractional numbers instead of times. How can I see the times?**

The fractional number that you see in the field is the serial value Access uses to represent a date or time. As you enter dates and times into Date/Time fields, Access stores the values internally as serial numbers, which can then be used in calculations. The integer part of the value you see in the calculation represents the number of days between the two dates, and the fractional value represents the portion of the day that passed between the two times entered.

If the values you are subtracting result in a difference that is *always less than one day in length*, there's an easy solution to the problem. You can simply change the format for the calculated field to display the value in Date/Time format. Click in the calculated field in the QBE grid. Click the Properties toolbar button, or choose Properties from the View menu to display the Field Properties for the calculated field. Click in the Format property, and type the characters **hh:mm:ss** into the property. Although this isn't one of the choices in the drop-down list, Access will accept the value and apply it to produce correct times.

If the calculated value may be more than one day in length, the solution gets considerably more involved. You'll need to create a function in Visual Basic for Applications and use that function in the expression for the calculated field. The function creates a string out of the time information stored as a fractional number. Use these steps to create this procedure:

1. Click the Modules tab in the Database window.

2. Click New.

3. Type the following code into the Module window that appears:

```
Function HrsMinsSecs(TimeVar As Double)
Dim Hrs As Long, Mins As String, Secs As String
If IsNull(TimeVar) Then
    HrsMinsSecs = Null
```

```
Else
  Mins = Format(DatePart("n", TimeVar), "00")
  Secs = Format(DatePart("s", TimeVar), "00")
  Hrs = (Fix(TimeVar) * 24) + DatePart("h", TimeVar)
  HrsMinsSecs = Hrs & ":" & Mins & ":" & Secs
  End If
End Function
```

4. Close the Module window. When asked whether you want to save the module, answer **Yes** and enter any name desired for the module.

5. Open the query in Design view, click in the Field cell for the calculated cell, and enter
   =**HrsMinsSecs(***value to convert***)**
   For this example, you might enter
   =**HrsMinsSecs([Last Date]−[First Date])**

6. Click the Datasheet View button to display the query's dynaset. The calculated field should now display as a time with the HH:MM:SS format. For example, if Last Date equals 12/25/98 22:30 and First Date equals 12/24/98 18:00, this function displays the result as 28:30:00 instead of 1.1875.

? I created a calculated field that divides two numbers, but the results don't show any **decimal places**, though they should. What's wrong?

There are two reasons why your calculated field may not show any digits to the right of the decimal place: using the wrong operator or using the incorrect DecimalPlaces property setting.

To find the cause of this problem, switch back to Design view for the query. Make sure that you used the forward slash (/) as the division operator in your formula, instead of the backslash (\ ). Among the Access operators, the backslash (\ ) is the symbol for *integer division*. This operator divides two integers and returns an integer result. If the values you divide with the backslash have decimal values, Access rounds them and then performs the division. Hence, 234.56\21.34 is the same as 235\21. If this is the cause of your problem, simply change the backslash to a forward slash (/), and the formula should work correctly.

If the problem isn't an incorrect operator, you may have set the DecimalPlaces property to zero. To check this, click in the calculated field while in Design view, and choose <u>P</u>roperties from the <u>V</u>iew menu. If the DecimalPlaces property is set to 0, change the entry to the desired number of decimal places.

? Can I get a query to return a specific number of the highest or lowest values in a field?

You can do this by changing the Top Values property for the query. (Doing so also can make your queries appear to run much faster if you are querying large amounts of data.) You can use the Top Values property to create a query that returns a specific number of the highest or lowest values in a field. As an example, you could create a query that returns the records of your top five salespeople. Use the following steps to do this:

1. Create the query to select the records you want included.

2. Sort the query by the field from which you want to select the top or bottom records. If you want to select the largest values in that field, sort in descending order. If you want to select the smallest values, sort the field in ascending order.

3. Open the Query Properties sheet by clicking the Properties toolbar button or by selecting <u>P</u>roperties from the <u>V</u>iew menu. If you see Field Properties at the top of the window, click an empty area of the query design.

4. Click in the Top Values property, and choose the desired option from the list, as shown here. For example, choose **5** to have the query return the top five values or **25%** to have the query return the top 25 percent of the values. You can also enter a different specific value, either as a number of records or as a percentage.

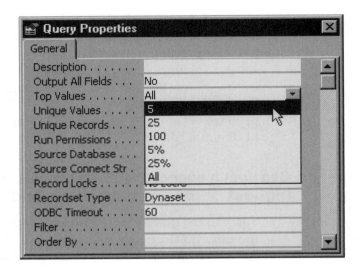

5. Click the Datasheet View toolbar or choose Data<u>s</u>heet View from the <u>V</u>iew menu to display the query's dynaset.

My query's calculated field displays too many places to the right of the decimal. How can I limit the decimal places it shows?

You can control the number of decimal places displayed in a number field of a query by changing the properties for that field. Use these steps:

1. Click the Design View toolbar button, or choose <u>D</u>esign View from the <u>V</u>iew menu to switch to Design view for the query.

2. Move to the calculated field whose decimal places you want to limit.

3. Choose <u>P</u>roperties from the <u>V</u>iew menu, or click the Properties button in the toolbar.

4. Click in the Format property, and choose one of the formats from the drop-down list.

5. Enter the desired number of decimal places.

6. Click the Datasheet View toolbar button, or choose Datasheet View from the View menu, to return to the query dynaset. You will see only the selected number of digits after the decimal point.

❓ How can I **round** the results of a calculation from four decimal places to two, so I can use the rounded results in another expression?

If you just needed to control how many decimal places appear in the Datasheet view, you could change the Decimal Places property. However, since you want to use the calculation again later, you need to control the actual number. To do this, combine the Val and Format functions. For example, enter

Val(Format(*expression*,"#.00"))

The Format property extracts the number by using only two decimal places. However, in the process, the Format property converts the number into text. The Val function converts the text back into a number.

❓ Why do I get **rounding errors** when I create a calculated field by using fields with the Currency format?

The calculated field is not inheriting the Format property of the table field. Therefore, the results of the calculated field often round improperly. You can correct this by changing the calculation you are using. (The following steps assume that you want to round to two decimal places.)

What you need to do is multiply the result of your calculated field by 100, then use the Int function to truncate the number (removing the decimal places), and finally divide the number by 100, giving the correct result. You can then use the Ccur() function on the resultant value to convert it back into a currency amount. In doing this, you are nesting the formula for the calculated field within another formula. To make the final formula easier to read, you may want to create two calculated fields, your original one and the one that does this. For example, if your calculated field is called Profits1, the new field's entry might be **Profits:Ccur(Int(Profits1*100)/100)**.

? **A calculated field in my query is based on a Number field that has a Scientific Format property. Why does the field in the resulting dynaset appear using a General format?**

Access does support *property inheritance* from the existing fields of underlying table to queries. Hence, the properties set for the fields in a table are automatically applied to those same fields used in queries. When a Number field uses a Scientific format in a table, it uses the same format in a query.

The problem with calculated fields is that they are not real fields, so they cannot support property inheritance from tables to queries. To format a calculated field correctly in the query, you need to set its Format property directly. To change this property, click in the calculated field in the QBE grid. Click the Properties toolbar button, or choose Properties from the View menu, to display the Field Properties for the calculated field. Click in the Format property, open the drop-down list, and select Scientific.

TROUBLESHOOTING

? **When I try to run my query, I get a message saying "Can't group on fields selected with '*'." What can I do?**

Here are some of the reasons you might get this message:

▷ The Output All Fields property is set to Yes. You will need to go into the properties for the queries and make sure that the Output All Fields property is set to No.

▷ The QBE grid for a crosstab query includes a * in the Field row. Remove the * from the QBE grid.

▷ You tried to change a select query into a crosstab query, and the QBE grid already has a * in the Field row. Remove the * before you change the query into a crosstab query.

▷ You are trying to execute a SQL statement that has an aggregate function or Group By clause as well as an *. Change the SQL statement to remove the asterisk, aggregate function, or Group By clause.

? **After I deleted the Format property settings for a field in my query, it still uses the same format instead of the one assigned in the table. What can I do?**

If the dynaset does not display data using the current property settings, Access has failed to refresh the display type for the query. To force Access to display the data properly, save the query, close it, and reopen it. When you reopen the query and run it again, Access will display the data according to the current property settings for the query.

? **Why do I get an "Out of Memory" error when I run my query, even though my computer has plenty of memory?**

When you get this error when trying to run a complex query, Access isn't complaining about any limitation of installed memory in your PC. The message actually refers to a shortage of memory in an internal amount of program space that Access sets aside to compose all the expressions used in your queries. In earlier versions of Access, this space was limited to 64K. In Access 97 and in Access 95, the old 64K limit has been replaced with a dynamic limit that provides more room, but it's still possible to build a query that is too complex to run. You can reduce the complexity of queries by using these steps:

➤ Remove any unneeded fields from the query.

➤ Shorten table names and column names.

➤ Minimize the expressions used in underlying queries.

➤ Avoid stacked queries: situations where query 1 and table 1 provide data to query 2, and query 2 and tables 2 and 3 provide data to query 3, and so on. Where possible, replace stacked queries with a single query that performs the operation.

Advanced Queries

Answer Topics!

Advanced Queries
@ a Glance

The previous chapter discussed general questions about queries, basic select queries, action queries, and parameter queries. This chapter covers more advanced areas involving the use of Access queries, including SQL-specific queries like the Pass-Through query.

Select queries are fairly straightforward, because they simply select the records to display in response to a question that you pose. The more advanced queries provide new options and new challenges. You'll find answers in this chapter to questions in the following areas:

➤ **Displaying Data** Answers in this area deal with unusual methods to control the ways in which data is displayed or edited in your queries.

➤ **Parameter Queries** Here you'll find answers that let you structure parameter queries to obtain more specific results, such as allowing for partial string searches.

➤ **Relational Queries** This part of the chapter provides answers regarding relational queries: queries that let you retrieve data from more than one table at a time.

➤ **Crosstab Queries** This portion of the chapter provides answers to questions about crosstab queries, which are used to provide a cross-tabulation of numeric data.

➤ **SQL and Programming** The answers provided in this portion of the chapter explore the advanced query topics of using SQL statements to directly manipulate data on a database server, and the use of Visual Basic for Applications (VBA) code to manipulate queries.

➤ **Working with Calculations** These answers detail how to use calculations in queries to obtain more varied and unusual results.

➤ **Troubleshooting** The answers in this part of the chapter help you deal with unexpected error messages and other general problems when using queries.

DISPLAYING DATA IN QUERIES

? **Is there a way to display all fields from a query's underlying tables without adding them all to the QBE grid?**

You can display all the fields without manually adding them by setting the query's OutputAllFields property to Yes. Use these steps:

1. Open the query in Design view.
2. Click in any blank area of the query, outside of the QBE grid.
3. Open the View menu and choose Properties to display the Properties window for the query.
4. Set the OutputAllFields property to Yes.

? **I want to display my query's dynaset but prevent edits. Can I do this without setting security on the query object?**

You can accomplish the same result by creating a form that displays your query as a datasheet with the form's editing capabilities disabled. Use these steps:

1. In the Database window, select the query and choose AutoForm from the New Object button on the toolbar to create a form that includes all the fields from the query.
2. Switch to the form's Design view.
3. Display the Property list for the form (open the View menu and choose Properties).
4. Set the Default View property to Datasheet.
5. Set the Views Allowed property to Datasheet.
6. Set the Allow Edits, Allow Deletions, and Allow Additions properties to No.
7. Save the form.
8. Now when you look at data through the form, you will see a datasheet containing data from the query. You cannot edit the datasheet.

▓▓▓▓▓▓ *Tip:*   If you are worried that users will open the query and not the form, you can copy the SQL statement from the query and paste it into the form's RecordSource property. Then you can delete the query, and the form still shows the correct data in its datasheet.

PARAMETER QUERIES

? **I want to create a parameter query in which users only have to enter part of a Text field's entry. Can I do this?**

Presumably, you want to create a parameter query in which the user does not have to enter the complete entry to have Access find matches. For example, you can enter part of a name when responding to the prompt for the parameter, but have the query return all records that include your response, even when it's only part of the name. You can do this by concatenating the * wildcard and the parameter value.

For example, suppose you want to find matching entries in your First Name field. You might enter the following criterion in the Criteria row:

Like [Enter first name:] & "*" Or Is Null

This criterion matches any entries with the complete parameter value or with the complete parameter value and trailing text. For example, if the user enters **Jo** in response to the parameter, Access searches the First Name field and returns all records containing "Jo" alone, or "Jo" combined with all other text (such as John, Joan, and Joseph).

Specifying "Or Is Null" allows the user to enter no parameter value and retrieve all records, including ones that have no entry for that field.

? **I want my parameter query to select all records when a user doesn't specify parameters. How can I do this?**

In parameter queries, users are prompted to supply entries each time you run the query. The entries often provide criteria. This lets you create a query with criteria that

change every time. For example, your parameter query
could present the invoices for a single week. The dates the
user enters determine which week's invoices are included in
the dynaset.

To produce a parameter query that displays all records
when no criteria are supplied, you need to create a criterion
that uses the wildcard character. This query either uses
the value provided by the user or matches everything. For
example, your criterion in the QBE grid might look like this:

Like "*" & [Enter a value:] & "*"

If the user does not enter a value to match, then the
criterion matches all entries in that field because of the *
wildcard character. If the user does enter the value, the
criterion matches only those values. The wildcard character
is ignored because the value entered is the entire content of
the field. When you run the query, you see a prompt like the
one shown here. If you type **Johnson**, the query's criterion
equals Like "*Johnson*". If you do not type anything, the
criterion equals Like "**".

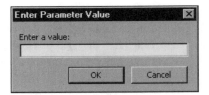

Can I create a parameter query that returns all records in which the Text field's entry starts with the **single letter** the query prompts for?

Yes, you can create a parameter query that returns all
records in which the entries in a Text field start with a single
letter provided by the user. You do this by combining the
letter entered with the * wildcard character for that field's
criterion. For example, you can make this entry in the
QBE grid:

Like [Enter first character:] & "*"

This criterion matches any entries starting with the letter
the user enters.

RELATIONAL QUERIES

? ### How do I **create a relational query?**

You can use a query to draw relationships between two or more tables. Here are the steps you'll need to do this:

1. Click the Queries tab in the Database window, then click New.

2. In the New Query window that appears, click Design view, then click OK. When you do this, a new Query window appears, containing a Show Table dialog box as shown.

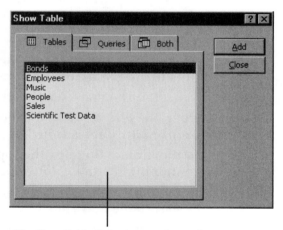

The Show Table dialog box can be used to add multiple tables to a query design.

3. In the Show Table dialog box, add each table needed in the query by selecting the table and clicking the Add button (or by double-clicking the table).

4. Create the relational joins needed between the tables by dragging the common field from one table to another. Once you do this, lines appear connecting the common fields in the tables. (If the database has default relationships set at the database level, Access will add the join lines automatically.)

5. Add the needed fields to the query by dragging the field names from the Field Lists to the columns of the query.

6. Add any needed sorting and selection criteria to the query design.

7. Save and run the query.

Tip: If you add more than two tables to a query, the join lines may cross in ways that make the relationships hard to follow. You can rearrange the Field Lists as desired to make the join lines easier to see.

Is there a way to join tables when one of the tables is in a different database?

You can join tables from different databases in a single query by linking to the table that's in the other database. Do this using the following steps:

1. Make the Database window the active window.

2. Open the File menu and choose Get External Data, then choose Link Tables from the next menu that appears.

3. In the Link dialog box that opens, find the database containing the table you want, and click Link.

4. In the Link Tables dialog box that appears next, select the desired table and click OK.

The linked table from the other database appears in the Database window of the current database, and you can use it along with the existing tables and queries while designing your relational query.

I can **edit some fields** in my relational query, but not others. Why?

There are some limitations in editing data through relational queries. If you've added referential integrity at the database level, you won't be able to edit any key fields used in the query that are on the "one" side of a one-to-many relationship.

? How can I create a relationship based on **more than one field** in a table?

You can create relationships based on multiple fields in a query's design. If no single field will work as a primary key, you can base the primary key on a combination of fields. The combination of fields, taken together, must uniquely identify each record in the table. For example, here a relationship between tables is based on a combination of last name and first name fields.

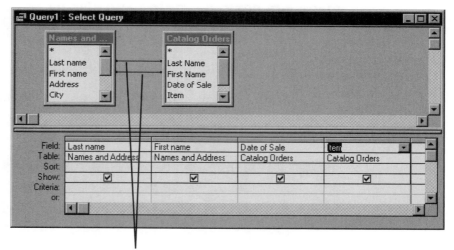

Combination of fields are linked to establish a relationship

This scheme would work as long as no two entries have the same name. To create the relationship, just drag and drop the fields from one table to the matching fields in the other table, one at a time.

? Why does my relational query fail to run while displaying the message "query contains ambiguous **outer joins**"?

Occasionally, Access gets confused when you join multiple tables and you define one of the links as an outer join. When this happens, Access displays the above error message. The way around this is to break the query into two queries, and use those two queries as the basis for the desired query. As an example, you could link the two tables with the outer join in one query and call it Query One, then create a second query containing the equi-joins and call that Query Two. Finally, you could create a query and add Query One and Query Two as data sources to that query, establishing the needed link between the related fields.

? **I want to use a query to show the relationship between employees and their managers, but all the employees and managers are in a single table. How can I do this?**

What you need to create is a type of join called a *self-join*. In Access, you create a self-join by adding the same table to the Query window twice, then linking one field to another field in the same table.

As an example, Figure 6-1 shows a self-join, with the Manager field in a table of employees related to

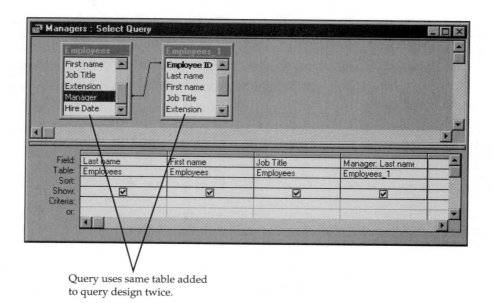

Query uses same table added
to query design twice.

Figure 6-1:   Example of a self-join in a query design

the Employee ID field in the same table. (Both the Manager field and the Employee ID field contain a 3-digit ID number used to identify each employee.) To show the employees and their managers, the name fields from the first Employee field list have been placed in the QBE grid, and the Last Name field from the second Employee field list (representing the manager's name) has also been placed in the QBE grid. (The field for the manager's name has been renamed by adding the label "Manager" and a colon ahead of the actual field name.) The resulting dynaset, shown in Figure 6-2, shows all employees and their managers.

? **I want to view all records in a relational query, including the ones that don't have a match between the two sides of the relationship. How can I do this?**

What you want to do is change the *join type* used for the query. By default Access makes any relationship you create in a query an *equi-join,* which is one of three possible join types (the others are *left outer join* and *right outer join*). With equi-joins, records appear only when the related field in one table matches an entry for the related field of the other table.

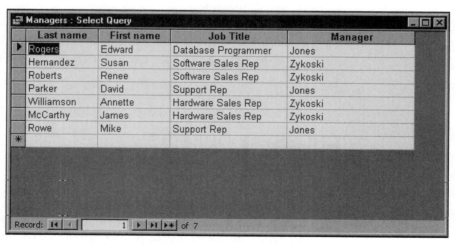

Figure 6-2:   The dynaset that results from a self-join

You can change the join type by performing these steps:

1. Open the relational query in design view.

2. Double-click the join line between the tables (or right-click on the line, and choose Join Properties from the shortcut menu). When you do this, the Join Properties dialog box appears, as shown here.

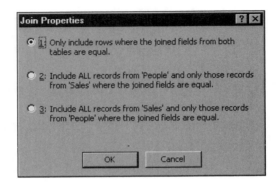

3. If you want a left outer join (a join that includes all records in the first table, whether records in the second table have a match or not), turn on the second option in the dialog box.

4. If you want a right outer join (a join that includes all records in the second table, whether records in the first table have a match or not), turn on the last option in the dialog box.

5. Click OK.

CROSSTAB QUERIES

How can I **cross-tabulate** numeric data?

The easiest way to cross-tabulate numeric data in Access is to create a query by means of the Crosstab Query Wizard. As an example of a crosstab, Figure 6-3 shows one table with a group of sales amounts for television sets, along with the results of a crosstab query that summarizes those sales by sales rep.

You can create a crosstab query by performing these steps:

1. Click the Queries tab in the Database window, then click New.

2. In the New Query dialog box that appears, select Crosstab Query Wizard, then click OK. When you do so, the first Crosstab Query Wizard dialog box appears, as shown in Figure 6-4.

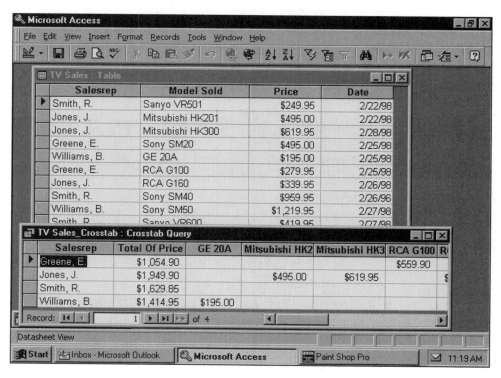

Figure 6-3:   A set of numeric data and the results of a crosstab of that data

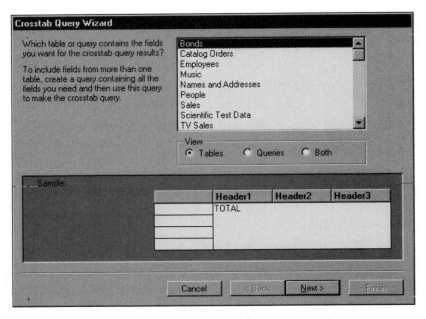

Figure 6-4:   The first Crosstab Query Wizard dialog box

3. In the list box, select the table or query that is to serve as the source of data for the crosstab, then click Next.

4. In the next dialog box that appears, choose the fields that should be used as row headings in the crosstab, then click Next.

5. In the next dialog box that appears, choose the fields that should be used as column headings. Select each desired field, then click the right arrow button to add the field to the list of column headings. When done selecting the column headings, click Next.

6. In the next dialog box that appears (Figure 6-5), choose the field or fields containing the numbers you want calculated at each column and row intersection. At the right side of the dialog box, choose the desired type of calculation. When done, click Next.

7. In the final dialog box that appears, enter a name for the query, then click View to view the query's dynaset.

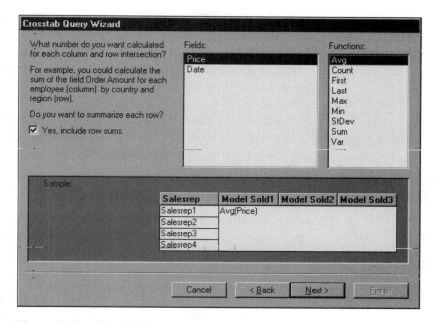

Figure 6-5:   The dialog box for fields and calculation types

? **When I press SHIFT-F9 in my crosstab query, it doesn't requery the underlying table to reflect changes. How can I get my crosstab query to display up-to-date information?**

A crosstab query displays a static snapshot of data rather than a dynamic dataset. It captures the data to show in the crosstab query at the moment when you show the crosstab's datasheet. This means that is does not automatically update when you change the data in the underlying table. To redisplay up-to-date information, close the query and reopen it.

? **Can I turn my crosstab query into a table?**

Yes, you can convert a crosstab query into a table. To do so, create the crosstab query and open it in Design view. Then convert it into a make-table query by opening the Query menu and choosing Make Table. Next, enter the name of the new table in the Table Name text box which appears, and click OK. Note that the table is not created until you run the query by choosing <u>R</u>un from the <u>Q</u>uery menu, or by clicking the Run button in the toolbar.

≡ *Note:*   The table you create with a converted crosstab query does not use the same layout as the crosstab query's Datasheet view. Instead, it presents the records as if you had converted the crosstab query into a select query, using the usual datasheet orientation and none of the summarizing available within the crosstab query.

 ### Why can't I **update** my crosstab query?

A crosstab query cannot be updated. A crosstab query produces a *snapshot* instead of a dynaset. A snapshot is a static picture of a set of records. You can edit the data in a dynaset; you cannot edit the data in a snapshot. This is simply a feature of how Access works and cannot be worked around. When you try to edit a crosstab query, the status line displays "This recordset is not updatable."

SQL AND PROGRAMMING

How can I use Visual Basic to **change the underlying SQL statement** a query uses?

You can use VBA code to change the SQL statement behind a query, thereby causing the underlying record source for the query to change. As an example, the following VBA code changes the underlying SQL statement for a query named Sales 98, so that the query selects all records in the table named Sales:

```
SELECT *
FROM Sales;
```

How can I **create** a pass-through query?

A pass-through query is a query that sends SQL commands directly to a database server according to the ODBC (Open Database Connectivity) standard. A pass-through query lets you work with tables on a database server without attaching the tables to an Access database. A pass-through query can also run procedures stored on the database server. You can use a pass-through query to change data in the database being edited, to create a database object, or to perform an action similar to an action query. You do this by entering the correct SQL commands for the desired actions, and these commands are passed directly to the database server. Since Access doesn't process the commands in a pass-through query, you need to use the syntax that the server expects when you enter the commands to send to the server. Use these steps to create a pass-through query:

1. Click the Query tab in the Database window, then click New.

2. In the New Query dialog box that appears, click Design View, then click OK. A new Query window opens, with the Show Table dialog box above it.

3. Click Close in the Show Table dialog box to avoid adding any field lists to the Query window.

4. Open the Query menu and choose SQL Specific, then select Pass-Through from the next menu that appears. A blank SQL Pass-Through Query window opens.

5. Enter the commands you want to send to the database server via the ODBC driver.

6. Open the Property window for the query by clicking the Properties toolbar button or by opening the View menu and choosing Properties.

7. Move to the ODBCConnectStr property and specify the information needed to connect to the database server. You may be able to enter this information by clicking the Build button and making selections.

8. Select Yes for the Return Records property if you want to get information back from this query or No if you just want to execute the commands without returning any information.

9. Choose Run from the Query menu or click the Run button in the toolbar to run the query.

≡   *Note:*   If you leave the connection string entry in the ODBCConnectStr property blank, Access prompts you for connection information each time you run the query.

Do I have to **link to the SQL tables** I want to work with in a pass-through query?

No, you do not have to link to the tables you want to work with in a pass-through query. This type of query allows you to work with the tables by using their server rather than Access.

Can I convert the pass-through query into a **make-table** query?

No, you cannot. If you convert a pass-through query to any other type of query, it loses its SQL statement. The query no longer produces a result.

▪▪▪▪▪   *Tip:*   If you want the data from a pass-through query placed in a table, create a separate make-table query that uses the pass-through query as its source of data.

How can I **print the SQL statement** for each of my queries?

Access converts all of your queries into SQL statements before they are run. To print the SQL statement for each of your queries, you use the Documentor feature built into Access. Use these steps:

1. Open the Tools menu and choose Analyze, then choose Documentor from the next menu that appears.
2. In the Documentor window, click the Queries tab.
3. Click Select All to report on all the queries.
4. Click Options.
5. Clear all the check boxes except SQL and select the Nothing radio buttons for both Fields and Indexes.
6. Click OK twice to create the report. The beginning of the report looks like the window shown in Figure 6-6.

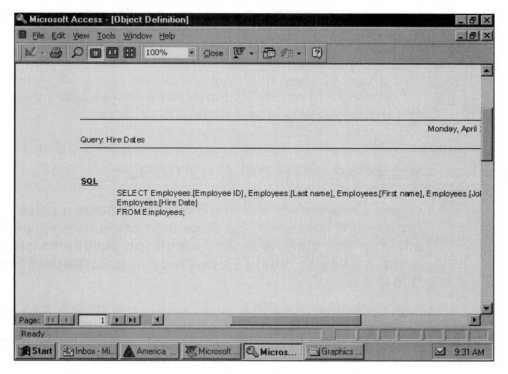

Figure 6-6:   A report containing SQL statements created with the Documentor

In the report, each query's SQL statement appears on a separate page.

❓ When I try to run a pass-through query, I get a **timeout error**. What can I do?

By default, Access waits 60 seconds to get a complete response to your pass-through query. If the response is not complete, it returns a timeout error. This is to prevent you from waiting a very long time for the result of the query. If you suspect that your pass-through query will take longer than one minute to run, open the query's property sheet. Move to the ODBC Timeout property and enter a new number of seconds to wait. If you set the property to zero, Access never prevents a timeout error.

? **Can I update the records returned by a pass-through query?**

No, you cannot edit the records returned by a pass-through query in Access, nor can you enter new ones. The data is a snapshot returned by the database server, rather than a dynaset of data in an Access table.

WORKING WITH CALCULATIONS

? **I need a calculated field in a query that shows a sales tax amount only when the State field contains a specific entry for one state, and shows zero for any other states. Is there a way to create a conditional calculation like this in a query?**

You can use the IIf() (Immediate If) function in a calculated field of a query, on those occasions when you want to perform a calculation in one way for some records and in another way for others. The syntax for this function is:

IIf(*condition,true,false***)**

where *condition* specifies the test you want to use to determine how to perform the calculation. *True* specifies the results you want if the condition is true, and *false* specifies the results you want if the condition is false. *Condition* is an expression, and *true* and *false* can be values, fields, or expressions.

As an example, if you wanted a calculated field in a query to display a sales tax of 6% of the Price field if the State field contained "NY" and zero for any other state, you could use an expression like this one in the Field row of a blank column:

Sales Tax:IIf([State]="NY",([Price]*0.05),0)

After entering the expression in the field of the query, you could change the formatting property of the field to Currency or Standard.

? **My query has separate date and time fields, but I want to use a parameter query to select records based on a combination of the date and time. How can I do this?**

You need to add a calculated field to your query that you use to select records, but which does not display. The query's parameters supply entries for this field. For example, create a calculated field by entering **New Time:[Date Field] & " " & [Time Field]** in the Field row, assuming your date and time fields are named Date Field and Time Field. Next, enter a criterion for this field, including the parameter prompts for where you want the dates and times placed. For example, you can enter **Between [Enter beginning date and time] and [Enter ending date and time]**. If you don't want this field displayed in the resulting dynaset, remember to clear the check box in the Show row of the QBE grid. When the query is run, the query prompts for the beginning and ending dates and times.

Tip: If you are uncertain that the query's user will correctly enter the dates and times, you can have separate parameter prompts. The criterion can join the dates and times, as in **Between [Enter beginning date] + [Enter beginning time] and [Enter ending date] + [Enter ending time]**.

? **My calculated fields are displaying numeric amounts that are actually dollars and cents, but the numbers appear as decimal values like "02.5." Is there a way to change the format for the display of a calculated field?**

You can change a calculated field's display in a query by changing the Format value in the Property window for that column in the QBE grid. Use these steps to do this:

1. Open the query containing the calculated field in Design view.

2. Open the View menu and choose Properties.

3. While the Properties window is open, click in the column that contains the calculated field.

4. In the Field Properties window, click the General tab if it isn't already visible.

5. Click in the Format property, and click the down arrow that appears to open the list box.

6. Choose the desired type of format from the list. If you want to see the calculations as currency amounts, choose Currency.

? **I need to calculate both a sum and an average for the same field, but I can choose only one calculation type from the list box in the Total row of the QBE grid. How can I obtain calculations of more than one type for the same field?**

When calculating totals, you can add the same field to the QBE grid more than once to obtain as many totals as you need. Once you choose Totals from the View menu to show the Totals row in the QBE grid, you can add any field more than once and choose the appropriate type of calculation in the Total row for each calculation type you need. As an example, Figure 6-7 shows a query's design with a Totals row, and totals based on Average, Minimum, and Maximum values have been added for the same field.

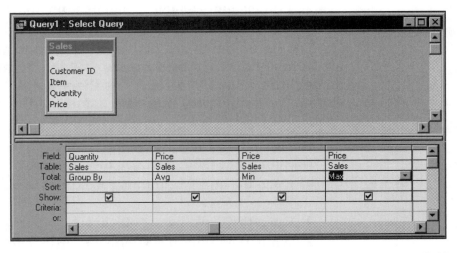

Figure 6-7:   A query design with different types of totals for the same field

TROUBLESHOOTING

? **Can my query extract just the day, month, or year from a Date field?**

You can do this by creating a calculated field containing the Day(), Month(), or Year() functions to extract just the day, month, or year, but there's an easier way. Create a custom format for the date field in the query that displays the element of the date that you want. Table 6-1 shows several custom formats you can use to do so, and the results of applying each format to the date December 8, 1998. To apply a custom date format, click anywhere within the field while in Design view, open the View menu and choose Properties, and click in the Format property. Enter the desired format, as shown in the table. The next time you run the query, you will see the new formats.

Tip: You can also use these custom formats as the Format property setting for report and form controls.

? **My queries print with a header and footer. Can I get rid of them?**

Yes, you can print your query from Access without including the default header and footer (which include the query name, the current date, and the page number). Run the query to display the data in a dynaset, open the File

Table 6-1:   Custom formats for limiting dates

Format	Returns
DD	08
DDD	Sun
DDDD	Sunday
MM	12
MMM	Dec
MMMM	December
YY	98
YYYY	1998

menu, and choose Page Set<u>u</u>p. In the Page Setup dialog box that appears next, turn off the Print Headings check box, then click OK. Finally, choose <u>P</u>rint from the <u>F</u>ile menu to print the data without the headings.

? My relational query is returning an impossibly **large number of records.** What's wrong?

With relational queries, this happens if you add multiple tables to the design but leave out one of the join lines between matching fields. Access then links every record in one table with every record in the other, resulting in what's called a *Cartesian product,* or cross product, of the two tables. To fix the problem, add the missing join line by dragging the field from the Field List of one table to the matching field of the other table.

? My query asks me for a **parameter,** but I didn't create it as a parameter query. What's wrong?

This problem usually occurs when you misspell a field name in the QBE grid. The problem can also occur if you have a field in the QBE grid that refers to a calculated field. If the field is performing a calculation based on a calculated field, make sure the Show check box for the calculated field is turned on in the QBE grid.

? My query runs too slowly. How can I improve the **performance** of my query?

Besides upgrading hardware (the common but expensive solution to slow performance), there are some steps you can take to speed up your queries. You can try any of these suggestions:

➤ Run the Performance Analyzer to obtain suggestions on how you might redesign your query to improve its performance. Open the <u>T</u>ools menu and choose Analy<u>z</u>e, then select <u>P</u>erformance from the next menu. In the dialog box that appears, click the Queries tab, turn on the check box beside the query you want to analyze, and click OK. If the Performance Analyzer is able to suggest any possible improvements to the design of your query, it will display these in a dialog box.

▷ In queries using multiple tables, try to index the fields on both sides of the join.

▷ Index fields as much as possible, and try to use indexes on any fields that contain selection criteria.

▷ Compact the database on a regular basis. Compacting a database speeds up queries, because it reorganizes records so that they are placed adjacent to each other by order of the primary key.

▷ Redesign queries that use the NOT IN operator, because Access has a hard time optimizing the use of NOT IN.

I get an error message about **S_Generation** when I try to run a query. What does this mean?

Access occasionally displays this message when you run an append query based on more than one table, and the query contains an asterisk in the Field Row to select all fields from one of the tables. Delete the asterisk, and add each field from the Field List individually to the QBE grid.

Why do my queries retrieve **too many columns**?

Open the Tools menu, choose Options, and click the Tables/Queries tab in the dialog box that appears. Under Query Design, make sure the Output All Fields option is turned off. (With this option turned on, every field appears in a query dynaset, whether you want it to or not.) This setting in Tools/Options won't change the corresponding setting for a query that you've already created. To change that setting, open the query in Design view, click in any blank area of the query outside of the QBE grid, open the View menu, and choose Properties. In the Query Properties window that opens, set the Output All Fields option to No.

? **When I try to run a query, I get a "type mismatch" error message. What's wrong?**

This error occurs when you try to use criteria that are of a different data type than the data stored in the underlying fields of the table. For example, if a table's field contains numbers and you type the criterion **"twenty"**, you see the error, because Access interprets the criterion as a text value and not as a number. If you enter the value as a numeric amount (such as **20**), the query works.

You also get this error if you include the dollar sign ($) in criteria you specify for a currency field. Remove the dollar sign to solve the problem.

Basic Forms

Answer Topics!

Can I add a button so that I can easily **add new records**?

How can I **center a form automatically** each time it opens?

Can I make one of the **command buttons** the default button?

Can I **disable the Datasheet view**?

Can I prevent users from **editing in a single control**?

How can I **filter the display of records**?

Can I **find a record by the record number**?

Can I **move between the header and detail sections** without using the mouse?

Can I **open any form** by selecting it by name?

Can I quickly **open a form** I use regularly?

Can I add a button to **print just the current record**?

Can I **prevent users from doing anything else** within Access while a form is open?

Can I easily create a **report based on the form**?

Can I **sort the records** viewed through my form?

How can I fix the **tab order**?

Can I change the title in the **title bar**?

Can I calculate a **total for one record**?

My form is **blank**. Why can't I see any data?

Why can't I **edit data** in my form?

Why does #**Error** or #**Name** appear in a control?

Why does my form run so **slowly**?

Basic Forms
@ a Glance

An Access form shows and lets you enter your data. You can create a form from a table or query, or combine data from a number of sources. Forms have a wide variety of controls that display data or add visual interest to the form.

You'll find that forms are especially important when you create an application for inexperienced users. With careful design, you can create forms that guide users through the steps to enter, edit, and get data from your database. Well-designed forms also limit the possibility of data error. The questions you'll see throughout this chapter cover the following areas:

➤ **Form Design**   In this area, you'll find answers to questions about common design techniques used with forms that display data from a single table or query.

➤ **Form Usage**   This portion of the chapter answers questions that arise about working with forms in common ways, such as providing the data that you want.

➤ **Troubleshooting**   In this part of the chapter, you'll find answers to problems that arise when using forms.

FORM DESIGN

 Should I base my form on a table or on a query?

Because Access lets you base forms on tables or queries, some advance planning may be a wise idea to make effective use of forms. If you intend to use the form to examine data from multiple tables, if you need to examine a selected subset of data, or if you want to sort the records in a particular order, base the form on a query. If you intend to use the form to examine any or all of the records in a single table, base the form on the table.

Note: When you base a form on a query, Access runs the query as the form opens. Hence, forms based on complex queries or on queries that process data from large tables can be slow to open.

 How can I quickly create a form?

The fastest way to create a form is to make use of the AutoForm menu option of the New Object toolbar button, shown here.

The AutoForm option builds a default single-column form for whatever table or query is selected at the time that you click the button. You can quickly build a default form with these steps:

1. In the Database window, click the desired table or query.
2. Click the down arrow to the right of the New Object button in the toolbar, and choose AutoForm from the menu that appears.

When you do this, Access builds a default form for the table or query. An example of such a form is shown in Figure 7-1.

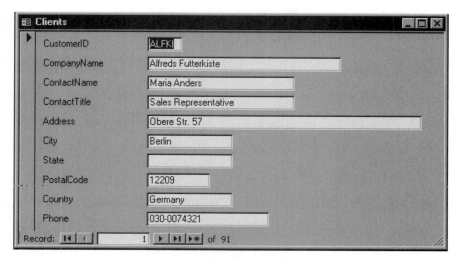

Figure 7-1:   An example of a default form created with the New Object toolbar button

What's involved in **creating a form with the Form Wizards**?

Like other Access wizards, the Form Wizards step you through the process of form creation by asking a series of questions about the desired forms. These are the steps you use to build a form with the Form Wizards:

1. In the Database window, click the Forms tab.
2. Click New to display the New Form dialog box.
3. In the Select a Table/Query portion of the dialog box, choose the desired table or query that you want to base the form upon.
4. Click Form Wizard in the list box, then click OK.
5. Follow the directions in the Wizard dialog boxes that appear. In the last dialog box, click Finish to begin entering or viewing data using the completed form.

What's involved in **creating a form manually**?

With the manual method of form design, you open a blank form and add desired fields and other design objects (labels, graphics, lines, and boxes) to the form at the desired location. These are the steps you'll need to create a form manually:

1. In the Database window, click the Forms tab, then click New.

2. In the New Form dialog box that appears, choose the name of the table or query that will provide data to the form.

3. Click Design view in the list box, and click OK. Access displays a blank form in Design view, as shown in Figure 7-2.

4. Add the desired objects (fields, labels, graphics, and any other types of controls) to the form. You can add fields by dragging them from the Field List to the form. To add other types of controls to the form, use the Toolbox. Click the desired tool in the Toolbox, and click in the form at the desired location to place the control.

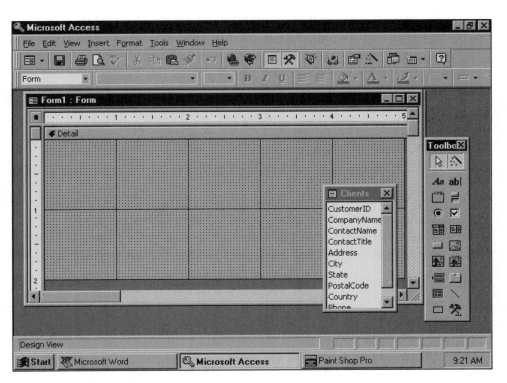

Figure 7-2:   A blank form in Design view

Design Tips for Forms

A perennial danger with any database is that users will enter data incorrectly. By carefully designing the forms that others use to enter, edit, or review data, you can avoid many problems. Some things to consider when designing a form are the following:

- ➤ If users will be entering data from a specific source, such as a paper form, match your form's design to the paper counterpart. Users are more likely to enter data correctly if they don't have to search for each piece of it.

- ➤ Use rectangles and lines to group sets of controls. That way, users enter related data (such as all of a product's identification information or an entire address) together.

- ➤ Don't crowd the controls together, making them hard to read. Users need to be able to identify easily which control they are working with.

- ➤ Make sure that the text on the form is meaningful and concise. Two text box controls labeled "Name" won't help a user enter an employee's first and last name correctly.

- ➤ Use validation rules to help ensure that entries occur in a logical range. For example, if you know that billing rates in your company vary from $50 to $300 an hour, you can assign validation rules to the Hourly Rate control to prevent a $5,000 entry.

- ➤ Use input masks on standardized entries. For example, since you know exactly how many characters are needed to enter a phone number, an input mask like the one you use in tables can make that entry easier.

- ➤ Use formatting to make numbers easier to read. It's easier to see that the salary of 1453920.20 is wrong when it looks like $1,453,920.20.

Tip: If you open a blank form and the Field List does not appear, you can choose Field List from the View menu to display it. Choose Toolbox from the View menu to display the Toolbox for adding controls other than fields.

5. Save the completed form by choosing <u>S</u>ave from the <u>F</u>ile menu.

? How can I add the current **date or time** to a form?

You can add the date or time to a form with these steps:

1. Open the form in Design view.
2. Open the <u>I</u>nsert menu, and choose Date and <u>T</u>ime. The Date and Time dialog box appears as shown here.

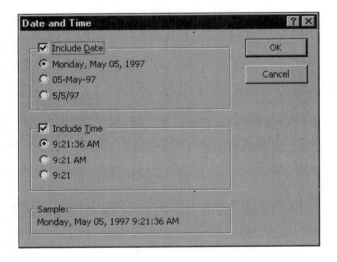

3. To include a date, turn on the Include Date check box, and choose a desired date format.
4. To include a time, turn on the Include Time check box, and choose a desired time format.
5. Click OK. The date or time field appears in the form, and you can drag it to its desired location.

? How can I add **graphics** to a form?

Graphic images as design elements can easily be added to forms using Windows cut-and-paste techniques. (This answer assumes that you want to add a graphic as a frame. If you want to use the graphic as a background for the form,

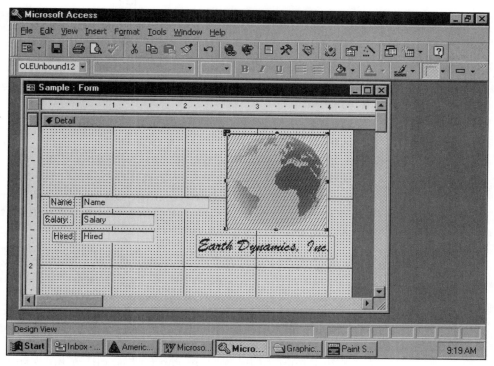

Figure 7-3: An example of a graphic placed in a frame in a form

see the question dealing with using an image of your own as a form's background, later in this portion of the chapter.) You can use the Unbound Object Frame tool of the Toolbox to insert an object, but if all you need is a graphic, it is usually easier to paste the graphic from the other Windows application. When you paste a graphic selection from another Windows program into a form's design, it automatically appears in an unbound object frame, and you can move or size the frame as desired. (Figure 7-3 shows the use of a graphic inside a frame in a form.)

You can use the following steps to paste a graphic into a form as a design element:

1. Open the desired form in Design view.

2. Switch to the graphics program you are running under Windows, and open the document containing the desired graphic.

3. Using the selection techniques applicable to the graphics program you are using, select the desired portion of the graphic.

4. From the graphics program's menus, open the Edit menu and choose Copy to copy the graphic to the Windows Clipboard.

5. Switch to Access (you can click the button labeled Microsoft Access on the Taskbar).

6. Click in the section of the form where you want the graphic to appear, open the Edit menu, and choose Paste.

7. Use the moving and sizing techniques common to form and report design to size the graphic and move it to the desired location in a form.

■■■■   *Caution:*   Before you resize an image, be sure that the Size Mode property for the frame containing the image is set to produce the effect you want. Clip keeps the image at the same size and shape, but some of its content can be lost both horizontally and vertically; Stretch keeps all the content of the image, but its shape can change; Zoom keeps the shape of the image, but some of its content can be lost either horizontally or vertically.

▦   *Tip:*   If you don't need to edit the graphic by means of OLE, you can convert it into a bitmap. You'll save on resources, and the form will open faster. Right-click the frame, choose Change To, and choose Image from the next menu.

? **Is there a way to hide the scroll bars or the record selectors that normally appear on a form?**

For small forms, or for forms that are to be used specifically for adding data, you may want to hide the scroll bars, the record selector buttons at the left edge of the form's window, or both. You can easily do this by opening the Properties window for the form (open the Edit menu and choose Select Form, then open the View menu and choose Properties), and setting either the Scroll Bars property or the Record Selector property, both found on the Format tab. With the Scroll Bars property, you can choose Both, Neither, Horizontal Only, or Vertical Only. With the Record

Selector property, your choices are Yes to display the record selectors or No to hide them.

How can I keep controls **horizontally or vertically aligned** as I move them?

You can keep controls aligned if you use the SHIFT key as you move them. When you hold the SHIFT key as you begin to move a control, the control moves horizontally or vertically, but not in both directions at once. Hence, you could keep horizontal alignment of a control while moving it vertically by selecting the control, holding the SHIFT key, and dragging the control vertically.

Can I use an **image of my own as background** for my form instead of the patterns the Form Wizards supply?

You can specify a graphic file as a form's background. Figure 7-4 shows an example of a form that uses a bitmap as the background for the form.

You can use files in .BMP, .ICO, .DIB, .WMF, or .EMF formats. You specify the file to be used as the background in the form's Picture property. Use these steps:

1. Open the form in Design view. If the form is already open, choose Select Form from the Edit menu to select the entire form.

2. Open the View menu and choose Properties to display the Properties window for the form.

3. Click the Format tab.

4. In the Picture property, enter a path and filename for the image file. (You can click in the property and then click the Build button at the far right to open an Insert Picture dialog box where you can locate a file.)

5. In the Picture Type property, specify whether the picture should be embedded or linked. (If you embed it, the image gets stored with the form, and your Access database increases in disk size to store the image— possibly by much more than the size of the image in the original file. If you link it, a link is created to the original file, and you must make sure the original file stays in its present location.)

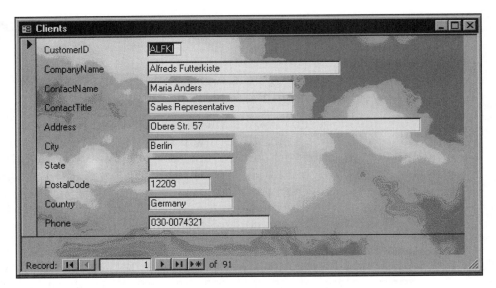

Figure 7-4:   A form using a bitmap as a background

6. In the Picture Size Mode property, choose Clip, Stretch, or Zoom as desired. (Clip displays the image at actual size, Stretch changes both the size and shape of the picture to fill the window completely, and Zoom resizes the picture to fit either the height or the width of the window, without distortion.)

7. If you want to change the alignment of the image, choose a desired setting in the Picture Alignment property.

8. If you want to repeat the image across the background of the form, set the Picture Tiling property to Yes.

9. Save the changes to the form. When you view the form in Form view, the image appears as a background in the form.

?   **How can I change the label of a control from the default that Access assigns based on the field name?**

If you wish to change the text within a label, click the label to select it, then click inside the label. When you do so, an insertion pointer appears within the text, and you can type the new text and use the BACKSPACE and DEL keys as needed to delete existing text.

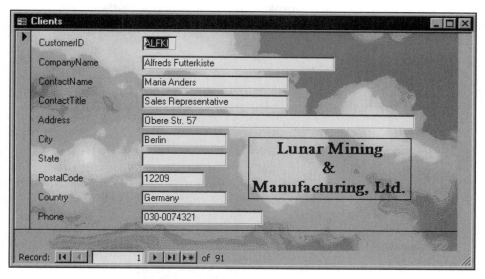

Figure 7-5:   An example of a label added to a form as a title

❓ How can I add a **label to a form**?

Besides fields, you will typically need to include text that's not attached to any object on forms. Such text may be descriptive or explanatory text, such as that used in titles or captions. Unattached text is added to forms with the use of a label tool. Figure 7-5 shows an example of a label in a form, used in this case as a title heading.

You can create a label with the following steps:

1. Open the form in Design view, and display the Toolbox (if it is not already visible).

2. Click the label tool.

3. To create a label that is automatically sized as you type, click where you want to start the label, and then type the label's text. Or, to create a label of any size, click where you want the label to start, drag the pointer until the label is the size you want, and then type its text.

❓ How can I add **lines or rectangles** to a form?

To add lines or rectangles to a form, click in the Toolbox on the Line or Rectangle buttons. Click in the form wherever you want to draw the line, and hold the mouse button. Move the pointer to wherever you want the line or rectangle to end. Release the mouse button, and the line or rectangle will appear on the form.

? How can I **manually add controls** to a form?

For manually designing forms, the Field List offers the easiest way to add controls based on fields. Click the Field List button in the Form Design toolbar or choose Field List from the View menu to display the Field List, shown here. Then, to create a control that displays data from the field, drag the field from the list to the desired location on the form.

To create a label, click the Label tool in the Toolbox. (If the Toolbox isn't visible, choose Toolbox from the View menu to display it.) Then on the form, click where you want to place the label; type the text for the label; and press ENTER.

To use a wizard to create a control (such as a list box or a combo box), make sure the Control Wizards tool in the Toolbox is pressed in. Next, click the tool for the type of control you want to create, and click in the form at the desired location for the control. Follow the directions in the wizard dialog boxes that appear.

? How can I **modify the colors** of a form?

It's very easy to change a form's colors in Access 97. Use these three steps:

1. Right-click a blank space in the form.

2. Choose Fill/Back Color.

3. Choose the color you want from the popup menu.

 Note: If a picture has been applied to the background of the form, the new color will not be visible. You can't have a background picture and a background color in effect at the same time.

? How do I **move** controls?

To move a control, first select it, then move the pointer near the edge of the control. When the pointer changes into an outstretched palm, drag the control to the desired location. To move a control apart from any attached label, first select the control (or label) by clicking it. Then place the pointer on the move handle (it is larger than the sizing handles and is in the upper-left corner of the control). When the mouse pointer changes to a hand with a pointing index finger, drag the control to the desired location.

? How can I change an **option button to a text box,** or vice versa?

You can change an existing control to another type of control. Open the form in Design view, and select the control you want to change. Then open the Format menu, choose Change To, and then choose the type of control you want to change to in the submenu.

? Is there a fast way to change the **overall appearance of a form?**

You can change the overall appearance of an entire form by changing the form's AutoFormat property. Open the form in Design view, click the AutoFormat button in the Form Design toolbar, and choose a new format from the dialog box that appears.

? How can I add a **page break** to a form?

In forms that will be printed often, you can add page breaks to indicate where one printed page should end and

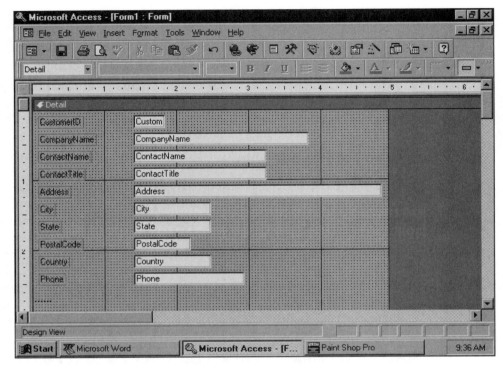

Figure 7-6:   A page break added to a form

another page should begin. To add a page break, perform the following steps:

1. In the Design view of the form, open the Toolbox if it isn't already open (choose T̲oolbox from the V̲iew menu).

2. Click the Page Break tool in the Toolbox, and then click the form where you want the new page to begin. The page break appears in the form's design as a short dotted line, as shown in Figure 7-6.

❓ Can I **prevent users from adding new records** in my form?

You can use the Allow Additions property of the form to prevent users from adding new records. To do so:

1. Open your form in Design view.

2. Display the Properties window for the form by clicking the Properties button in the toolbar, or by choosing Properties from the View menu.

3. Click the Data tab.

4. Move to the Allow Additions property and set it to No.

5. Save the form, and then switch back to Form view. You can no longer add records using this form.

❓ Can I **prevent users from updating records** in my form?

Yes, you can easily prevent users from updating the records displayed in your form by setting the Allow Edits and Allow Deletions properties to No in the form's Design view. This prevents users from editing the contents of controls that are bound to a table or query. Use these steps:

1. Open your form in Design view.

2. Display the Properties window for the form by clicking the Properties button in the toolbar or by choosing Properties from the View menu.

3. Click the Data tab.

4. Set both the Allow Deletions and Allow Edits properties to No.

5. Save the form.

❓ How can I **print the data in a form** without printing all the records in the underlying table?

To print the data without printing all the records in the underlying table, you need to select the desired record within the form and then print just the selection instead of all pages. Use these steps:

1. Open the desired form in Form view.

2. To print a single record, find the desired record, then click the Record Selector bar at the left edge of the form, or open the Edit menu and choose Select Record.

3. Open the File menu and choose Print. When you do so, the Print dialog box appears. Click Selected Record(s) in the Print Range portion of the dialog box.

4. Set any other desired options in the dialog box. Then click OK to begin printing.

? Is there a quick way to **select every control on a form** so that I can move them as a group?

You can quickly select every control on a form by displaying the form in Design view, and then choosing Select All from the Edit menu (or pressing CTRL-A). (You can deselect all selected controls by clicking anywhere outside of a control.)

? How do I change the **size of a control**?

To resize a control, select the control; move the pointer to any of the control's sizing handles (the eight small boxes that surround the control); and drag the handle until the control is the desired size.

? How can I change the **size of my form**?

You can increase or decrease the height of form sections individually, but the entire form has just one width. If you change the width of just one section, you change the width of the entire form. (Also remember that you can try changing the size of the window to fit the form while in Form view.) Use these steps to change the size of your form:

1. In the form's Design view, change either the height or the width by placing the pointer on the bottom edge or right edge of the section. The pointer changes to a double-headed arrow.

2. Drag the pointer up or down to change the height of the section.

3. Drag the pointer left or right to change the width of the section, as shown in Figure 7-7.

4. To change both the height and width of a form at the same time, place the pointer in the lower-right corner

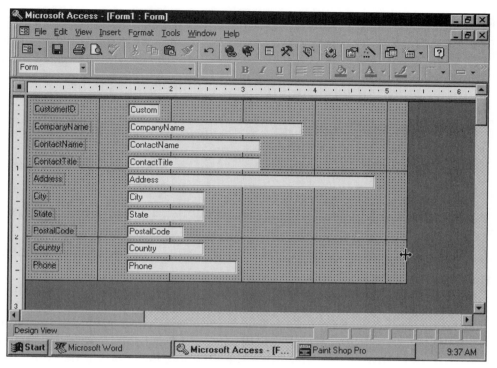

Figure 7-7:   Changing the height or width of a form

of the section, until the pointer takes the shape of an arrow with four heads. Drag the pointer in any direction to adjust the size of the form.

? Is there a way to change the **spacing of the grid** used in form design?

You can change the grid spacing (the number of dots per square inch or per square centimeter). To do this, open the form in Design view, and open the Edit menu and choose Select Form. Next, open the View menu and choose Properties. Click the Format tab, and change the Grid X and Grid Y settings. The higher the numbers, the finer the grid.

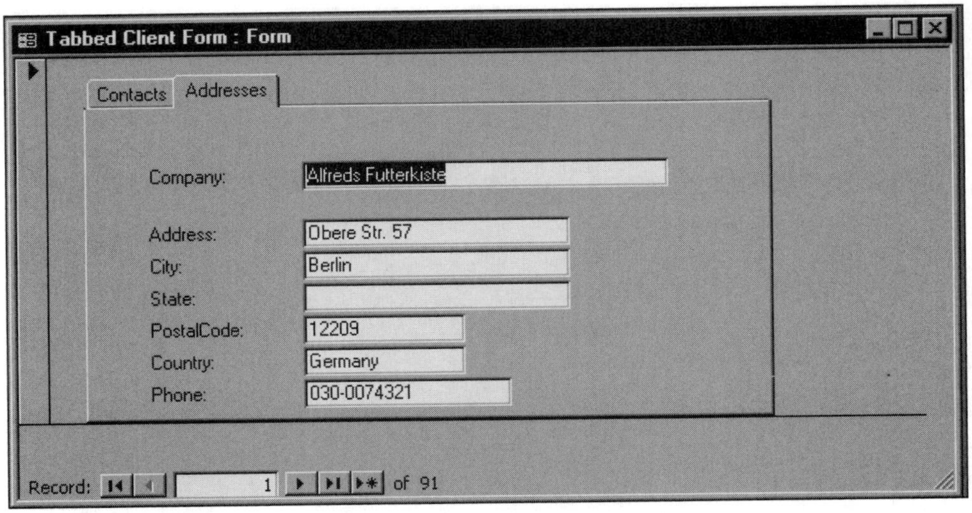

Figure 7-8:   The use of a tabbed form in Access

❓ How can I create **tabbed forms** in Access?

You can use the Tab control of the Toolbox to create tabbed forms that resemble the tabbed dialog boxes used in many programs designed for Windows 95. Figure 7-8 shows the use of a tabbed form; in this type of form, different controls are placed on each tab of the form.

Use the following steps to create a tabbed form:

1. Create a new form in Design view.

2. Click the Tab control in the Toolbox. (If the Toolbox isn't visible, choose Toolbox from the View menu to display it.)

3. In the form, click at the point you want to place the upper left corner of the tab control, and drag to the desired location for the lower right corner of the control. When you release the mouse button, Access creates a tabbed control containing two tabs, as shown in Figure 7-9.

4. Add the desired controls to each tab by first selecting the tab, then dragging fields from the Field List to the tab or adding controls from the Toolbox.

5. To change the name of a tab, double-click the tab to open its Properties window, click the Format tab, and enter a desired name in the Caption text box.

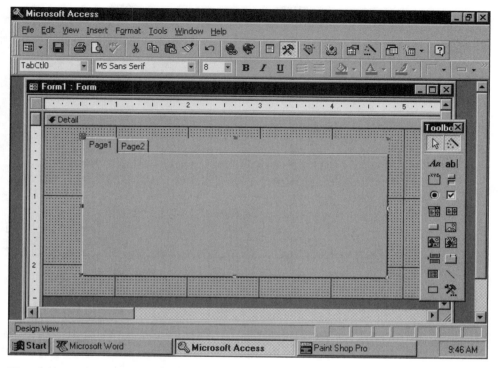

Figure 7-9:   A new tabbed control

6. To add more tabs, select the tab that the new tab should appear after, and choose Tab Control Page from the Insert menu.

USING FORMS

How can I add **buttons to perform tasks** (like printing or closing the form) to a form?

Command buttons can be added to forms in Access for numerous common tasks. These include records management (navigating to records and updating them), opening and closing forms, and printing forms and reports. You can add a command button to perform tasks such as these by performing the following steps:

1. In the Design view of the form, turn on the Control Wizards if they are not already on (click the Control Wizards tool in the Toolbox until it is highlighted).

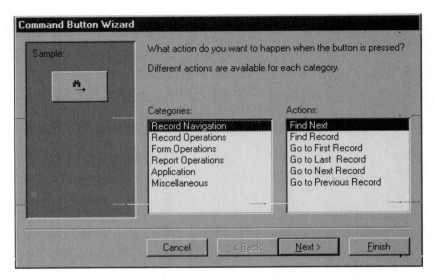

Figure 7-10:   The first Command Button Wizard dialog box

2. Click the Command Button tool in the Toolbox.

3. Click in the form where you want to place the command button. In a moment, Access displays the first Control Wizards dialog box for a command button, shown in Figure 7-10.

4. Follow the steps outlined in the wizard dialog boxes. (The exact steps will vary, depending on what action you want the button you place to perform.) In the last dialog box that appears, click the Create button to display the command button while in Design view.

Can I add a button to a form to move to the end of the table so that I can easily **add new records**?

Yes, you can easily create such a command button in your forms. In fact, Access will give you a hand in doing this with the Command Button Wizards. Use these steps to add this button to the form's design:

1. Open the form in Design view.

2. If the Control Wizards are turned off, click the Control Wizards button in the Toolbox to turn them on (the button should look pushed in).

3. Click the Command Button tool in the Toolbox.

4. Click in the form at the location where you want the button to appear. In a moment, the first Command Button Wizard dialog box appears, as shown earlier, in Figure 7-10.

5. In the Categories list box, choose Record Operations. In the When Button is Pressed list box, choose Add New Record.

6. Click Finish.

7. Right-click the new button, and choose Properties to display the Properties window for the button.

8. Click the Event tab.

9. Move to the On Click property, and then click the Build button at the right. The form's Module window opens and displays the event procedure created by the Command Button Wizard.

10. Move to the end of the line that reads DoCmd GoToRecord , , AcNewRec and press ENTER.

11. Type **Forms![**_form name_**]![**_control name_**].SetFocus** where _form name_ is the name of your form and _control name_ is the name of the first control in your tab order.

Now when you select the button in the form, Access moves you to a new blank record and moves the focus to the first control in your tab order; that is, the user begins entering information in that control.

? How can I **center a form automatically** in the Access window each time it opens?

You can do this by setting the Auto Center property for the form to Yes. Open the form in Design view, and choose Properties from the View menu. Click the Format tab in the Properties window that opens, and set the Auto Center property to Yes.

? How can I make one of the **command buttons** on a form the default button?

You can make any command button the default button by changing its Default property. Open the form in Design view, right-click the desired button, and choose Properties. Click the Other tab, and set the Default property to Yes.

? How can I **disable the Datasheet view** (or the Form view) for a form?

You can disable users' ability to switch between Form view and Datasheet view for any form. Use the following steps to do this:

1. Open the form in Design view.
2. Choose Properties from the View menu, to open the Properties window for the form.
3. Click the Format tab.
4. Set the Views Allowed property to Form if you want to disable the viewing as a datasheet, or to Datasheet if you want to disable the viewing as a form.
5. If you set the Views Allowed property to Datasheet, set the Default View property to Datasheet.
6. Save the form.

? I know how to make an entire form read-only. But how can I prevent users from **editing in a single control**?

Access gives you the ability to restrict editing in a form at the control level, by changing the editing properties for the control. In Design view, right-click the desired control; choose Properties; then click the Data tab in the Properties window that opens. If you want to make the data readable but prevent editing, set the Locked property to Yes. If you want to disable the control so that it is dimmed and cannot receive the focus (that is, so that the user cannot get to the control by clicking on it or tabbing), set the Enabled property to No.

? How can I **filter the display of records** while using a form?

You can use a feature called *filter by form* to restrict the records you can view in a form. Use these steps to do so:

1. Open the form in Form view.
2. Click the Filter by Form button on the toolbar. Or open the Records menu, choose Filter, then choose Filter By Form.

3. Click in the field for which you want to enter a criterion that records must meet to be included in the filtered records.

4. Enter the criterion you want to use to select the records, or choose an entry from the drop-down list. (You can do this using more than one field, if needed.)

5. If a search based on an "Or" criterion is desired, click the Or tab that appears at the bottom of the form, then choose another entry from the drop-down list.

6. Click the Apply Filter button in the toolbar, or open the Filter menu and choose Apply Filter/Sort.

The form will show only those records meeting your filter criteria. To clear the effects of the filter, click the Remove Filter button on the toolbar, or open the Records menu and choose Remove Filter/Sort.

Tip: If you want to find records where a check box, toggle button, or option button is selected or deselected, turn the box or button on or off until it appears the way you want to use to filter the records. To cancel the filtering effects of the box or button, continue clicking the box or button until it is grayed out.

Is there a way I can **find a record by the record number** while in Form view?

It may not be intuitively obvious, but you can easily do this. Click in the Record Number box (between the navigation buttons) at the bottom of the form or press F5. Delete the existing entry, type a new value, and press ENTER to go to that record.

Can I **move between the header and detail sections** of a form without using the mouse?

Yes, while in Form view you can press F6 to move between sections of a form. (This assumes that the header contains one or more controls. If there are no controls in the header, Access won't let you move into that section of the form.)

? Can I **open any form** in my database by selecting the form by name from a combo box in another form?

Yes, you can open one form by selecting its name from a combo box in another form. You first need to create a combo box that will display the names of all the forms in your database. Then you need to set up the combo box so that selecting a name from the box opens the selected form. To do this, you use VBA (Visual Basic for Applications).

1. Create the combo box from which you want to select the form to open on the first form.

2. Right-click the combo box and choose Properties to open the Properties window for the box.

3. On the Other tab, enter **ListOfForms** in the Name property of the combo box.

4. On the Data tab, select Value List as the Row Source Type property setting.

5. On the Event tab, move to the On Enter property, then click the Build button at the end of the field.

6. Select Code Builder in the list box that appears, then click OK.

7. Enter the following code:

```
Private Sub ListofForms_Enter()
Dim MyDb As Database
Dim MyContainer As Container
Dim I As Integer
Dim List As String
Set MyDb = DBEngine.Workspaces(0).Databases(0)
Set MyContainer = MyDb.Containers("Forms")
List = ""
For I = 0 To MyContainer.Documents.Count - 1
        List = List & MyContainer.Documents(I).Name & ";"
Next I
Me![ListofForms].RowSource = Left(List, Len(List) - 1)
End Sub
```

8. Close the Module window.

9. Move to the After Update property of the combo box, and click the Build button again.

10. Select Code Builder in the list box that appears, then click OK.

11. Enter the following code:

```
Private Sub ListofForms_AfterUpdate()
        DoCmd.OpenForm Me![ListofForms]
End Sub
```

12. Close the Module window.

13. Open the form in Form view and select a form name from the combo box. The form you select is opened.

? How can I quickly **open a form** that I use on a regular basis?

There are two ways to do this. You can create an Autoexec macro that has an Open action for the form as its first event, in which case the form automatically appears whenever you open the database. The second method is to create a shortcut directly to the form on the Windows desktop.

To create an Autoexec macro that opens the form, create a new macro (click the Macros tab in the Database window, then click New). In the Action column of the macro, choose OpenForm. Under Form Name in the Action Arguments pane, choose the desired form from the list. Save the macro under the name **Autoexec**. From then on, when you open the database, the form will load automatically.

To create a shortcut from the Windows desktop, size the Access application window so that you can see a portion of the Database window and your Windows desktop simultaneously. Then click the Forms tab in the Database window, and drag the desired form onto the Windows desktop. A shortcut to the form appears on the desktop, and you can double-click the shortcut to launch Access and open the form.

Tip: Of the two methods, the first is more advantageous if you want to perform other actions in the macro, such as maximizing the form that you want to open or opening other forms or reports. The second method works best if you don't always want to open the same form; you can add desktop shortcuts for each of your commonly used forms. (If you have a large number of them, you can create a new folder and store the shortcuts inside the folder.)

? **How can I add a button to a form to print just the current record?**

You can use the Command Button Wizards to add a button that prints the current record. You need to be careful about the selection that you make in the wizard dialog boxes to get the desired results, because choosing Form Operations followed by Print Current Form gives you a button that prints every record in the underlying table or query, which is *not* what you want. Use these steps to add a button that prints a single record:

1. Open the form in Design view.
2. If the Control Wizards are turned off, click the Control Wizards button in the Toolbox to turn them on (the button should appear pushed in).
3. Click the Command Button tool in the Toolbox.
4. Click in the form at the location where you want the button to appear.
5. In the first Command Button Wizard dialog box that appears, click Record Operations under Categories, and click Print Record under Actions.
6. Click Next, and follow the directions in the successive wizard dialog boxes to choose a picture or caption for the button. In the last dialog box, click Finish to add the button.

? **How can I prevent users from doing anything else within Access while a form is open?**

You can force users to stay in the form until they close it by setting the form's Modal property to Yes. Use these steps:

1. Open the form in Design view.
2. Open the Edit menu, and choose Select Form.
3. Open the View menu, and choose Properties.
4. In the Properties window which opens, click the Other tab.
5. Set the Modal property to Yes.

? I regularly print data using a form. Is there an easy way to create a report based on the form?

It doesn't get much easier. In the Database window, right-click the desired form and choose Sa<u>v</u>e as Report. In the Report Name dialog box that appears, enter a name for the new report and click OK.

? Can I sort the records viewed through my form?

You can do this through the form, although you are limited to sorting on only one field at a time. Click in the field that you want to sort on; then click the Sort Ascending or Sort Descending button on the toolbar as desired.

Tip: If you want to view the data based on a sort involving more than one field, create a query that sorts your data as desired. Then use the query as the data source for the form.

? When I tab through my form, the tab order isn't from top to bottom. How can I fix this?

This often happens when you add a new field to a form, because Access tabs through the fields in the order in which you added them. When you add a new field, it becomes last in the tab order, regardless of the field's location in the form. Use these steps to change the tab order:

1. Open the form in Design view.
2. Open the <u>V</u>iew menu, and choose Ta<u>b</u> Order. You next see the Tab Order dialog box, shown here.

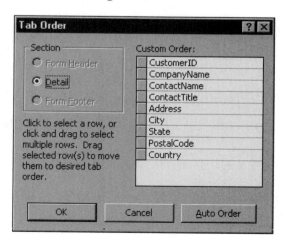

3. Click each field you want to change the order of, then drag the field in the Custom Order List Box into the order you want to move between the fields.

4. Click OK to save the changes.

? How can I change the title that appears in a form's **title bar**?

This title is stored in the form's Caption property. If you don't like the default title that the AutoForm button or the wizard assigns, you can easily change it. Use these steps:

1. Open the form in Design view.

2. Choose _P_roperties from the _V_iew menu, to open the Properties window for the form.

3. Click the Format tab.

4. Under the Caption property, enter a new title.

5. Switch to Form view to see the title.

? How can I calculate a **total for one record** in a form?

You do this by adding a _calculated field_ to the form. The field is simply a text box that performs the necessary calculation. What expression you place in the text box will depend on what fields you are attempting to total. For example, if you wanted to display the total of two fields called **Cost** and **Shipping**, you would use the expression =[Cost] + [Shipping] in the text box. To add the calculated field to the form, use these steps:

1. Open the form in Design view.

2. Click the Text Box tool in the Toolbox.

3. Click in the detail section of the form where you want to place the calculated field.

4. Click in the field, and type the expression needed to calculate the total.

TROUBLESHOOTING

? **My form is blank. Why can't I see any data?**

There are two likely causes for this problem. One is that the form is based on a query that's not returning any data. If the form is based on a query, double-click the query in the Database window to run the query. If it is empty, the form will also be empty. Restructure the query's criteria to provide the needed data.

The other likely possibility is that you are in Data Entry mode. When a form is in Data Entry mode, it displays a blank record you can use to add data. To see all your records, open the Records menu and choose Remove Filter/Sort.

? **Why can't I edit data in my form?**

If you can't edit data in a form, check for any of the following possibilities:

▷ The form was created as a read-only form. If the Allow Additions, Allow Editing, and Allow Deletions properties for the form are set to No, you won't be able to make any additions or changes to the data.

▷ The Locked property for some or all of the controls in the form may be set to Yes.

▷ Another user on a network may be editing the same record.

▷ The form may be based on a table or query that's not updatable (such as a query based on linked SQL tables).

? **Why does #Error or #Name appear in a control in my form?**

This problem can be due to a number of causes. Check for any of these possibilities:

▷ Check for proper spelling of field names in the Control Source property for the control.

▷ If field names used as parts of expressions contain spaces, make sure that brackets surround the field names. As an example, **[Last name]** is a valid reference to a field name within an expression.

▷ If you are using a built-in function as part of an expression, make sure that the syntax is correct, and the arguments are in the proper order.

▷ Make sure any fields named in the Control Source property for the control haven't been renamed or removed in the underlying table or query.

❓ Why does my form run so slowly?

If your form is slow to open and use, you may be facing the natural challenges of working with large amounts of data. You can run the Performance Analyzer, both on the form and on any underlying query, to obtain a report on how you might redesign the form or the query to speed performance. To run the Performance Analyzer, close the form, then open the Tools menu, choose Analyze, then choose Performance from the submenu that appears. Next, turn on the check box for the form or underlying query in the Performance Analyzer dialog box that appears, then click OK. If the Performance Analyzer is able to make any suggestions for the improvement of the form or query design, it will display these in a dialog box.

In addition to using the Performance Analyzer, you can try the following suggestions:

▷ Close any other forms you aren't using.

▷ Avoid the use of bitmaps, graphic backgrounds, or other unnecessary graphics in the forms' design.

▷ If your form has any unbound object frames containing graphic images, convert these to image controls. (In Design view right-click the frame, choose Change To, then choose Image.)

▷ Avoid sorting records in an underlying query unless the order of the displayed records in the form is important.

▷ Index any fields in subforms that are used for criteria in underlying queries.

▷ If records in a subform won't be edited, set the subforms' Allow Additions, Allow Edits, and Allow Deletions properties to No.

chapter

8 Answers!

Advanced Forms

Answer Topics!

Advanced Forms
@ a Glance

The previous chapter discussed general questions about the design and
use of basic forms. This chapter picks up among the more advanced
topics of that same subject. When you want to take the design and
usage of forms past the ordinary, you often run into the kinds of
questions highlighted in this chapter. The questions you'll see here
cover the following areas:

☛ **Form design**   In this area, you'll find answers to questions about
unusual design techniques and accomplishing useful tasks with list
boxes and combo boxes.

☛ **Form usage**   This portion of the chapter answers questions that
arise about working with forms in more complex ways, such as
validation, limiting user manipulation of forms, and exporting data
from forms.

☛ **Relational forms**   In this part of the chapter, you'll find answers
that help you make effective use of *relational forms*: forms that
display data from multiple tables.

☛ **VBA and forms**   The answers provided in this portion of the
chapter explore the use of Visual Basic for Applications (VBA) code
to manipulate forms.

FORM DESIGN

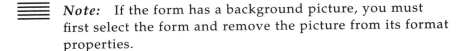

Can I make a form that **changes colors** as I tab through the fields?

You can do this by modifying the BackColor property for the form's detail section through the use of VBA code. Your code would need to be attached to the OnEnter event for each field in the form. You'll also need the numeric values equivalent to your desired colors. The easiest way to obtain these is to look at the value stored in the Back Property entry of the Properties window for any section of a form, once you've changed that section's color in Design view. Once you know the numeric values for the desired colors, do this:

1. Right-click the first field in the form and choose <u>P</u>roperties.
2. In the Properties window that opens, click the Event tab.
3. Click in the On Enter property; then click the Build button at the far right of the property.
4. Click Code Builder in the next dialog box that opens, and click OK.
5. In the Module window that opens, enter code like this:
   Forms![_formname_**].Section(0).BackColor=**_nnn_
   where _formname_ is the name of the form, and _nnn_ is the numeric value of the background color.

Repeat steps 1 through 5 for each field in the form, using a different numeric value for the BackColor property, and save the form. When you run the form, its background color will change as you move through the fields.

Note: If the form has a background picture, you must first select the form and remove the picture from its format properties.

I have a list box with two columns, and I'd prefer that one of the columns remain hidden. Is there a way to hide a column in a list box?

Using the properties for the list box, you can hide any column that you don't want displayed. This can prove useful when you have a list box that's bound to a field, and you want the field's contents hidden. You do this by changing the Column Widths property for the list box so that the width of the column you want to hide is zero. The Column Widths property contains a width value for each column in the box, and the values are separated by semicolons. Hence, a three-column list box would have three values in the property, separated by semicolons. In Design view, right-click the list box and choose Properties to open the Properties window for the box. Click the Format tab, and change the entry under Column Widths. Assuming the list box contained three columns each 3/4" wide and you wanted to hide the second column, you would change the Column Widths property to .75";0;.75".

 How can I add a list box or a combo box to a form?

List boxes and combo boxes are often useful in Access forms. You can use list boxes to present a number of available values from a list, and you can use combo boxes to allow users to enter a value by typing it or by choosing it from a list of items. You can easily add list boxes or combo boxes to forms with the aid of the Control Wizards. Use the following steps:

1. Open the form in Design view.
2. Turn on the Control Wizards in the Toolbox if they are not already on (if the Control Wizards are on, the Control Wizards button in the Toolbox will appear depressed).
3. In the Toolbox, click on the List Box tool if you want a List box, and click on the Combo Box tool if you want a combo box.

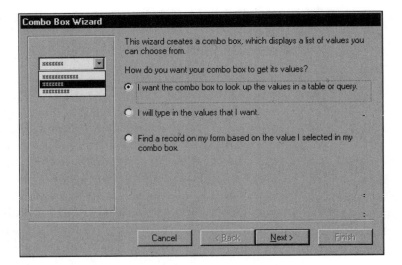

Figure 8-1:   Control Wizard dialog box for placing a
combo box

4. Click in the form where you want to place the control.
   In a moment, Access displays the first Control Wizard
   dialog box for a list box or a combo box, as shown in
   Figure 8-1.

5. Follow the steps outlined in the Control Wizard dialog
   boxes. (These steps will differ, depending on the type of
   box you add and the sources you choose for the choices
   that appear in the list box or combo box.) In the final
   dialog box that appears, click the Finish button to add
   the list box or combo box to the form.

**I print forms regularly to obtain quick reports of selective
data, and most of my forms have command buttons
on them. Is there a way to prevent the buttons from
printing?**

You can prevent command buttons (or any other objects
placed on a form) from printing by changing the Display
When property for the object. Use these steps to do this:

1. Open the form in Design view.

2. Right-click the command button or other object you want to prevent from printing, and choose Properties.

3. In the Properties window which appears, click the Format tab.

4. Set the Display When property to Screen Only.

5. Save the form.

6. Test your changes by printing one page of the form.

How can I change a text label to display as **reverse video**?

Text stands out if you create white text against a black background, an effect also known as *reverse video*. (Figure 8-2 shows a form containing a label with its shading formatted as reverse video.) You can apply this effect to a text label with the following steps:

1. Right-click the label, choose Fill/Back Color from the submenu, and click Black in the color box that appears.

2. Right-click the label, choose Font/Fore Color from the submenu, and click White in the color box that appears.

Figure 8-2:   A form with a text label displayed as reverse video

? Can I create something on my form like the ScreenTips that appear when I point the mouse at a toolbar button?

Yes. This took some doing in earlier versions of Access, which may be why Microsoft added a property that lets you easily create customized ScreenTips for any control on a form. Use these steps to do this:

1. Open the form in Design view.

2. Right-click the control you want to create a ScreenTip for.

3. Choose Properties from the menu that appears, and click on the Other tab of the Properties window.

4. Click in the ControlTip Text property, and type the message you want for your ScreenTip.

5. Repeat this process for any other controls you want to have ScreenTips for.

6. Save the form.

When you open the form and leave the mouse pointer stationary over any control with an entry in the ControlTip property, the custom ScreenTip appears, as shown in the example in Figure 8-3.

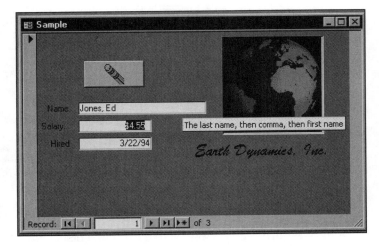

Figure 8-3:   An example of a custom ScreenTip

How can I use a combo box to **search for records** in a form?

You can use the Control Wizard to add a combo box that displays a drop-down list. When the user types a few characters of a search string and presses ENTER, Access finds and displays a matching record in the form. Use these steps:

1. Open the form in Design view.

2. Turn on the Control Wizards in the Toolbox if they are not already on (if the Control Wizards are on, the Control Wizards button in the Toolbox will appear depressed).

3. In the Toolbox, click on the Combo Box tool.

4. Click in the form where you want to place the control.

5. In the first Combo Box Wizard dialog box that appears, turn on the last option, titled "Find a record on my form based on the value selected in my combo box," and click Next.

6. In the next dialog box that appears, add the field you want users to search on, then click Next.

7. In the next dialog box that appears, set a desired width for the combo box column, then click Next.

8. In the final Combo Box Wizard dialog box, enter a desired label for the field, then click Finish to add the combo box to the form.

9. Save and run the form.

As you type part of a search string into the combo box, Access displays matching entries in the underlying table or query. When you press ENTER, the form moves to that record.

 ### How can I create a **shadow box** on a form's controls like the ones created by the Form Wizards?

The shadow boxes that the Form Wizard creates are actually two controls. One control is a text box used to display or edit the data, and the other is a rectangle that serves as a shadow. You could manually create a rectangle, set its background color to gray, and place it underneath the control, but in this latest version of Access there's an easier

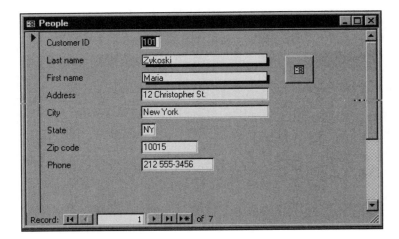

Figure 8-4: The result of the Shadow effect added to the Last name and First name controls

way to give controls a shadow effect. Open the form in Design view, and right-click the control. From the menu which appears, choose Special Effect, then choose the Shadow option from the submenu. Figure 8-4 shows the appearance of two controls with the shadow added using this menu option.

? We have a personnel database with employee photos, and when we paste the photos into an OLE Object field in a form, large parts of the images are cut off. If we make the field substantially larger to accommodate the photos, it takes up too much room on the form. How can we show the entire photo?

You need to change the default setting for the Size Mode property of the OLE Object field. By default this setting is Clip, which clips any image that's larger than the control. Use these steps:

1. Open the form in Design view.

2. Right-click the OLE Object frame used to display the photos, and choose Properties.

3. Click the Format tab.

4. In the Size Mode property, choose Zoom to display the entire object with no distortion, or choose Stretch to size the object to fill the control (some distortion may result).

Tip: If your photos are all the same size, it's usually best to choose Zoom and then resize the field slightly to eliminate any extra blank space in the field when the photos are displayed.

FORM USAGE

Can I let users easily **cancel editing** of a record?

You can add a command button to a form that lets the user cancel edits made to the record; the command button uses a VBA procedure to simulate choosing Undo from the Edit menu. Use these steps to add a button that cancels edits to a record:

1. Open the form in Design view.

2. Turn on the Control Wizards in the Toolbox if they are not already on (if the Control Wizards are on, the Control Wizards button in the Toolbox will appear depressed).

3. In the Toolbox, click on the Command Button tool.

4. Click on the form where you want to place the button.

5. In the first wizard dialog box that appears, select Record Operations, and select Undo Record. Then click Next.

6. In the next dialog box that appears, choose one of the available pictures for the button, or enter text of your choosing to be displayed on the front of the button.

7. Click Finish to add the button to the form.

Can I **close a form** automatically after a certain period of time?

Yes, you can have a form close itself after a certain amount of time. Use the following steps.

1. From the Database window, click the Macros tab and click New to open a new Macro window.

2. Click the drop-down list button in the Action column of the first row of the macro, and choose Close.

3. Open the File menu and choose Save to save the macro (give it any name you want).

4. Open the form in Design view.

5. Open the View menu and choose Properties to open the Properties window for the form.

6. Click the Event tab.

7. Move to the Timer Interval property, and set it to the number of milliseconds that you want the form to stay open. Remember, there are 1,000 milliseconds to 1 second. For example, enter **10000** if you want the form to stay open for ten seconds, or enter **60000** if you want the form open for a minute.

8. Click in the On Timer property, and choose the macro you just saved from the list.

9. Save and close the form.

Now, when you open the form, it displays for the time set in the Timer Interval property, and then it closes.

When I double-click an OLE object in Form view, nothing happens. How do I **edit an OLE object?**

The reason you can't edit the OLE object is that the control's Enabled property is set to No. Access sets the Enabled property differently for OLE objects that are part of the form design versus those stored in a table. The object you double-clicked is probably an unbound OLE object. To edit the unbound OLE object while in Form view, you need to return to the form's Design view. Select the control containing the OLE object, open the View menu, and choose Properties. In the Properties window click the Data tab, move to the Enabled property, and set it to Yes. Move to the Locked property and set it to No. From now on, you can edit your unbound OLE objects in Form view. The bound object frames that display OLE objects stored in a table already have their Enabled property set to Yes.

Tip: You can tell in Form view whether you can edit an OLE object. When you can edit the object, it has black marks (handles) around the inside of the frame after you click it, as you can see here:

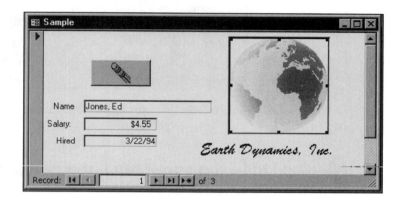

? When I choose Save As/Export from the File menu and export a form's data to an RTF file or an XLS file for use with Microsoft Word or Microsoft Excel, the exported file is missing the data from the subform. What's wrong?

The Export command does not output the data from subforms or subreports. This is simply a part of Access' design and cannot be worked around. If you need the related data that is displayed in the subform, create a relational query that contains the subform fields, then export the results of that query.

? Why doesn't the **header** that I created appear in Form view?

The header that you created was probably a page header. There are two headers available on forms: form headers and page headers. A form header appears both on the screen and when printed, but a page header displays only if the form is printed. The same is true for the page footer.

Tip: To display the Page Header and Page Footer sections, choose Page Header/Footer from the View menu. To display the Form Header and Form Footer sections, choose Form Header/Footer from the View menu.

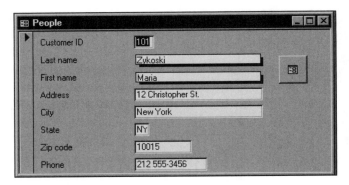

Figure 8-5:   A form lacking scroll bars and navigation
selectors

? Can I **hide the scroll bars and navigation buttons** in my forms?

Yes, on forms you can hide these elements by changing the
Scroll Bars and Navigation Buttons properties. Open the
View menu and choose Properties to display the form's
Properties window. Click the Format tab, move to the
Scroll Bars property, and choose Neither. Then select the
Navigation Buttons property and enter No. When you save
and view the form, your form might look like the example
shown in Figure 8-5.

Besides hiding the scroll bars and navigation buttons, you
can hide the record selectors by setting the Record Selectors
property to No. You can remove the Minimize, Maximize,
and Restore buttons in the upper-right corner of the form by
changing the MinMax Buttons property to None.

Tip: If you want to hide the navigation buttons and scroll
bars on a subform, you must modify the subform's design and
change the properties there. You cannot hide the navigation
buttons and scroll bars for a subform from the Design view for
the main form.

? Can I **prevent users from closing my form** with the Control-menu box?

Yes, in fact, you can remove the Control-menu box from the
Form window. That way you can make sure that users

exit the form only the way you intended. To do so, open the form in Design view. Open the View menu and choose Properties to display the form's Properties window. Click the Format tab, and set the Control Box property to No.

? I use different validation rules for certain fields in my form and the underlying table. Which one actually gets used when I enter data in the form?

Actually, both of them apply when you enter data in the form. Access tests the data you enter using both the form's and the table's validation rules. If the data violates either rule, you can't save the record containing the offending data.

Access evaluates a validation rule when you move the focus to another control or record after entering or editing data. If you leave a field without entering or altering any data, the validation rule is not evaluated. Access also tests entries against the validation rules when you leave the form, switch views, or close the form.

RELATIONAL FORMS

? How do I change the column widths of a subform?

To change the column widths, you'll need to view the subform in Datasheet view. Find the subform by name in the Database window, and double-click it to open the subform. Open the View menu and choose Datasheet View to switch to Datasheet view, then change the width of the columns as needed. Finally, open the File menu and choose Save to save the new column widths.

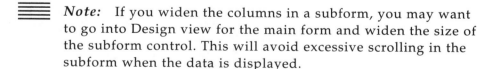

Note: If you widen the columns in a subform, you may want to go into Design view for the main form and widen the size of the subform control. This will avoid excessive scrolling in the subform when the data is displayed.

? ### How can I **create a relational form**, or a form that displays data from more than one table?

There are two ways that you can create relational forms in Access. One way is to create a relational query and then create a form based on the data in that query. (See Chapter 6 for specifics on creating relational queries.) The other way, which is more common with one-to-many relationships, is to create a form containing a subform. The main part of the form displays the records on the "one" side of the relationship, while the subform displays the records on the "many" side of the relationship. Figure 8-6 shows an example of a relational form that uses a subform.

While you can create this type of form manually, the easiest way to create a form with a subform is to use the Form Wizards. (Note that in order to use the Form Wizard to create relational forms, you must first establish default relationships at the table level; see Chapter 4 for specifics

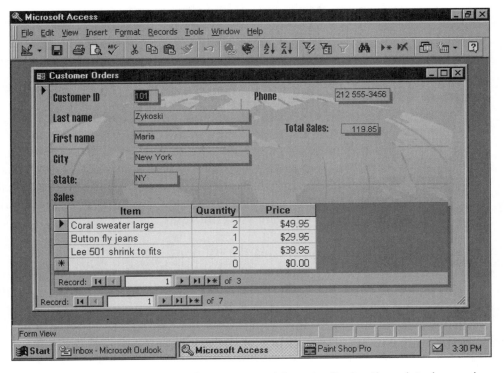

Figure 8-6:   A relational form that uses a subform to display the related records

on creating a relationship.) Use these steps to create a relational form:

1. Click the Forms tab in the Database window, then click New.

2. In the New Form dialog box that appears, click Form Wizard.

3. In the list box at the bottom of the dialog box, choose the table or query that will supply the data for the main form. (This is the data from the "one" side of the one-to-many relationship.)

4. Click OK.

5. In the first Form Wizard dialog box that now appears, choose the fields that will appear in the main part of the form (but don't close this dialog box when done).

6. Click in the Tables/Queries list box, and choose the table or query that will supply the data for the subform. (This is the data from the "many" side of the one-to-many relationship.)

7. Select the fields that are to appear in the subform, then click Next.

8. In the next dialog box that appears (Figure 8-7), make sure that the desired table or query is selected in the

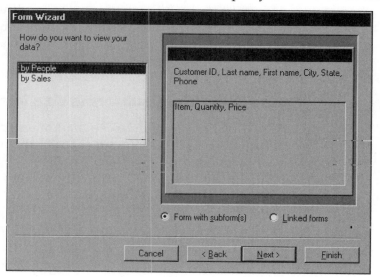

Figure 8-7:   The Form Wizard dialog box asks which table/query should be used to view data

list box for viewing your data in the main form. (The table or query that contains the data for the "one" side of the one-to-many relationship should be selected.) Leave the Forms with Subforms option turned on at the bottom of the dialog box, and click Next.

9. In the next dialog box to appear, choose a desired layout for the subform (tabular or datasheet), and click Next.

10. In the next dialog box to appear, chose a desired style for the form, and click Next.

11. In the final dialog box that appears, enter the desired titles for the main form and the subform, then click Finish.

When I open a relational form in Design view, I can change the design of the main form, but I can't change any aspects of the subform except its size. How do I modify the subform?

The subform is saved as a separate form, so you must specifically open it in Design view to make changes to it. You can find the subform by name in the Database window and open it in Design view, but if you already have the main form open in Design view, there's a faster way. Just double-click on the subform control (the blank rectangle that represents the subform). When you do this, the subform opens in Design view, and you can make any desired changes to its elements.

Can I use multiple subforms on a form?

Yes, you can include more than one subform on a single form. You'll need to get more into the manual methods of form creation instead of trusting the wizards. Create the desired subforms manually, using the same design methods that you would use to create any form. Then open the main form in Design view, and drag the subforms from the Database window onto the main form to add subform controls. You'll need to open the Properties window for the subforms (click each subform, open the View menu, and choose Properties), and check the Link Master Fields and Link Child Fields properties, to be sure that Access has selected the proper fields to be used for the relationship between the main form and the subform. The Link Master Fields property must contain the name of the field to link to in the main form, and the Link Child Fields property must contain the name of the field to link to in the subform.

? **I often print my relational forms to show all the data related to an entry in the main form. Is there a way to print all the records in the subform, even when they don't fit on the screen?**

You can do this by changing the Can Grow property for the subform. This property allows the size of the subform to expand as needed during printing to accommodate all the records. Open the form in Design view, right-click anywhere in the subform, and choose Properties. Click the Format tab, and set the Can Grow property to Yes. If you also want to omit the subform from printing if there are no related records, you can set the Can Shrink property to Yes.

? **How can I make a subform a read-only subform, while allowing changes to the data in the main form?**

You can use these steps to make a subform read-only:

1. Open the form containing the subform in Design view.
2. Right-click the subform control, and choose Properties from the shortcut menu that appears.
3. In the Properties window that opens, click the Data tab.
4. Set the Locked property to Yes.
5. Open the File menu and choose Save to save the changes to the form.

How can I synchronize two forms, so that data in the second form shows records that are related to the record shown in the first form?

We'll assume that for one reason or another, you don't want to use a relational form containing a subform to do this. (If you do want to use a form with a subform, you can easily create one with the Form Wizards.) You may want to examine related records on two forms at the same time. As an example, when looking at a customer's record in a Customer form, you might want to see another form containing all sales for that customer. You can create a command button that, when pressed, opens a second form and synchronizes that form so it displays data related to the record on the first form. Use the following steps to do this:

1. Open the first form in Design view (the form that will contain the button).

2. Turn on the Control Wizards in the Toolbox if they are not already on (if the Control Wizards are on, the Control Wizards button in the Toolbox will appear depressed).

3. In the Toolbox, click on the Command Button tool.

4. Click on the form where you want to place the button.

5. In the first Form Wizard dialog box that appears, click Form Operations in the Categories box, and click Open Form in the Actions box, then click Next.

6. In the next dialog box that appears, choose the form you want to open and synchronize to the first form, then click Next.

7. In the next dialog box that appears, select the option titled "Open the form and find specific data to display," then click Next.

8. The next dialog box to appear, shown in Figure 8-8, asks which field contains the matching data used to synchronize the forms. Click the desired field on both sides of the dialog box, then click the <-> button in the center, then click Next.

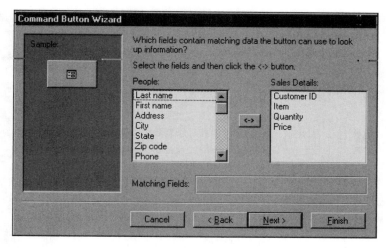

Figure 8-8:   Dialog box asking for fields used to synchronize the data in the forms

9. In the next dialog box to appear, choose text or a picture for the face of the button, then click Finish to add the button to the form.

Once the button has been added, you can open the form and click on the button. When you do so, the second form will open, displaying data related to the record shown in the first form, as shown in Figure 8-9.

? Is there a way to **total values in a subform** and display that total amount on the main form?

Many times you may want to total an amount contained in a subform (such as a number of items ordered, or a total number of hours worked by an employee), and display that total on the main form. You can't add a control on the main form that directly calculates a total from the data in the subform. However, you can accomplish the desired goal by creating a control on the subform to provide the totals, hiding that control, and referencing the hidden control in

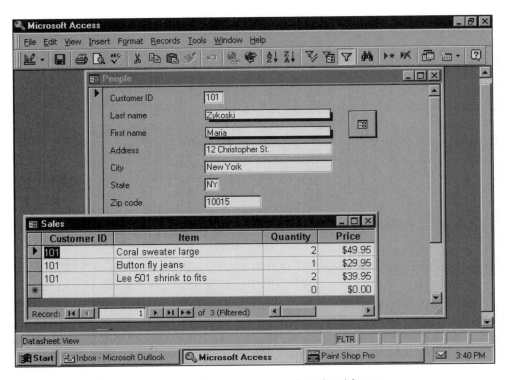

Figure 8-9:   Example of data displayed in synchronized forms

the subform from another control on the main form. Use the following steps to do this:

1. Open the subform in Design view.

2. Open the View menu and choose Properties to display the Properties window for the subform.

3. Drag the border of the subform's footer until there is room to place a control. (If the subform has no footer, open the View menu and choose Form Header/Footer to add one.)

4. Add a text box to the footer section of the subform. In the Control Source property for the control, enter an expression that totals the desired field. As an example, the Price Subtotal control shown in the footer of the following form contains the expression =**Sum([Price])**.

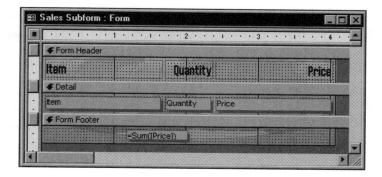

5. Enter a name for the control in the Control Name property (and make a note of this name, as you'll need to refer to it later).

6. Set the Visible property for the control to No.

7. Open the File menu and choose Save to save the subform.

8. Open the main form in Design view.

9. Open the View menu and choose Properties to display the Properties window.

10. Add a text box to the form that will contain your total. In the Control Source property for the text box, you'll need to enter an expression that refers to the hidden control in the subform. The syntax is =[*subform control name*].**Form!**[*subtotal control name*], where *subform control name* is the control name for the subform and *subtotal control name* is the name that you gave to the hidden control you added to the footer of the subform. Our example uses the expression =[Sales Subform].Form![Price Subtotal] to provide the needed results.

11. Set the Format property for the new control you added to Fixed or Currency, set the Decimal Places property to whatever is appropriate for the type of value you are totaling (for example, 2 for currency), and set the Visible property to Yes.

12. Save the main form by opening the File menu and choosing Save.

? Data in my subform appears as a datasheet, but I want to view the related records one at a time. How can I view the subform data in Form view?

By default, relational forms you create using the Form Wizards display your subform data in a datasheet. If you want to change the way you view the data during one specific use of the form, you can switch back and forth between Form view and Datasheet view. Just click anywhere in the subform, open the View menu, and choose Subform Datasheet. This command is a toggle, so each time you choose it, the data shown in the subform alternates between a form and a datasheet.

If you want to make the subform always display its data in a form, you'll need to change the Default View and Views Allowed properties for the subform. Use these steps to do so:

1. Open the subform in Design view.

2. Open the View menu and choose Properties.

3. In the Properties window that opens, click the Format tab.

4. Change the Default View property to Single Form.

5. Change the Views Allowed property to Form.

6. Open the File menu and choose Save to save the changes to the form.

VISUAL BASIC FOR APPLICATIONS (VBA) AND FORMS

? If I export a form to another Access database, are the procedures that the form uses also exported?

When you export a form, the form's design includes its *module*, containing all the event procedures. If the form uses only event procedures, your form design has all the ones you need. If the form uses procedures from other modules, these procedures are not included. To get those procedures into the other database, export the module they are contained in.

? Can I **look at the VBA code** behind a particular form?

While in the form's Design view, choose Code from the View menu or click the Code button in the toolbar. A Module window appears. To show the code for a specific object, select it from the Object drop-down list at the top left portion of the window. To see the VBA code associated with a specific event for that object, select the event from the Procedure drop-down list box at the top right portion of the window.

? Can I **run VBA code** within a form?

Yes, you can execute VBA code within a form. To do this for a Function procedure, you need to call the function from a property of the form or a control in it. To do so, move to the property, and enter
=*FunctionName*( )
where *FunctionName* is the name of the function. You can also perform VBA code in a form by attaching event procedures to the form or to controls on the form.

? Can I **test to find the view** my form is in?

You may need to know a form's current view while running a VBA procedure or a macro. The CurrentView property indicates which view the form is using. This property is only available in macros or in VBA code. The possible settings for this property are

0	Design view
1	Form view
2	Datasheet view

As an example, a macro could have a condition to test the current view. This entry might look like:
[Forms]![*Form Name*]**.[CurrentView]**=**1**
Then when the current view is the Form view, the macro will perform some action.

Basic
Reports

Answer Topics!

Basic Reports @ a Glance

Reports in Access are descriptions of how you want to print the data in a table or a query. Unlike forms, they cannot be used to enter data. You can create a report manually, or you can use one of the Report Wizards to guide you through the process. The questions you'll see throughout this chapter cover the following areas:

▷ **Designing Reports** In this area, you'll find answers to questions about common design techniques used with reports that display data from a single table or query.

▷ **Using Reports** This portion of the chapter answers questions that arise about working with reports in common ways, such as sorting and grouping data, and printing reports in challenging ways.

▷ **Working with Mailing Labels** In this portion of the chapter, you'll find answers to questions that are specific to the use of reports formatted as mailing labels.

▷ **Troubleshooting** In this part of the chapter, you'll find answers to common problems that arise when using reports.

DESIGNING REPORTS

? **How can I quickly create a report?**

The fastest way to produce a report in Access is to settle for a default tabular report or a default columnar report. Producing either of these reports is a matter of these simple steps:

1. In the Database window, click the Reports tab.
2. Click New.
3. In the New Report dialog box that opens, click AutoReport: Columnar or AutoReport: Tabular, as desired.
4. In the list box, select the table or query you wish to base the report on.
5. Click OK.

The columnar AutoReport Wizard creates a report with the data arranged in a single column of successive fields, as shown in Figure 9-1. Each field appears on a separate line, with the corresponding label to the left.

The tabular AutoReport Wizard creates a report with the data arranged in the form of a table, as shown in Figure 9-2. Each record appears on a separate line, and the labels print once at the top of each page.

? **What's involved in creating a report with the Report Wizards?**

The Report Wizards in Access 97 let you create columnar reports, tabular reports, relational reports with subreports, and reports with charts, using just a few steps. These are the steps you can use to create reports with the Report Wizards:

1. In the Database window, click the Reports tab.
2. Click New to display the New Report dialog box, shown at the bottom of the next page.

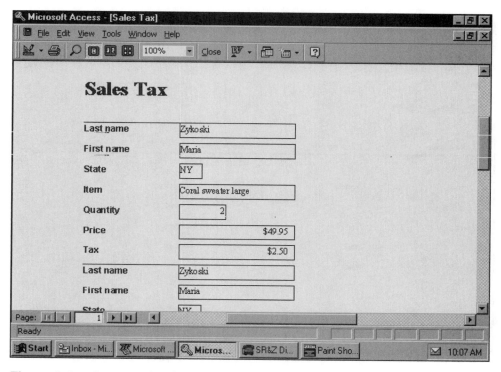

Figure 9-1:   An example of a columnar report created with the AutoReport Wizard

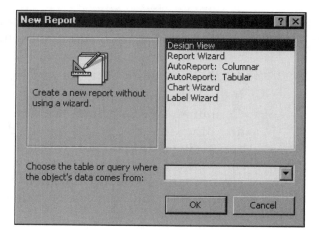

3. Choose the desired wizard from the dialog box.

4. In the list box, choose the table or query you wish to base the report on. (If you want to base the report on more

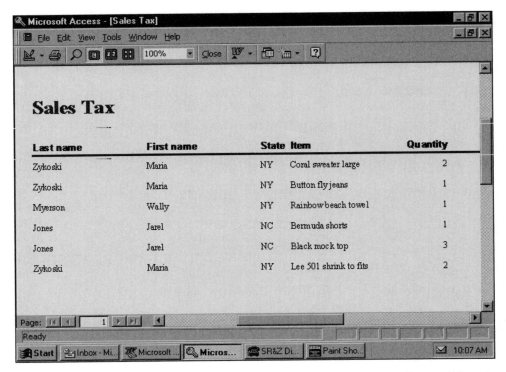

Figure 9-2:   An example of a tabular report created with the AutoReport Wizard

than one table, choose the primary table that will supply data to the main part of the report. You'll be able to choose fields from other tables in dialog boxes that appear later.)

5. Click OK.

If you selected AutoReport Tabular or AutoReport Columnar, Access creates the desired report. If you selected any other report type, follow the directions that appear in successive dialog boxes. (If you are creating a report based on more than one table, the first dialog box that appears will require you to select the desired fields from the first table, then choose another table by name, then select the desired fields from that table.)

What's involved in **creating a report manually?**

With the manual method of report design, you open a blank report and add desired fields and other design objects

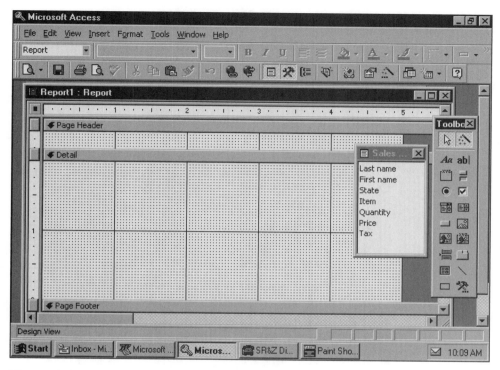

Figure 9-3: A blank report in Design view

(labels, graphics, lines, and boxes) to the report at the desired locations. You also specify sections, such as page header and page footer or group header and group footer sections, that identify groups of data to help divide your report. These are the steps you'll need to create a report manually:

1. In the Database window, click the Reports tab, then click New.

2. In the New Report dialog box that appears, choose the name of the table or query that will provide data to the report.

3. Click Design view in the list box, and click OK. Access displays a blank report in Design view, as shown in Figure 9-3. (If the Field List is not visible, you can choose Field List from the View menu to display it.)

4. Add the desired objects (fields, labels, graphics, and any other types of controls) to the report. You can add fields by dragging them from the Field List to the report. To

The Nuts and Bolts of Report Sections

Because reports contain many specific sections, understanding what these sections are and how they relate to each other is essential in designing reports. Once you know where and in what order the sections of a report print, you'll find it much easier to create an effective report. A report can contain the following sections:

- A *report header* appears once at the beginning of the report.
- A *page header* appears at the top of every page and below any report header.
- A *group header* appears above the detail section of the first record in every group.
- *Detail sections* contain the individual records in the report.
- A *group footer* appears below the detail section containing the last record of every group.
- A *page footer* appears at the bottom of every page.
- A *report footer* appears once at the end of the report.

When Access assembles your report for display or printing, it starts by printing the report header and page header sections. Then it prints detail sections until the page is full. Next, Access prints the page footer section, a page break, and the page header section on the next page. Each page contains the page header section, as many detail sections as can fit, and the page footer section. On the last page of the report, the report footer prints before the page footer section.

When a report has group sections, the printing order is basically the same. The difference is that Access prints the group header section before the first record of each group and the group footer section after the last record of each group.

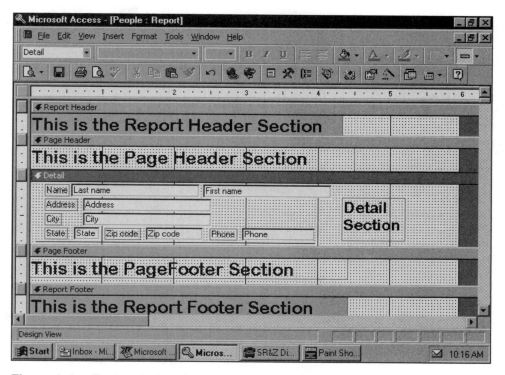

Figure 9-4:   Report design showing the different sections of a report

add other types of controls to the form, click the desired tool in the Toolbox and click in the report at the desired location to place the control.

5. Add any necessary sections to provide sorting and grouping in the report. You choose Sorting and Grouping from the View menu to open a Sorting and Grouping dialog box, where you can specify levels of sorting and enable sections in the report for groups of data.

6. Save the report by choosing Save from the File menu.

In Figure 9-4, you can see a report design that prints the report previewed in Figure 9-5. You can see how the sections in the report design are added to the final report.

How can I add the current **date or time** to a report?

You can add the date or time to a report with these steps:

1. Open the report in Design view.

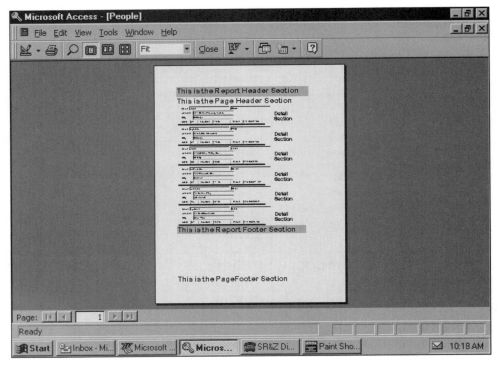

Figure 9-5:   Preview of report showing how the different sections actually print

> **2.** Open the Insert menu, and choose Date and Time. The Date and Time dialog box appears, shown here.

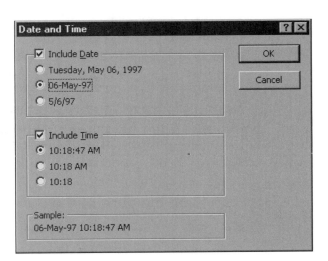

3. To include a date, turn on the Include Date check box and choose a desired date format.

4. To include a time, turn on the Include Time check box and choose a desired time format.

5. Click OK. The date or time field appears in the report, and you can drag it to its desired location.

? How can I add **descriptive text** to a report?

To add descriptive text to a report, click the label tool in the Toolbox, then click in the report at the desired location and begin typing the text. As you add text, the text box expands as necessary to accommodate it. You can also create a label of a fixed size; to do so, click the label tool in the Toolbox, then click at the upper-left corner for the label and drag the pointer to the desired lower-right corner. When you create a label in this manner, you can make the label's container deep enough for multiple rows of text. The text will wrap as you reach the right border; you can also press CTRL-ENTER within the text box to force a new line. When done entering text, press ENTER or click outside of the text box to finish the text entry. Figure 9-6 shows a label added to a report using this technique, in this case at the top of the page. You can resize the label at any time by clicking on its border and dragging the label's sizing handles (the eight small boxes that surround the label's border). An easy way to change the font or font size for the text box is to click the text box to select it, then choose the desired font or font size in the Formatting toolbar.

? How can I add **graphics** to a report?

You can add a graphic image to a report as a design object, using the object frame tool of the Toolbox. As an example, Figure 9-7 shows a report that uses a graphic pasted from a Windows Paint file.

To add a graphic, first click the Unbound Object Frame tool of the Toolbox. (Choose Toolbox from the View menu to display the Toolbox.) Then click in the desired starting location in the report, and drag the pointer until the frame reaches the desired size.

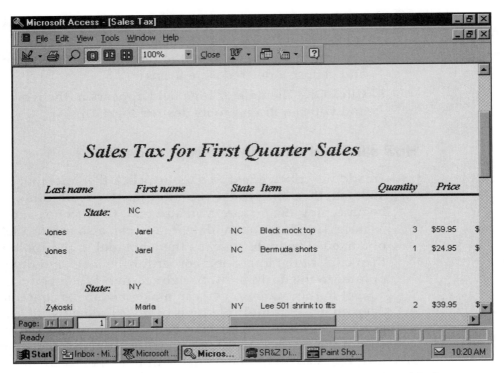

Figure 9-6:   An example of descriptive text added to a report as a label

When you release the mouse, an Insert Object dialog box appears, as shown in Figure 9-8. In the Object Type list box, click the name of the Windows program that is used to create the graphic. If the image exists in a file, click the Create from File button and use the Browse button to find the desired image file; after you click Open in the Browse dialog box and OK in the Insert Object dialog box, the graphic is pasted into the report. If you are creating a new graphic, click Create New; when you click OK, you will be taken into the Windows program where you can create the desired graphic, and when you are done, you can choose Exit from the File menu to return to Access.

•••••• *Tip:* If you don't need to edit the graphic by means of OLE, you can convert it into a bitmap. You'll save on resources, and the report will open faster. Right-click the frame, choose Change To, and choose Image from the next menu.

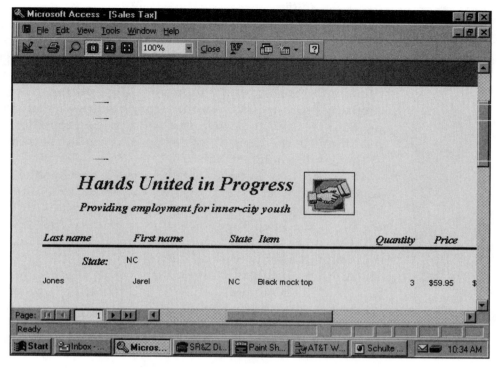

Figure 9-7:   An example of graphics within a report

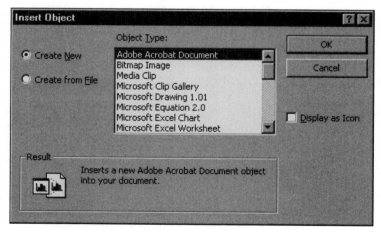

Figure 9-8:   The Insert Object dialog box

? **Can I keep groups together on a page,** rather than letting them split between pages?

You can keep groups of records together on a single page. To do this, open the Sorting and Grouping dialog box by clicking the Sorting and Grouping toolbar button, or by choosing Sorting and Grouping from the View menu. Select the field creating the group you want to keep together, and then move to the Keep Together property in the bottom half of the window and set it to Yes.

The Keep Together property here is the same as the Keep Together property in the Properties window, except that here you have one more option. You can choose With First Detail for the Keep Together property from the Sorting and Grouping window when you want the group's header section on the same page as the first record in the group. This option prevents the unpleasant result of a group header at the bottom of one page and the group's records on the next.

? **How can I manually add controls** to a report?

The Field List provides the easiest way to add controls to a report based on fields. Click the Field List button in the toolbar, or choose Field List from the View menu, to display the Field List, shown here. Then, to create a control that displays data from the field, drag the field from the list to the desired location in the report.

To create a type of control other than a text box based on a field, click the tool for the desired control in the Toolbox. (If the Toolbox isn't visible, choose Toolbox from the View menu to display it.) Then click on the report where you want to place the control.

? How do I get my report to print on **multiple columns**?

First decide how many columns you want and how much room you have on the page. Once you are sure that all the columns will fit on the page, perform these steps:

1. Open the report in Design view.

2. Open the File menu and choose Page Setup, and click the Columns tab in the dialog box that appears (shown here).

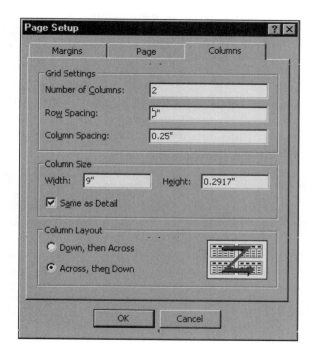

3. Enter the number of columns you want to create in the Number of Columns box.

4. Enter the space you want between the columns in the Column Spacing box.

5. Choose whether you want the items arranged first down, then across, or first across, then down. When you arrange them across, then down, you are creating a layout like mailing labels. If you use down, then across, they are arranged like columns of text in a newspaper.

6. Click OK.

≣   *Note:*   If you add more than one column to a report and the
new column either does not appear or only partially appears,
you need to fix the report design. The report is not wide
enough to accommodate the added columns.

?   **I want my report to use multiple columns for only
the detail sections and a single column for the other
sections. How do I do this?**

To create a report that uses different numbers of columns
for different sections, you need to use subreports. Figure 9-9
shows a report with a text box at the top occupying a single
section, and a two-column middle section.

Use these steps to create such a report:

1. Create a report that shows only the detail sections you
   want to appear in the final report. Turn off the Page
   Header/Footer and Report Header/Footer options in

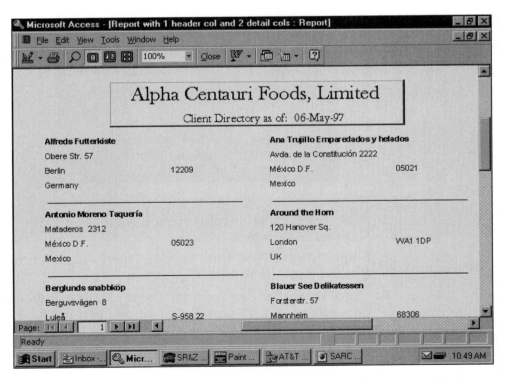

Figure 9-9:   A report that uses a subreport control to vary the number of columns

the <u>V</u>iew menu, so that the report has no headers or footers.

2. Choose Page Set<u>u</u>p from the <u>F</u>ile menu, and click the Columns tab in the dialog box that appears.

3. Enter the number of columns you want to create in the Number of Columns box.

4. Enter the space you want between the columns in the Column Spacing box.

5. Choose whether you want the items arranged down, then across, or across, then down. When you arrange them across, then down, you are creating a layout like mailing labels. If you use down, then across, they are arranged like columns of text in a newspaper.

6. Click OK, then save the report. If you used a "down, then across" orientation with two columns, your first report might look like Figure 9-10.

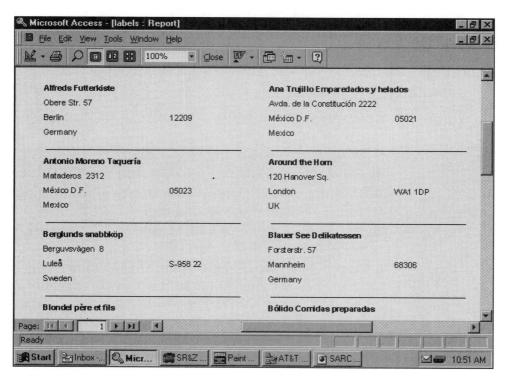

Figure 9-10:   A multicolumn subreport in Print Preview

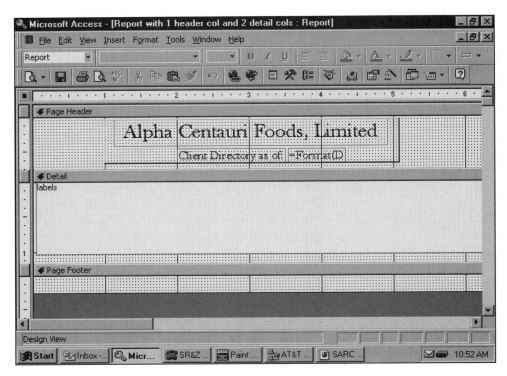

Figure 9-11: The report with varying numbers of columns in Design view

7. Create another report.

8. Create the headings and footings that span the columns in the first report.

9. Switch to the Database window, but don't maximize it.

10. Drag the first report from the Database window to the Detail section of the second report.

11. Resize the subreport control, if necessary, so that it is as wide as the second report.

12. Right-click the subreport control and choose Properties, then click the Format tab in the Properties window that opens. Change the Border Style property to Transparent.

Figure 9-11 shows the completed report design. You can see how this report contains the page header section that you want to span the columns. When you switch from here to preview, your final report might look like the example shown earlier, in Figure 9-9.

•••••• *Tip:* If you have a problem with obtaining the correct data in the main report, make sure the Record Source property for the main report is empty. You do not want a table or query associated with this report. For the subreport control, make sure that the Link Child Field and Link Master Field properties are empty.

How can I **number the records** in the detail section of my report?

You can number records within each group or across the entire report. To do so:

1. Add an unbound text box control to the detail section of the report.
2. Display the properties for this control by clicking the Properties toolbar button or by choosing Properties from the View menu.
3. Click the Data tab, then move to the Control Source property and enter =1.
4. Move to the Running Sum property and set it to Over All.

If you have grouped the records in your report and want to start numbering records again at the beginning of each group, set this property to Over Group instead. The records in your report are numbered, as shown in Figure 9-12.

How do I add **page numbers** to a report?

You can add page numbers to a report by using the Page Numbers option of the Insert menu. Use these steps to add page numbers:

1. Open the report in Design view.
2. Open the Insert menu and choose Page Numbers. The Page Numbers dialog box appears, as shown at the bottom of the next page.

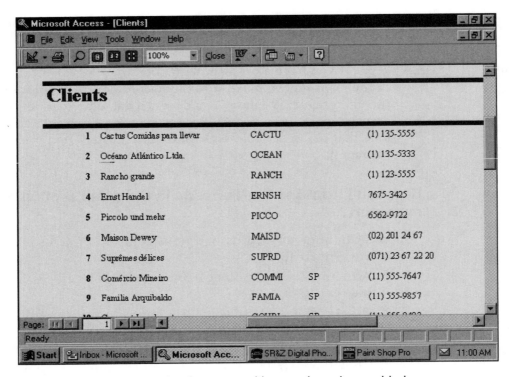

Figure 9-12:   An example of a report with record numbers added

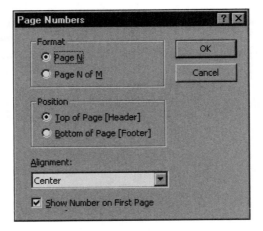

3. From the options shown in the dialog box, choose the desired format, position, and alignment for the page numbers.

4. If you want to include page numbering on the first page, turn on the Show Number On First Page check box.

5. Click OK.

❓ How can I start **page numbering with a number other than 1** on a report?

You can start numbering pages at any number you choose. You do this by manually adding a control that uses an expression to display the desired page number. If the report doesn't already have a page header or footer, add one by choosing Page Header/Footer from the View menu. Then add a Text Box control to the page header or page footer where you want the page numbers to appear. Click inside the control, and type the expression

=[Page] + *first page number − 1*

where *first page number − 1* has a value that is one number less than your desired starting page number. For example, if you wanted to begin page numbering with 40, you would enter the expression =[Page]+39 in the text box.

❓ Is there a way to have Access **prompt me for a value** and use that value as a title in my report?

You can in much the same way that you have Access ask for values when running a query. Using this trick, you can specify information—such as a report's title—that you want to change each time you run the report. Use these steps to include a parameter in a report's design:

1. Create a text box (*not* a label control) that will be used to store the parameter. Place it where you want the information to print. (Usually, you will want to place the control in the page header or in the report header.)

2. Click in the text box, and type the expression =[Enter the title:] into the box.

3. Format the text box as desired. (You will probably want to increase the font size to be displayed or printed prominently as a title.) To produce a centered title, widen the box so it is as wide as the report's width, and click the Center button in the toolbar while the text box is selected.

When you run the report, you will see an Enter Parameter Value dialog box asking you to enter the title for the report. Type an entry and click OK, and that entry appears as the report's title.

? How can I include a **running sum** in a report?

Often, with reports containing numeric values, you want to include a running sum. For example, you may want to see a running total of sales besides the sale amount for each sale. You can include a running sum by using these steps:

1. Open the report in Design view.
2. Add a Text Box control to the Detail section of the report.
3. Right-click the text box and choose Properties to open the Properties window.
4. Click the Data tab, and in the Control Source property, enter the name of the field you wish to sum.
5. In the Running Sum property, choose Over All if you want the running sum to keep a running total throughout the entire report. Or, choose Over Group if you want the running sum to reset to zero for each group.

? How do I **summarize calculated fields** on a report?

To summarize a calculated control, use the Sum( ) function with the control's formula in a text box control in the report footer section. For example, suppose you have a control named Total Billing that has a Control Source property of =[Billing Rate]*[Hours]. The control in the report footer section that totals this field has a Control Source property of =Sum([Billing Rate]*[Hours]).

USING REPORTS

? Can I use a report from **another database** in my current database?

You can easily copy a report that exists in a different database, and use the copy in your current database. It may not be intuitively obvious, but the Windows Clipboard can be used to copy reports (or other Access objects) from one database to another. Open the database that contains the report you want to copy, select it in the Database window, open the Edit menu, and choose Copy. Close the database and open the database in which you want to place the copy, open the Edit menu, and choose Paste. In the dialog box that appears, enter a name for the report.

If the report should use data from a table or query that has a different name than the original report's data source, remember to open the Properties window for the copied report, and change the Record Source property to the current table or query that will be used to supply the data.

Note: You can't use this trick to copy reports from earlier versions of Access into the current database. To use reports from earlier versions of Access, you'll have to convert the database created in the earlier version to Access 97 format, then copy the report from the other database.

How can I print reports using **double-spacing**?

This is something you'll have to do in the design of the report, not in the printing process. To double-space a report, include one row of controls for each record in the Detail section. Then leave a space of the same height as the controls below the row containing the controls. Figure 9-13 shows a report design for a listing of company names and phone numbers, double-spaced.

How can I change the default print **margins**?

To change the default print margins for all new reports, open the Tools menu and choose Options, then click the General tab in the window that appears. Enter the new margins in the text boxes under Print Margins and click OK. Access now uses these default print margins for all new reports as well as for printing datasheets, open queries, forms, and modules.

If you want to change the print margins for existing reports, you'll have to do so for each individual report. Open each report in turn. Choose Page Setup from the File menu. Then set the print margins, and click OK.

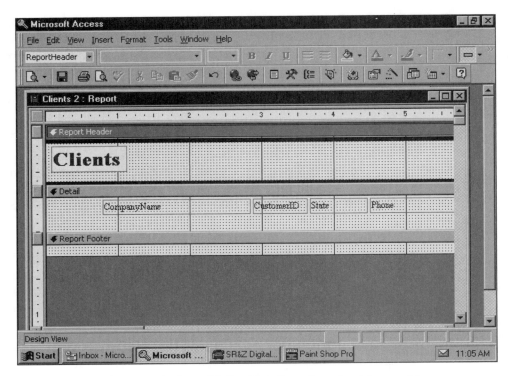

Figure 9-13:   A report design with the Detail section sized to provide
double-spacing

❓ Can I choose **not to print a section of my report,** depending on a certain condition?

Yes. You can attach a macro to the On Format property of the section that executes the CancelEvent action when a condition is met. Since the CancelEvent action prevents Access from formatting this section, it doesn't print with the rest of the report.

For example, suppose you don't want to print the Month of Order footer when there is less than $1,000 in sales that month. To do this, you could create a macro that has a CancelEvent action and the following entry in the Condition column:

DSum("[Sale Amount]","[Invoices]","[Month of Order Date] = Reports![My Report]![Month Text Box]") < 1000

This condition sums the Sale Amount field in the Invoices table when the Month of Order Date field entry is the same as the contents of the Month Text Box control in the header of the report. When this sum is less than 1,000, Access executes the CancelEvent action, so that this section is neither formatted nor printed.

? I have a report that prints invoices, and I need to restrict each record to print on a single page. How can I force a report to print one record per page?

With this type of report, don't use a page header or page footer section. Instead, place any page header information at the top of the Detail section. Then, click the Detail section to select it, and choose Properties from the View menu to open the Properties window for the Detail section. Click the Format tab, and set the Force New Page property to After Section.

? I'm using a parameter query as the basis for my report. How can I display the parameters used in the actual report?

When you create a parameter query, include the parameters themselves as fields in the QBE grid. For example, if you are entering a start date and an end date as the parameters for the Date field, you should create Start and End fields in the QBE grid, as shown in Figure 9-14. (Be sure to use the exact same name and case when naming the fields in the grid as you used in the criteria for the parameter.)

Now when you create your report, the field list for this query displays the two new fields. These fields contain the entries you made for the parameters. You can add them to your report just as you would add any other field from the query.

For example, a text box control can join text and the parameter entries to tell readers what dates are covered by the data in the report. In this case, the expression entered for the control's Control Source property is

= "For the Fiscal Quarter Beginning " & [Start date] & " and Ending " & [End date]

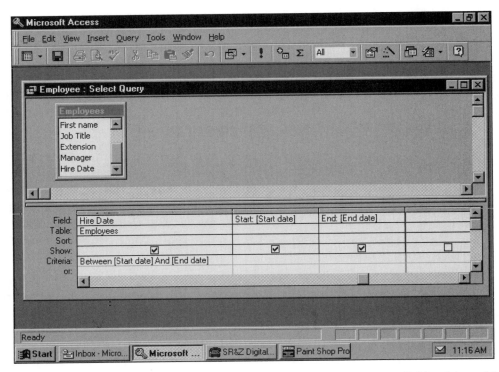

Figure 9-14:   A parameter query with the parameters included as fields of the grid

? How can I **print a report based on the current record shown in a form?**

You need to create a macro that opens a report by using the contents of a control on your form to choose which records display. Attach this macro to a command button on the form so that you can open the report by clicking the button.

This macro uses the OpenReport action. Set a Where condition argument to make the report display the same record currently displayed in the form. For example, this macro might contain the following information:

Action: OpenReport
Arguments: Report Name: *Name of report*
           View: Print
           Where condition: [*Field name*] =
           Forms![*FormName*]![*FormControlName*]

Field name is the name of the table or query field that selects which records appear in the report. It must equal the same entry as one of the controls in the form. You can automatically attach this macro to the On Click property of a command button by dragging the macro from the Database window to the form while the form is in Design view. When you change to Form view and click the command button on the form, Access prints a report using all the records with the same value as the one on the form. If you want the report to show only the record in the form, make sure the field name contains an entry that is unique to the record. You could use an AutoNumber field, which is unique for each record.

❓ How can I change the **record source** used for a report?

Each report has a Record Source property that tells Access the name of the underlying table or query providing the records. You can change this property in Design view to base the report on a different table or query. Use these steps:

1. Open the report in Design view. (If the report is already open, choose Select Report from the Edit menu.)
2. Open the View menu and choose Properties.
3. Click the Data tab.
4. Click in the Record Source property, open the list box, and choose a table or query as the report's source of data.
5. Save the report.

❓ How can I add **sorting and grouping** to a report?

You can print the data in your reports in a specified order by sorting it. And to highlight or summarize certain information, you also divide the data into individual groups, and sort the records within the groups. To add sorting or grouping to a report, perform these steps:

1. Open the report in Design view.
2. Open the View menu and choose Sorting and Grouping, or click the Sorting and Grouping button in the toolbar

to display the Sorting and Grouping dialog box, shown here.

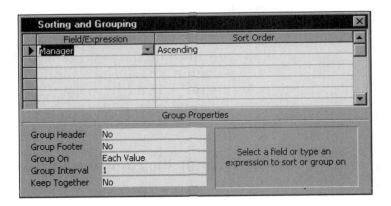

3. In the first row of the Field/Expression column, select a field name or type an expression. The field or expression in the first row becomes the first sorting level. The second row becomes the second sorting level, and so on. (You can sort or group up to 10 fields or expressions.)

When you fill in the Field/Expression column, Access sets the Sort Order to Ascending (A through Z, 0 through 99) by default. To change the sort order, select Descending from the Sort Order list. Descending order sorts from Z through A or from 99 through 0.

To add grouping to the report, use these steps:

1. Set the sort order for the data in the report, as described above.

2. In the upper half of the dialog box, click the field or expression that you want to add grouping for.

3. In the lower half of the dialog box, set the group properties as desired. Use the Group Header property to add or remove a group header for a field or expression, and use the Group Footer property to add or remove a group footer for a field or expression. Use the Group On property to indicate how you want the values grouped.

❓ Do I have to **sort by a field I use to group data** in a report?

In Access, you can use either a field or an expression to group records within a report. The field or expression that the group is based on must be sorted as well; it's not possible to have a grouping in a report and not sort the field or expression used for that grouping. If you think about it, this requirement makes sense. If Access didn't sort the records by the same expression used for grouping, your report would have several groups for the same field or expression value.

❓ Can I **sort data** by a field that's not shown on the report?

You can sort by a field not displayed in your report, as long as that field is included in the table or query that you based the report on. To sort on an undisplayed field, simply open the Sorting and Grouping dialog box (choose Sorting and Grouping from the View menu), and include the field in that dialog box.

If the field you want to sort by is not included in the table or query you are using, you need to add it. If you are using a table, you will need to restructure the table to include the field you want to sort on, and add the needed data. If you are using a query, redesign the query to include all the fields you want to use in the report, including the field you want to sort on. Then open the report in Design view, open the Sorting and Grouping dialog box, and include the field needed to perform the sort in that window.

When working with reports that are based on queries, keep in mind that you have a choice when it comes to determining the sort order. You can define the sort order in the design of the query and leave the Sorting and Grouping dialog box for the report blank, or you can fill in the Sorting and Grouping dialog box in the report to control the sort order from within the report. If you try to use both approaches simultaneously, the settings in the Sorting and Grouping dialog box for the report will take priority over the sort order established in the query.

? **How can I print my report to a text file?**

Printing your report to a text file in Access is very easy. Right-click the report in the Database window, and choose Save <u>A</u>s/Export. In the Save As dialog box that appears, leave the To an External File or Database option selected and click OK. In the dialog box that appears next, change the Save As Type option to Text Files, and enter a desired name in the File Name box. Click Export to produce the file.

WORKING WITH MAILING LABELS

? **Why do I get a block of blank mailing labels?**

You may have blank records in the underlying table on which the report is based. If all of the blank records are printing together, they all contain the same entry in whichever field you are using for sorting. You'll need to check whether these blank records are the result of a data entry error or whether these records just don't have entries in those fields. If the records share a trait that causes them not to have entries in these fields, you can define a query that excludes them.

? **How can I create mailing labels?**

Mailing labels are a simple matter, thanks to the Mailing Label Wizard that's built into Access. It supports a variety of mailing label formats, including the popular Avery® label types. You can use these steps to create mailing labels:

1. In the Database window, click the Reports tab, then click New.

2. In the New Report dialog box that appears, select Label Wizard.

3. In the list box at the bottom of the dialog box, choose the table or query that contains the data for the labels, and click OK.

4. In the first Label Wizard dialog box (shown next), choose the size and type of mailing label desired, then click Next.

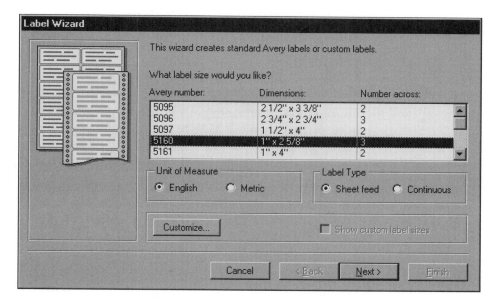

5. In the next Label Wizard dialog box that appears, choose the font and colors you want for your label, then click Next.

6. The next Label Wizard dialog box, shown here, asks which fields should appear in the label. Select the first field that should appear on the first line of the label, and click the > button.

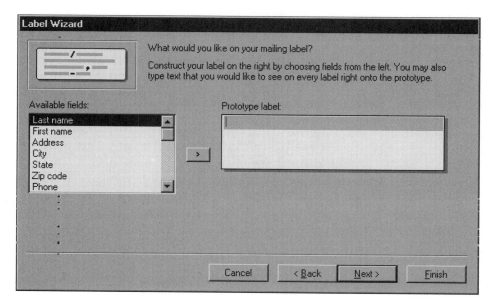

7. To follow the field you just added with a space or other punctuation, type the space or the punctuation character.

8. To have another field appear on the same line, select that field and click the > button.

9. To place the next field on the next line, press ENTER.

10. Repeat steps 6 through 9 for each successive row of the label. As you build the label, the right half of the dialog box shows a representation of how the label will appear.

11. When done adding fields, click Next. Access displays the next Mailing Label Wizard dialog box (shown here), asking how you want the labels sorted.

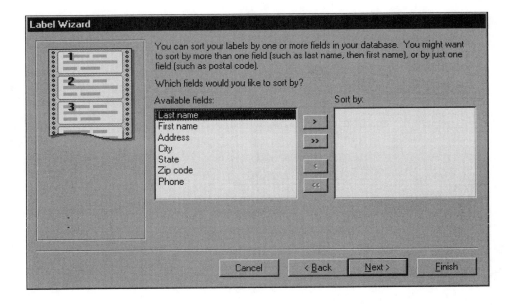

12. Select the first field to be used in any sort order, then click the > button.

13. If desired, select the next field to be used in any sort order, and click the > button. Repeat this step for each additional field you want added to the sort order. (You can remove fields from the sort order by selecting them in the right half of the dialog box and clicking the < button, and you can remove all fields from the sort order by clicking the << button.)

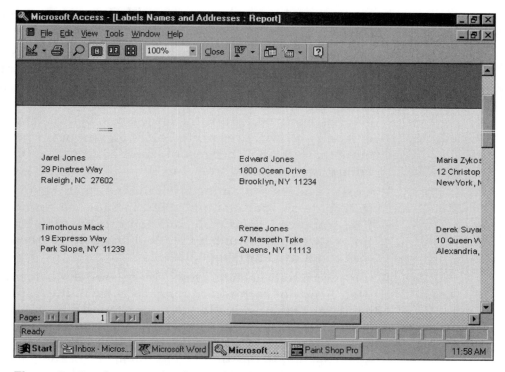

Figure 9-15:   An example of completed mailing labels

14. Click Next. Access displays the final dialog box of the Mailing Label Wizard, which asks whether you want to see the labels as they will be printed, or modify the labels (open them in Design view). Make your desired choice, then click Finish.

Figure 9-15 shows an example of completed mailing labels in a preview window.

How can I print a report that contains a specific number of mailing labels for each record?

You can create a report that lets you choose how many copies of each label you want to print. To do so, create a parameter query that makes as many copies of each record as you need. Use these steps:

1. Create a table that contains a single Number type field, with a field size of Long Integer. For this example, assume that you named the field Number and the table Copies.

2. Create a series of records in the Copies table. The first record should contain 1 in the field, and each record after it should equal the preceding entry plus 1. For example, enter 1, 2, 3, 4, 5, and so forth. You will only need to enter as many records as the largest number of copies of labels you will ever print. So, if you will never print more than 10 labels per record, enter 10 records in the table with the values from 1 to 10.

3. Create a query containing all of the information you want to include on your mailing labels. Include the Number field from the Copies table, but don't try to establish any link between the Number field and any fields of the table that contains your label data.

If you switch to Datasheet view, you can see that Access has created a copy of each record for each entry in the Copies table. Because the two tables are unrelated, Access creates a *Cartesian product*, by matching every record in the Copies table to every record in every other table. To print all copies of one label before printing any of the next, sort on a field in the address, such as a Last name field. Otherwise, you will print one of each label, and then start again.

4. Enter a parameter criterion for the Number field that equals the number of labels you want to print, such as **<=[How many copies?]**. "How many copies?" is the message Access displays each time this query is run, requesting the entry for this criterion.

5. Create your mailing label report by using the query you just created, or change the Record Source property for an existing mailing label report to use the new query.

Whenever you attempt to print your report, Access first runs the query. Because it is a parameter query, you get the prompt that lets you choose how many labels to create.

 Note: If you use this method to print multiple labels, you'll need to enter as many records in the Copies table as copies you'll expect to need. If you only add ten records but you want to print 20 copies of labels, you'll have a problem. You'll get no more than the number of labels indicated by the highest value in the Copies table.

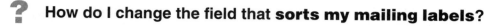

How do I change the field that **sorts my mailing labels?**

The same sorting and grouping features that change the order of records in a report also set the order of mailing labels when that is what the report prints. With the report in Design view, open the <u>V</u>iew menu and choose <u>S</u>orting and Grouping, or click the Sorting and Grouping button in the toolbar to display the Sorting and Grouping dialog box. Enter the name of the field you want to sort by in the Field/Expression column of the first line. Select the kind of sort you want (ascending or descending), in the Sort Order column of the same line. Include any other fields you want to sort by in the following lines.

TROUBLESHOOTING

There's too much **blank space in my report.** What can I do?

When a report contains too much blank space, you can reduce this excess of white space by reducing the space between sections of the report and by reducing the space between controls. Reduce the height of the controls to the minimum necessary to display the data, and move the controls up against the top edge of the detail section. Then pull the bottom edge of the detail section as close as reasonably possible to the controls. Also, reduce the height of any header and footer sections in the report by as much as possible. (If every other page of the report is blank, see the question, "Why is **every other page** of my report blank?" later in this section.)

Why are some of my report's **calculated fields** empty?

If some calculated fields on your report are empty but others are not, the calculations with empty results are based on fields where the field entry equals Null. (In Access, Null means the absence of data.) Calculated fields that use math operators (+, -, *, /, \, ^ or Mod) return Null when part of the expression equals Null. To correct this, convert the nulls to zeros by using a NullToZero function that you can write using VBA code. The NullToZero function looks like this:

```
Function NullToZero (anyValue as Variant) As Variant
If IsNull(anyValue) Then
     NullToZero = 0
Else
     NullToZero = anyValue
End If
End Function
```

This function converts any null values into zeros so that they will not affect the calculation. To create the function, click the Modules tab in the Database window, then click New. In the Module window that opens, type the code exactly as shown above. Save the module (give it any name you want), and close the Module window.

To use this function, display the Properties window for the calculated control (right-click the control and choose Properties). Under the Data tab, edit the Control Source property so that the NullToZero function converts the entries that contain null values. For example, if a control displays the results of =[Price] + [Tax], change the Control Source property to contain the expression =NullToZero([Price]) + NullToZero([Tax]).

? Why aren't the **column headings** in my subreport printing?

Access does not print page headers and footers that are in subreports. If you included the labels for your column headings in the page header of the subreport, they won't appear when you print the report. You have two ways around this:

➤ In cases where the subreport always fits on a single page, put the labels for the columns in the Report Header of the subreport.

➤ In cases where the subreport may span several pages, put the labels for the columns in the Group Header of the subreport, and set the Repeat Section property of the group header to Yes.

? **Why is every other page of my report blank?**

If every other page of the report is completely blank, the report is too wide for the width of your printed page, minus the page margins. (Remember to subtract the combined width of the left and right margins from the width of the paper in trying to calculate how wide your report sections can be.) Try reducing the report's width by dragging the right edge of the report inwards. Also, you can reduce the size of the report's margins by choosing Page Setup from the File menu, clicking the Margins tab, and reducing the amount shown in the Left and Right boxes.

? **I want to show a total at the bottom of each page in my report, but I keep seeing the message "#Error" instead. What's wrong?**

Your problem is that Access does not allow the Sum( ) function in a page footer. To place a total in a page footer, create a control in another section of your report that performs the calculation. Set the Visible property for the control to No to hide it. You may also need to set its Running Sum property from No to Over All or Over Group to choose when you want the calculation reset. Then create another unbound text box in the page footer. Enter the name of the control containing the calculation as the text box's Control Source property setting.

As an example, suppose you want to total the billings in the page footer section. Part of your report design might look like the one in Figure 9-16. This detail section includes a calculated control that totals the billings; it has a Visible property set to No, and its Running Sum property is set to Over All. This control is named Total Calc. The control containing =[Total Calc] in the page footer section returns the value of the Total Calc control for the last record printed on the page, which also is the total up to that point in the report.

Tip: You can get similar results by adding a macro to the page footer section's On Format property. The Item argument equals the control in the page footer section, and the Expression argument equals the control in the other section.

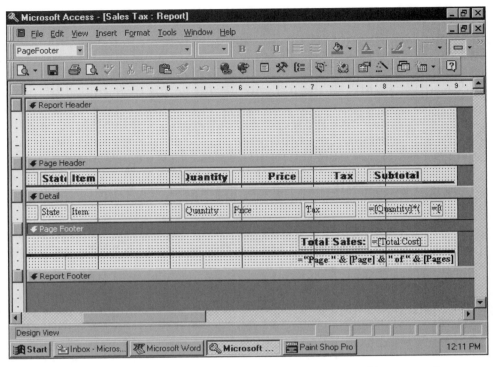

Figure 9-16: An example of a control used to provide a total in a page footer

Why does the **message "#Error or #Name"** appear in a control within the body of my report?

This problem can be due to a number of causes. Check for any of these possibilities:

☞ Check for proper spelling of field names in the Control Source property for the control.

☞ If field names used as parts of expressions contain spaces, make sure that brackets surround the field names. As an example, **[Last name]** is a valid reference to a field name within an expression.

☞ If you are using a built-in function as part of an expression, make sure that the syntax is correct, and the arguments are in the proper order.

☞ Make sure any field named in the Control Source property for the control hasn't been renamed or removed in the underlying table or query.

? **When I run my report, it prompts me for unexpected parameters. Why is this happening?**

This problem occurs when you misspell a field name in the Control Source property of a control or in the Sorting and Grouping dialog box. Access can't find a field by that name in the underlying table or query, so it thinks you are referring to a variable that doesn't currently exist in memory. Check to make sure all field names in the Control Source properties of fields and in the Sorting and Grouping dialog box are spelled correctly. Also, if field names manually entered in any Control Source properties contain spaces, make sure that brackets surround the field names.

Controls Used with Forms and Reports

Answer Topics!

Controls Used with Forms and Reports @ a Glance

Controls are the basic elements behind the appearance of your forms and reports. They shape the appearance of your data and add other visual elements. With the use of various properties, they can control how your data is displayed or perform certain types of validation. The controls that you use in forms and reports are basically the same. Throughout this chapter, you'll find answers to questions about either type of design. The questions in this chapter fall into the following areas:

▷ **Form and Report Design**   In this portion of the chapter, you'll find answers dealing with the general use of controls in both forms and reports.

▷ **Placing Controls**   This portion of the chapter provides answers to questions about the sizing, alignment, and placement of controls on forms and reports.

▷ **Using Controls in Forms and Reports**   Here, you'll find answers to questions about how your controls display and print data when you use your forms and reports.

▷ **Calculations and Controls**   This portion of the chapter provides answers that help you solve problems with calculated controls used in forms and reports.

▷ **Troubleshooting**   The answers in this part of the chapter help you deal with unexpected error messages and other general problems that arise with controls.

● ● ● ● ● ● ● ● ● ● ●

The Nuts and Bolts of Forms and Reports

Controls are the building blocks of your forms and reports, and Access offers many types of controls for your use. Some controls work better in forms than in reports. Others are chosen because they work best at displaying a specific type of data. Here are the types of controls you can add to forms and reports, along with some ideas about when to use them.

▷ A *label* adds text that doesn't change from record to record. You can use labels to add fixed information, such as a company or department name, or to identify data.

☞ A *text box* accepts or displays text that changes from record to record. This type of control is commonly used to display and enter data. The control is often used to display the contents of a single field, just as you would see it in a table's datasheet. Text boxes are also commonly used to store or display expressions.

☞ An *option group* contains a group of toggle buttons, option buttons, or check boxes.

☞ A *toggle button* shows a button that can look pushed in or released. A toggle button, like a check box, often represents a Yes/No field. Toggle buttons may also be used like option buttons to show a field that has a limited number of possible values.

☞ An *option button* shows an open circle that has a black dot in the center when selected. Option buttons usually show which of a limited set of possible values a field has, like the station selector buttons on a car radio, so they are also known as *radio buttons*. Like a toggle button or a check box, an option button can also be used for a Yes/No type field.

☞ A *check box* shows a square box that contains a check mark when selected. Check boxes or toggle buttons frequently display the setting of a Yes/No type field. However, you can also use them in place of option buttons to show the selected value for a field.

☞ A *combo box* shows a drop-down list box like the ones in Windows dialog boxes. Forms frequently use them to give you a choice of typing an entry or selecting one from a list. They also use less space than a list box. Reports seldom use this type of control.

☞ A *list box* shows a list with the current selection highlighted. List boxes work well in forms when a user can only select from a predefined set of choices.

☞ A *command button* adds a button that does something when clicked, such as executing a macro or module. Unlike toggle buttons, command buttons don't stay pressed.

▷ An *image* adds a control used to display a picture. The resulting picture is in display-only format; that is, you cannot double-click it to edit the picture in an OLE application. If you want to be able to edit the picture, use an unbound object frame instead.

▷ An *unbound object frame* adds a control that contains an OLE object that is not linked to any underlying field of an Access table. Use this control when you paste data from another application into your form or report design as a decorative object.

▷ A *bound object frame* adds a placeholder that displays the contents of OLE Object fields of a table. Use this control to store embedded and linked OLE data.

▷ A *page break* divides the form or report into pages. Divide a form into multiple pages when you have lots of data to show or enter and breaking the form into smaller chunks makes it easier to understand. Divide reports into pages when you have more data than can fit on one page and you want to control where the page break occurs. Reports have several page break options, so you can place page breaks by section properties instead of with controls that are in the detail band.

▷ A *tab control* adds a tabbed form control to the form. Clicking one of the tabs causes its own set of controls to be displayed so that the user can enter a particular set of data fields.

▷ A *subform* or *subreport* adds a control representing another form or report. This subform or subreport appears in the form or report you are designing. Use subforms and subreports to show records from a related table that are associated to the record currently displayed in the main form or report.

▷ A *line* adds a line. Use lines to divide or decorate the form or report.

▷ A *rectangle* adds a box. Add boxes to your design to visually group controls or other elements of a form or report.

FORM AND REPORT DESIGN

? **Access underlines the next letter when I enter an "&" in a label. How do I display an ampersand "&"?**

The ampersand (&) is a special character in Access. It identifies the letter that you want underlined. Underlining a letter lets you move to the attached portion of a compound control by pressing ALT and the letter; therefore, if you were to enter an ampersand beside the letter "N" in "Name" in a label attached to a text box, pressing ALT-N would move you to that text box when in Form view. To tell Access that you want to use the ampersand as an ampersand and not as an underlined letter, type two ampersands next to each other. For example, type **Renee && Benjie's Cycle Shop** to display "Renee & Benjie's Cycle Shop."

? **How can I display information from another table in my form or on a report?**

You can do this with the use of the Dlookup function. Dlookup returns the value of a field from any table. You can add this function as a calculated field to show a value from another table. Dlookup makes use of three arguments: an expression, a domain, and criteria. The expression argument is the name of the field that contains the data you want to display. The domain argument is the name of a table or query that is the source of the data. The criteria argument tells Access which matching record or records should be selected by the function. In most cases you will want to compare a value in the table or query to a control on your form or report.

As an example, suppose you have a form for a Payroll table that you use to enter weekly payroll information. When you use the form, you enter the employee's ID number. To make sure that you enter the correct number, this form has a calculated control that displays the employee's name from the Employees table. The entry that

you would use for the Control Source property is
**=DLookUp("[Employees]![First name] & " &
[Employees]![Last name]", "[Employees]",
"[Employees]![Employee ID] =
Forms![Payroll]![Employee ID]")**
This formula uses Dlookup to return the first name and the
last name from the Employees table and separates them
with a space. You can see this in both the form and its
design, shown in Figure 10-1.

The other domain functions, such as Dcount, Dlast,
Dfirst, and Dsum, work the same way. They use the
same arguments but perform different tasks with the
selected data.

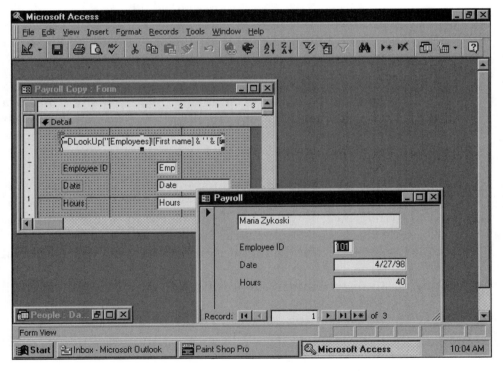

Figure 10-1:   A form and the form's design that make use of the Dlookup function

Note: A limitation to the use of the Dlookup function is that you can show data from only one field at a time. If you want to show data from several related fields, you'll need to use a subform or subreport control instead.

How can I make a text box **change colors** depending on the value of its data?

You can do this by using Visual Basic for Applications (VBA) code to modify the value of the Fore Color property for the control. In the On Enter property for the control, add an event procedure that contains code that sets the Fore Color property to the desired value. For example, the following code changes the foreground colors of a Salary field depending on whether the amount stored in the field is greater than $6.00 or not. (The Me! operator, used in this code, tells Access that the value assigned refers to the object in whatever form is currently open.)

```
Private Sub Salary_Enter()
   If Salary > 6 Then
       Me!Salary.ForeColor = 255
   Else
       Me!Salary.ForeColor = 8421440
   End If
End Sub
```

If you want to change the color of the background, use the term **BackColor** in place of the term **ForeColor** in your VBA code.

How can I attach a bitmap picture to my **command button**?

To display the contents of a bitmap graphic on a command button, switch to the Design view of the form, and use the following steps.

1. Right-click the command button and choose Properties.
2. Click the Format tab in the Properties window, and click in the Picture property.

3. Click the Build button that appears to the right of the property to display the Picture Builder dialog box, shown here.

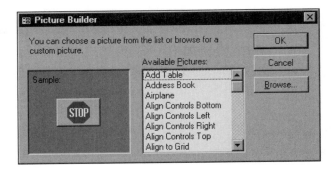

4. Choose one of the available pictures in the list box, or to use your own bitmap file, click Browse and find the file in the dialog box which opens.

5. Click OK.

Figure 10-2 shows an example of a form that uses bitmaps on various command buttons.

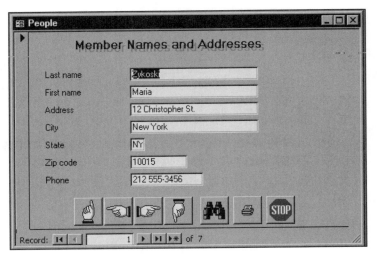

Figure 10-2:   A form containing buttons with bitmaps

Tip: If you are using your own bitmap files as images for the buttons, you should size and position the image in the file as desired before you add it to the button. You cannot perform any scaling of an image that's added to a button as a bitmap, so if the image is too large to fit on the button, you must change the size of the image (or resize the button).

Do I need to set the **Control Source property** for a combo box?

You need to set the Control Source property for a combo box only when you use the combo box to enter data rather than to search for records. When you use a combo box for data entry, the Control Source property tells Access where to store the data that you enter. However, if you use the combo box to find records instead, then you don't want to set the Control Source property—there is no new data to store.

How can I prevent Access from running a **Control Wizard** every time I create a button, combo box, or list box?

You can turn off the Control Wizards. To turn off these wizards, display the Toolbox while in Design view for the form or report. Then click the Control Wizards button in the Toolbox, shown here, so that it no longer appears pushed in.

With the Control Wizards turned off, when you create a command button, option group, combo box, or list box, you simply add an empty control to the form or report design. You must then enter the desired settings in the Property window for the new control.

? **How do I format numbers in my form or report as currency?**

You can change the Format property for the control that displays the data to display it as a currency value. Use these steps to do so:

1. Open the form or report in Design view, and right-click the control used to display the currency amounts.
2. Choose Properties and click the Format tab.
3. Click in the Format property and choose Currency from the list box.

▪▪▪▪▪▪ *Tip:* When you change the Format property, you may also want to change the Decimal Places property. This property sets how many digits appear after the decimal point.

? **I created a form with shadowed text. When I edit the text, however, its shadow doesn't change. How do I edit the shadow text?**

Many of the Form and Report wizards create labels that appear as shadowed text. This text is actually a combination of two labels. The second label is darker and is placed slightly to the right of and slightly below the first to create the "shadow" effect. If you change the text of the top label, the text of the shadow does not change. To change the text for both controls easily, click and drag around both controls so they are both selected, then right-click either control and choose Properties. Click the Format tab in the Properties window and enter the desired caption under the Caption property. This will change the text for both controls.

? **My text displays extra characters that I can't find in Design view. How do I remove the extra characters?**

Usually, these extra characters are a result of a control that you can't see because it is behind a text box or other object. Check to see if anything, such as a label, lies behind the text box when in Design view. Click the text box, open the Format menu, and choose Send to Back. If a control was behind the text box, you can now see it. At this point, you can select the control that causes the problem and delete it.

? **I can hide a control in a subform by setting its Visible property to No, but when the subform appears in Datasheet view, the field is still visible. How can I hide a control's field in Datasheet view?**

The Visible property of a control affects only the control itself, which is viewed through the form when in Form view. To hide the column when in Datasheet view, you'll have to save the datasheet with the column hidden. Open the subform and switch to Datasheet view, then right-click the header of the column you want to hide, and choose Hide Columns from the menu. When you close the subform, and later save the form's design, you will also save the Column Hidden property of the form's datasheet.

? **Can I have page breaks in my report that occur only when certain conditions are met?**

Yes, you can have conditional page breaks in a report. You can get away with this because a page break is a control with a Visible property, like all controls. But the Visible property works differently with page breaks, because you don't "see" them when a report is printing. When a page break control's Visible property is true (which is the default), the page break occurs. If a page break's Visible property is set to false, the page break does not occur. So the secret to creating a conditional page break is to change the value of the Visible property for the page break as the report prints. You can do this with Visual Basic for Applications (VBA) code or with a macro.

As an example, assume that in a report of sales from many countries, you want to force a page break for one particular country. You can add a page break control and use the Property window for the control to give the control a specific name. You can then refer to that control in VBA code that you attach to the On Format property of the report's group band for the Country field. Here's an example of code attached to the On Format property for such a report:

```
Private Sub GroupFooter0_Format(Cancel As Integer,
FormatCount As Integer)
If Country = "USA" Then
    CountryBreak.Visible = True
Else
    CountryBreak.Visible = False
End If
End Sub
```

In this case, the page break control has been named
"CountryBreak" in its Properties window and has been
added to the group band for the Country field. The code
placed in the On Format property for the Country footer
band of the report causes the page break's Visible property
to be set to false unless the Country field for the group
currently printing contains the characters "USA", in which
case the property is set to visible and a page break occurs
during printing.

How can I make small changes to the **position or size of a control** on a form?

In Design view, select the control that you want to adjust.
To change the size of the field, press SHIFT and use the
arrow keys to adjust the size. To move the control, press
CTRL and use the arrow keys. Note that you can also type
measurements for the Top and Left properties, to move the
control to that location. Typing values for the Height and
Width properties sets the size of the control.

Can I change the **properties of a group of controls** without having to change each one individually?

Yes, you can change properties for controls as a group. Use
these steps to do this:

1. Open the form or report in Design view.

2. Select the first control you want to change the
   properties for.

3. Hold the SHIFT key and select each additional control desired. (As an alternative, you can click and drag around a group of controls to select them all if they are adjacent to each other.)

4. Right-click on any of the selected controls, and choose Properties from the shortcut menu. Notice that the Properties window that opens is titled "Multiple Selection."

5. Make the desired changes to the properties. When you close the Properties window, the changes will be applied to each of the selected controls.

? Is there an easy way to draw **rectangular borders** around controls?

When you want a border surrounding a text box or a label, there's an easier way than using the rectangle tool to draw them. Right-click the label or control and choose Properties, then click the Format tab. Set the Border Style property to Solid rather than the default of Transparent, and change the Border Color and Border Width properties as desired.

? How do I **remove lines** created by a Report Wizard that I cannot find in the report's design?

The Report Wizards routinely add lines as borders at the bottom of report sections, and often these lines are hard to see because of where they are placed. The easiest way to remove these lines is to drag the bottom of the section down, so that the lines become clearly visible. Select the line and press DEL to delete it; then drag the bottom of the section back to its previous size.

If you can't locate the line at the bottom of the section, click on any text box in the section. Then press TAB repeatedly to move through all the controls until you get to the line that you did not find. Press DEL.

? Why won't my report become narrower when I drag the **right margin** to the left?

The report has a control somewhere on the right side of the report. This control is preventing you from moving the margin. Access will not let you relocate controls by dragging the margin. You must move the control first, then drag the margin.

▬▬▬▬ *Tip:*   If a report doesn't appear to have any controls in the way and you still can't drag the right margin to the left, check to see that there are no lines extending to the right margin. You must also shorten any lines that are adjacent to the right margin before you can narrow the margin.

? What's the difference between the **Row Source and Control Source** properties for a combo box?

The Row Source property specifies where the combo box gets the options to display in its drop-down list. For example, in a form for entering customer addresses, the State combo box might get its list from the State Code field of a table of valid states.

The Control Source property specifies where the data selected or entered in the combo box is stored. In the above example, the selection in the combo box might be stored in the State field of the Customer table. The field entered for the Control Source property also sets the entry that appears in the combo box when you look at an existing record (that's why it's called a "source").

? I have a paper form that is used as a basis for entering records. Is there a way I can **scan the existing form and use the scanned image as a background for a form in Access?**

You can scan a paper form and use the scanned image as a background for an Access form. (This provides a form with a more familiar environment to your data-entry operators, assuming they are accustomed to looking at the paper version of the form.) You can use the following steps to do this:

1. Scan a blank form and save the resulting graphic image in Windows Bitmap (.BMP) format.

2. Open a new blank form in Design view.

3. Open the Edit menu and choose Select Form, then open the View menu and choose Properties.

4. Click the Format tab of the Properties window that opens.

5. Click in the Picture property, and enter the name (including the path) for the bitmap file.

6. Set the Picture Size Mode property to Stretch.

7. Set the Picture Alignment property to Form Center.

8. Set the Picture Tiling property to No.

9. Close the Properties window to display the form with the bitmap as a background.

10. Add the desired controls and labels to the form, using the usual design techniques for designing forms in Access.

Tip: To size text boxes so that they match the size of boxes drawn on the form you scanned, you may want to disable the Snap to Grid setting that is normally turned on during form design. Open the Format menu, and choose Snap to Grid.

❓ How do I refer to my controls in my **subforms and subreports**?

The syntax for a control on a subform is
Forms![*Form name*]**!**[*Subform Name*]**.Form!**[*Control Name*]
The syntax for a control on a subreport is
Reports![*Report name*]**!**[*Subreport Name*]**.Report!**[*Control Name*]
For example, suppose you want to identify the Last Name control that appears on the Name Entry subform. The main form is Names and Addresses. The correct syntax is
Forms![Names and Addresses]![Name Entry].
Form![Last Name]
If Names and Addresses were a report and Name Entry were a subreport on the Names and Addresses report, you could enter
Reports![Names and Addresses]![Name Entry].
Report![Last Name]

▰▰▰▰▰ *Tip:*   The Expression Builder helps you avoid misspellings in control, form, and report names when entering a needed syntax.

? What syntax do I use to refer to controls on my sub-subforms?

You can extend the same syntax that you use to refer to a control to refer to a control in a subform that is in another subform. The syntax is
Forms![*Form Name***]![***Subform Name***].Form![***Sub Subform Name***].Form![***Control Name***]**
As an example, suppose you have a form named Divisions. This form has a subform named Departments. In the Departments subform is a subform named Employees. The Employees subform has a control named Employee Name. To identify the Employee Name control, you can use the syntax:
Forms![Divisions]![Departments].Form![Employees]. Form![Employee Name]

▰▰▰▰▰ *Tip:*   If one of the levels of the reference to the control is for a subreport, change the **Form!** in front of the report name to **Report!**. If the main object is a report rather than a form, replace **Forms!** with **Reports!**.

? When I tab through my form, the order isn't from top to bottom. How can I fix the **tab order**?

This problem commonly occurs when you add a new field to a form, because Access tabs through the fields in the order that you added them to the form. When you add a new field, by default it becomes last in the tab order, regardless of where you put it. You can change the form's tab order using these steps:

1. Open the form in Design view.
2. Open the View menu, and choose Tab Order. The Tab Order dialog box opens showing the current order, as shown on the next page.

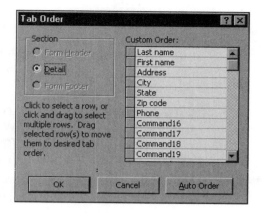

3. Drag the fields in the Custom Order list box into the order in which you want to move between them.

4. Click OK to save the changes.

•••••• Tip: You can quickly organize the tab order for controls from top to bottom again, by clicking the Auto Order button in the dialog box.

? How can I choose a check box or a radio button to display the contents of a **Yes/No field** in a form?

You can choose to add a check box or a radio button to indicate the contents of a Yes/No field, by clicking the desired tool in the Toolbox before adding the field from the Field List. In Design view, open the View menu and choose Field List to display the field list, if necessary. Then open the View menu and choose Toolbox to display the Toolbox, if necessary. Click the desired tool (the radio button or the check box); then drag the Yes/No field from the Field List to the form. The control that gets created will be the type you selected in the Toolbox.

PLACING CONTROLS

? Can I **add controls to a form** without creating associated labels each time?

You can disable the automatic addition of labels to new controls by setting the Auto Label property to No for the desired type of control. Use the following steps to do this:

1. Open a form or report in Design view.

2. Open the View menu and choose Properties, to open the Properties window.

3. Click the tool in the Toolbox that you want to disable the addition of labels for. When you do this, you will notice that the title of the Properties window changes to "Default *xxx*", where *xxx* is the type of control you selected.

4. Click the Format tab, and set the Auto Label property to No.

From here on, when you add new controls of the type that you selected in the Toolbox, Access will not automatically add new labels attached to the controls.

Tip: You can always delete the label portion of a compound control. Select the label portion of the control, and press DEL. The rest of the compound control remains on the form or report design.

? In forms created with the wizards, the control and the attached label move together. When I add a text box control and later create a label for it, they move separately. How can I attach the label to the control?

Text box controls added by the wizards are *compound controls.* You can create a compound control by adding a label to the text box control. To do this, select the label control, and press CTRL-DEL (or choose Cut from the Edit menu) to cut the control to the Windows Clipboard. Select the text box control you want to attach the label to, and press SHIFT-INS (or choose Paste from the Edit menu). Both controls in a compound control move together, unless you drag either control separately by dragging the largest handle at the upper-left corner of the control.

❓ How can I **move controls as a group**?

To move controls as a group, you must first select all of them. There are three ways to select multiple controls in a form or report design.

- ☞ Hold down the SHIFT key while clicking on each desired control (this method is recommended if the controls are not adjacent to each other).

- ☞ If the desired controls are adjacent to each other, click above and to the left of the first control and drag below and to the right of the last control. When you release the mouse button, the controls will appear selected as a group.

- ☞ If the desired controls are all aligned with each other either horizontally or vertically, you can click the ruler above or to the left of the controls to select them as a group.

Once the desired controls have been selected, you can move, size, or align them as a group.

❓ How can I **move just the label** for my text box? They keep moving together.

The trick in moving a label separately from the text box lies in how you select the label. When you select the label, it is surrounded by eight small squares, called *handles*. The one in the upper-left corner is larger than the others. When you point to the larger handle, the pointer turns into a hand pointing with its index finger, like the one shown here. Drag this larger handle to move the label. The text box stays where it is.

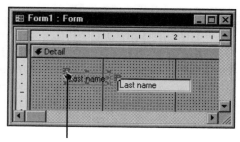

Pointer in shape of a finger

? How can I assign a **shortcut key** to a control?

You can assign an ALT-key combination, also known as a *shortcut key*, to the control's attached label by placing the ampersand (&) immediately in front of the character you want used as the shortcut key in the Caption property for the control's attached label. In Design view, right-click the label for the control, and choose Properties. Click the Format tab. Then, in the Caption property, place an ampersand in front of the character you want to use as the shortcut key. For example, if you wanted to allow the use of ALT-C to move to a City field in the form, you would enter **&City** in the Caption property for the label.

▪▪▪▪▪▪ *Tip:*   If you have a control with no label attached to it, you can add one by creating a label, choosing Edit/Cut, selecting the control you want to attach the label to, and choosing Edit/Paste.

? Why doesn't the To Fit command, from the submenu that appears when I select Size from the Format menu, adjust the **size of my controls** to fit the text in them?

Choosing Size from the Format menu and then choosing To Fit does adjust the height and width of labels and command and toggle buttons. However, it adjusts only the *height* of text boxes, combo boxes, and list boxes to fit the font of the text it contains. This command does not change the *width* of these controls, because the width depends on the control's contents. If you want to change the width of these objects, you must do so manually.

? How can I draw **straight lines** on forms and reports?

You can use a little-known keyboard technique to keep your lines straight. Select the Line tool in the Toolbox, then hold the SHIFT key depressed as you click and drag in the form or report to draw the line. When you hold the SHIFT key while drawing a line, Access restricts the line to perfectly horizontal, perfectly vertical, or to a 45-degree angle.

USING CONTROLS IN FORMS AND REPORTS

? **How do you open a combo box on a form without a mouse?**

Move to the combo box and press ALT-DOWN ARROW.

? **My Date field has a Long Date format in its table and a Short Date format in a query. When I add the field from the query to my form, what date format does it use?**

When you set field properties in a query, they override the field properties that are set for the table. So, if you add the field with the Short Date format from the query rather than the field with the Long Date format from the table, the control displaying the date field in the form has the Short Date format by default.

Tip: Regardless of what format is used by the table or query, you can change a form or report control to whatever format you want. Open the form or report in Design view, right-click the control, and choose Properties from the shortcut menu. In the Properties window that appears, click the Format tab, then click in the Format property and choose the desired format from the list.

? **How can I avoid having to click the down arrow to display the choices in my combo box?**

You can create a macro that simulates pressing the DOWN ARROW key as the user moves into the combo box. Use the following steps:

1. Create a new macro.
2. In the Action column, choose SendKeys.
3. Under Action Arguments, enter %{Down} in the Keystrokes entry, and leave the Wait entry set to the default of No.
4. Save and close the macro (give it any name you want).

5. Right-click the combo box in Design view, and choose Properties.

6. Click the Event tab in the Properties window.

7. Click in the On Enter property, and choose the macro you just created by name from the list box.

8. Save the form.

When you tab to the combo box field in Form view, the macro sends the keystroke ALT-DOWN ARROW, which opens the combo box.

❓ Can I set a **memo field's control** so that the insertion point goes to the end of the entry when I move to the control?

When you move to a field's entry, initially the entire entry is selected. This makes it easy to delete a long entry accidentally by typing a single character. If you want to automatically deselect the entry and place the insertion point at the end of the text, you can do this with a macro that simulates pressing F2. Use these steps to do this:

1. Create a new macro. In the Action column, choose SendKeys. Under Action Arguments, enter {F2} in the Keystrokes entry, and leave the default of No in the Wait entry.

2. Save the macro (you can name it whatever you want).

3. Open the form in Design view.

4. Right-click the memo field, and choose Properties from the shortcut menu.

5. In the Properties window, click on the Event tab.

6. Click in the On Enter property, and choose the macro you just created from the list.

7. Save the form.

▪▪▪▪▪▪ *Tip:* This macro works for any type of field, not just Memo fields. If you want the insertion point to be at the beginning of the field instead of at the end, replace {F2} with {F2}^{HOME}. ^{HOME} represents pressing the CTRL-HOME key combination.

❓ I have a lot of single-character codes to enter. Can I get the form to move to the next field when I complete an entry?

To do this, use the Input Mask and Auto Tab properties. The Input Mask property restricts the entry to just the number of characters set by the property. (Right-click the field and choose <u>P</u>roperties, then click the Data tab to get to the Input Mask property, or the Other tab to get to the Auto Tab property.) As an example, you might enter **LL** as the input mask for a field containing state abbreviations, **00000-0000** for ZIP codes, or **A** for a field containing a single letter or number. Next, set the Auto Tab property for each of the fields to Yes. When the AutoTab property is set to Yes, the focus automatically moves to the next control when the field is filled in.

▰▰▰▰▰ *Tip:* You can also have the Input Mask property set the style of capitalization. Use the < symbol to make letters after this point lowercase and > to make them uppercase.

❓ How can I prevent users from moving to a control on a form?

Forms have *tab orders* that set the sequence in which you move through the controls on the form by pressing TAB. You can remove a control from the form's tab sequence so that pressing TAB never moves the user to that control. Right-click the control in Design view, and choose <u>P</u>roperties. Click the Other tab in the Properties window, and set the Tab Stop property to No. Note that regardless of the setting in the Tab Stop property, users can still move to a control by clicking in it. If you want to disable the control completely from user access, click the Data tab in the Properties window, and set the Enabled property to No.

CALCULATIONS AND CONTROLS

❓ How can I have a text box that combines text along with one or more fields?

You can add a calculated control that uses the *concatenation operator* (&) to concatenate, or combine, the text and the field contents. You enter an expression that joins the text and the field contents into the Control Source property for the text box. As an example, if you wanted to combine the First name and Last name fields along with some text, you might have this expression stored in the Control Source property for the text box:

= "The Employee of the month is " & [First name] & " " & [Last name]

If the First name field contains "Michael" and the Last name field contains "Jones", the output of this control will show "The employee of the month is Michael Jones".

❓ How can I give a **default value** to a calculated control?

You can't. If you think about this, you'll realize that you really don't want to. The whole reason for the calculated control is that it equals the value of a calculation.

❓ How do I put an **upper limit on the value entered** into a field in my form?

You can use the Validation Rule property for a control to specify a maximum value that will be accepted when entering data into that control. Right-click the control, and choose Properties. In the Properties window that opens, click the Data tab, and enter an expression in the Validation Rule property. As an example, if a field should have a date prior or equal to today's date, you can enter <=**Date( )** as the Validation Rule property. If you want users to enter a number less than 750, you can enter <**750**.

▰▰▰▰▰ *Tip:*   When you enter a validation rule, make sure the person using the form knows what the appropriate limits are. Either add a label beside the field that describes acceptable entries, or include an explanation in the Validation Text property. Access displays a message box with the contents of the Validation Text property when you try to leave the field and the validation rule is not met.

? **How can I add expressions to count Yes/No responses in a Yes/No field in a report?**

For some reports, it may be helpful to have a sum total of responses in a Yes/No field. You can use expressions in text boxes to calculate the number of Yes or No responses and include the Sum() function to produce a sum total. The following expressions can be used in a report group's footers or in the report footer to count the number of occurrences of Yes and No in a field whose data type is Yes/No and whose field name is "Insured." Use the same expression, and substitute the name of your field for the example "Insured" in the expressions shown:

This expression	Sums this:
= Sum(IIF([Insured],1,0))	Number of Yes responses
= Sum(IIF([Insured],0,1))	Number of No responses

TROUBLESHOOTING

? **Why does #Error appear in my text box when the source of data for the control is a formula that uses a field to supply one of the values?**

The most likely reason for this error message is that the control has the same name as one of the fields you are using in its formula. In such cases, Access gets confused because it thinks that the formula refers to the control rather than the field, resulting in a circular reference. For example, you might see this error if a text box is named Unit Price and one of the fields you are using in the calculation is named Unit Price. To fix the problem, change the name of the control.

? **I've added a new record to the underlying table that's supplying data to a combo box on a form, but the choice doesn't appear in the combo box when I open it. What's wrong?**

All you need to do is refresh your screen. Once you do this, the new item you added to the source table will appear in the combo box. To refresh the screen, open the Records menu and choose Refresh.

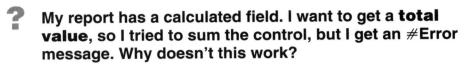

My report has a calculated field. I want to get a total value, so I tried to sum the control, but I get an #Error message. Why doesn't this work?

To sum the values from a calculated field, you must reference the entire calculation. Access will not correctly interpret your attempt to sum the control name when it refers to a calculated field. Access successfully totals the fields in a table or a query, but in that case the names of the controls used to display the data are the same as the field names, so Access really is summing the fields. When you want to sum a calculated field, enter the entire calculation within the argument for the Sum function. As an example, assume that you have a calculated control named Year_Total, and it has a Control Source property of [Amount Owed] − [Amount Paid]. To get a total, you could not use the expression =Sum(Year_Total), as this would produce the error. Instead, you would use the expression =Sum([Amount Owed] − [Amount Paid]) to total the calculation for all records in the report.

Sharing Data

Answer Topics!

How do I edit my database that was created by a **previous version** of Access?

How can we transfer some data stored in **Rbase** to Access?

Can I export **selected records** from a table?

How can I export a **table or query** as an Excel worksheet or as a FoxPro or dBASE database file?

WORKING WITH OLE AND DDE 293

When I double-click an OLE object, I see a message that the **file can't be opened**. What do I do?

Instead of the content of my OLE object, all I see is an **icon**. How can I change this?

Can I use **OLE** to paste an Access table into another application?

How can I prevent users from editing a **Paintbrush image** stored as a decorative object in a form?

When the original data used to create a linked OLE object has changed, how do I **update the link**?

How can I play **video or sound** that's displayed in an OLE object field in a form?

Sharing Data
@ a Glance

One of the greatest advantages of Windows is that you can easily exchange data between different applications using the Windows Clipboard or OLE (Object Linking and Embedding) features. A simple cut-and-paste operation makes it easy to combine graphics, spreadsheet data, and text into a single, attractive document. With OLE features, you can enter and format data in whatever application is the most suitable, and then use the data in any of your other applications that support OLE. Access also shares data with other applications through importing, exporting, and attaching. In fact, the very name of the program, *Access,* comes from the original intent of Microsoft to provide a database product that would work with data stored in a wide variety of formats. These features are all designed so that you can make use of existing data without the tedious process of rekeying it. The questions covered in this chapter are all related to the following two areas:

➡ **Importing, Exporting, and Linking**   In this part of the chapter, you'll find answers to questions about importing data, exporting data, linking to tables stored outside of Access, and working with data from earlier versions of Access.

➡ **Working with OLE**   This area of the chapter will provide answers to questions that deal specifically with Object Linking and Embedding (OLE) and with OLE objects that are stored in your Access tables and appear in your forms and reports.

IMPORTING, EXPORTING, AND LINKING

? Why are dates imported from an Excel worksheet four years off?

The date fields that you've imported from the Excel worksheet originally came from Excel for the Macintosh. Excel for Windows uses the 1900 date system, where serial numbers from 1 to 65,380 represent dates from Jan 1, 1900, to Dec 31, 2078. Excel for the Macintosh uses the 1904 date system, where numbers from 0 to 63,918 represent dates from Jan 1, 1904, to Dec 31, 2078. You can correct this in Excel for Windows or in Access. From Excel, change the date system for the Excel worksheet, then save the worksheet and import it into Access. (In Excel, open the Tools menu and choose Options. Click the Calculation tab, and turn off the 1904 Date System check box.) Or to correct the problem from Access, create an Update Query. Use the expression [*date field name*] + **1462** (the number of days between the two systems) to correct the dates.

? What is a delimited text file?

A delimited text file is a text file of data with the fields delimited, or separated, by specific characters. Delimited files can use any character as the delimiter; most commonly, the comma is used to separate the fields, text fields are surrounded by quotation marks, and lines are separated by carriage return characters. A delimited file open in the Windows Notepad is shown here.

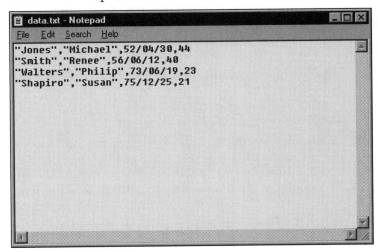

Many programs running on larger computers (such as mainframes) can produce files containing data in delimited format, and these can be imported into Access.

? Why are **errors** reported when I append a spreadsheet or a text file to an existing table?

Appended records must match the structure of the existing table: each field must have the same data type as the matching field in the existing table, and the fields must be in the same order (unless you are using the entries in the first row of the incoming table as field names, in which case the field names must match). For every record that causes an error, Access adds a record to a table it calls Import Errors. You can open this table and examine the data it contains to see why the errors are occurring. Here are some common reasons that errors occur when appending data as part of an import process:

➪ The data stored in a field of the incoming table doesn't match the data type for the destination field. For example, if the destination field is a Date/Time field, the incoming data may be composed of characters that Access does not recognize as valid dates or times.

➪ The data in a numeric field of the incoming table is too large for the data type of the destination field in the Access table. For example, if the Field Size of a number field in Access is set to Integer, the incoming data may contain a number value greater than 32,767.

➪ One or more rows in the imported table contain more fields than are in the destination table.

➪ You are attempting to import records that have the same values as existing primary key values in the existing table.

In some cases, you can get around the errors by editing the data in the tables you are importing so that the data does not cause problems. In other cases, you may need to redesign the structure of the destination tables in Access. You may need to change field sizes or field types or rearrange fields to match the layout of the tables you are importing.

? Is there a fast way to import an **Excel worksheet** into an Access table?

If you just want to bring a worksheet into a new table, the easiest way, believe it or not, is with the Windows Clipboard. Access is sufficiently intelligent to recognize Excel data pasted into the Clipboard, and Access will automatically create a new table based on that data when you do a cut-and-paste operation. When you do this, it is helpful to include field names in the top row of the selected data of your Excel worksheet. Access will automatically assign those worksheet column headings as field names in the new table. Use these steps:

1. Open the Excel worksheet, and select the data you want to use to create the table in Access. If possible, include column headings in the selection that can be used as field names. (Figure 11-1 shows an example of data in an Excel worksheet, selected for pasting into an Access table.)

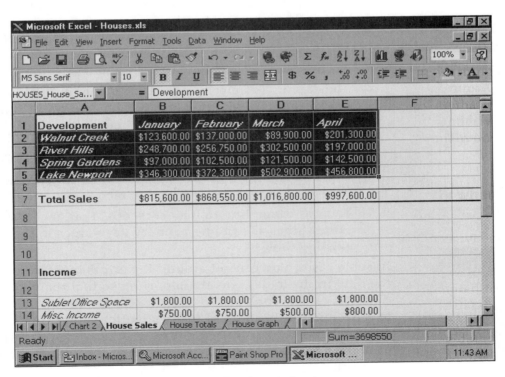

Figure 11-1:   Selected data in an Excel worksheet

2. Open the Edit menu, and choose Copy.

3. Switch to Access, and with the Table tab of the Database window active, choose Paste from the Edit menu.

4. When Access asks whether the first row of your data contains column headings, answer **Yes** if your selection included column headings.

5. When Access prompts that the table was successfully imported, click OK.

Access will create a new table with the same name as the worksheet in Excel, as shown in Figure 11-2. If you included column headings in your selection, Access will assign field names that are the same as those column headings; if not, Access assigns field names of 'F1', 'F2', 'F3', and so on. Access assigns field types and formats based on how the

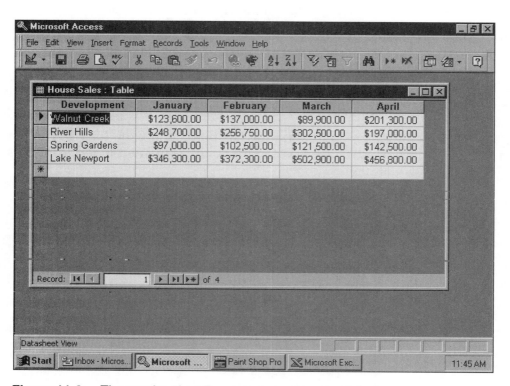

Figure 11-2:   The results of an Excel worksheet pasted into Access as a new table

data was stored in Excel. For example, if a column consists of date values, Access creates a Date/Time field; if a column contains numbers formatted as currency, Access creates a Currency field.

? Which databases can Access **export** to?

Access can export to the following databases:

- ▷ Paradox 3.*x*, 4.*x*, and 5.0
- ▷ FoxPro 2.*x* and 3.0
- ▷ dBASE III, III+, IV, and 5
- ▷ SQL databases via ODBC
- ▷ Earlier versions of Access

Access can also export files in the following formats:

- ▷ Microsoft Excel 3.0, 4.0, 5.0, 7.0/95, and 8.0/97
- ▷ Lotus 1-2-3 in .wk1 and .wk3 formats
- ▷ Text (delimited)
- ▷ Text (fixed-width)
- ▷ HTML and IDC/HTX

? What is a **fixed-width** text file?

A *fixed-width* text file has fields of a fixed length. Here, a fixed-width text file is shown as opened in the Windows Notepad.

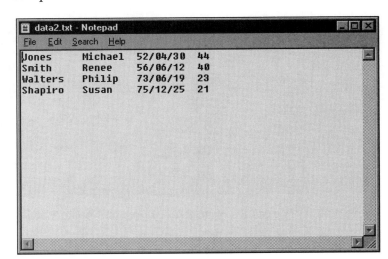

Each row, which is a single record, has the same fields. Each field is the same length in all records. In this example, each line contains a last name, first name, date of birth, and age. Many programs running on larger computers (such as mainframes) can produce files containing data in fixed-width format, and these can be imported into Access.

? Which databases can Access **import** from?

Access can import data from the following sources:

- ⮞ FoxPro 2.*x* and 3.0
- ⮞ dBASE III, III+, IV, and 5
- ⮞ Paradox 3.*x*, 4.*x*, and 5.0
- ⮞ Microsoft Excel 3.0, 4.0, 5.0, 7.0/95, and 8.0/97
- ⮞ Lotus 1-2-3 spreadsheets .wks, .wk1, .wk3, and .wk4 (linked files are read-only)
- ⮞ Delimited text files
- ⮞ Fixed-width text files
- ⮞ HTML 1.0 (list only), 2.0, or 3.*x* (table or list)

? Can I **import an entire Access database?**

You can import all the objects in a closed database into a database that's open. Use the following steps to do this:

1. Open the database that you want to import the other database into.

2. Open the File menu and choose Get External Data. From the submenu that appears, choose Import.

3. In the Files Of Type box that appears, make sure Microsoft Access is the selected file type.

4. Click the arrow to the right of the Look In box, choose the drive and folder where the Access database you want to import from is located, and double-click the icon for that database.

5. To import all the tables, click Select All. If you only want to import the table definitions (and not the data in the tables), click Options, and under Import Tables, click Definition Only.

6. Click the Queries tab to display the available queries, then click Select All to import all queries. If you want to import queries as tables, click Options; then, under Import Queries, click As Tables.

7. For forms, reports, macros, and modules, click the respective tab in the Database window, then click Select All. If you want to include relationships, custom menus and toolbars, or import/export specifications, click Options, and then, under Import, choose the items you want included.

8. Click OK.

? How do I **import a text file**?

You can import a text file with the Get External Data command of the File menu. During the process, dialog boxes presented by the Import Text Wizard will prompt you for the information needed for an import specification for the text. Use these steps to import the file:

1. Open the File menu, and choose Get External Data. From the submenu that appears, choose Import.

2. In the Import dialog box that appears, change the Files Of Type entry to **Text Files**.

3. Enter the file name in the File Name box, or find it in the list box and select it, then click Import. In a moment, the first dialog box of the Import Text Wizard appears, as shown in Figure 11-3.

4. Click Next, and follow the directions that appear in the successive dialog boxes. Depending on whether your data is fixed or delimited, you will be asked to confirm field locations and to indicate a new or existing table where the resulting data should be stored.

? What are **import/export specifications**?

Import/export specifications are the entries needed to either import or export delimited and fixed-width text files. For fixed-width text files, they precisely describe each field's name, data type, starting point, and ending point for any given record. For delimited text files, they describe the characters separating field entries and enclosing text

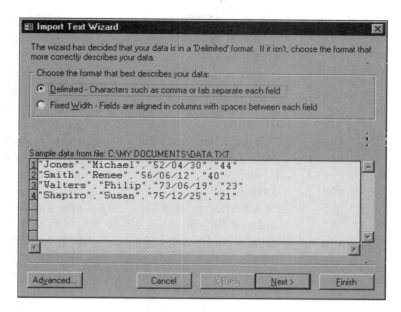

Figure 11-3:   The first dialog box of the Import Text Wizard

entries. You provide the entries needed to the import/export specifications during the process of running the Import Text or Export Text Wizards.

? In earlier versions of Access, I used the Import/Export Specification command from the File menu to design a specification for importing ASCII text files. This command doesn't exist in Access 97. How can I create an import/export specification?

Access 97 still makes use of import/export specifications, but they are treated differently. They are now created as you run the Import Text Wizard or Export Text Wizard, and they are saved along with the database you import to or export from. When you use the Save As/Export or the Get External Data command and specify a file type of text, the Wizard dialog boxes that appear can be used to provide your import or export specification.

? I can't open a linked Paradox table. Why?

The likely cause of this problem is Access' inability to find an associated Paradox index (.PX) file or an associated

Paradox memo field (.MB) file to go with the Paradox table. If you link to a Paradox table that has a primary key, Access must find the Paradox index file in the same directory. And if you link to a Paradox table that has memo fields, Access must find the Paradox memo field file in the same directory. If these files have been deleted or moved, Access can't open the table.

If you link to a Paradox table that lacks a primary key, Access cannot update the data. You'll need to go into Paradox and add a primary key before you can update the data from Access.

Another possibility is that the Paradox table (.DB) and index (.PX) files are set to read-only. Use My Computer or Windows Explorer to open the folder where the files are located, right-click the file, choose Properties, and click the General tab. If the Read-Only check box is turned on, clear it and click OK.

Finally, if the Paradox table is stored on a network, you may have insufficient access rights at the network level. Check with your network administrator to be sure that you have rights to any directory where the Paradox tables and indexes are stored.

? Why are my **linked SQL tables** read-only, when I haven't specified them as such?

Linked SQL tables must have a unique index before you can edit them. Access requires that a unique index be defined for each table. SQL views and synonyms are also read-only when there is no unique index. To fix this problem, create a unique index for your table from your SQL server. Then relink the tables to implement the changes.

? Why does Access not **lock records** in my linked SQL table when I have record locking set?

When you work on a linked SQL table, the SQL database controls the locking. Therefore, the locking does not change, regardless of what your setting is in Access. Access always acts as if this is set to No Locks. To change how the records are locked, change them from the SQL database.

? I want to import and export data for use with Lotus 1-2-3 and Paradox, but Lotus 1-2-3 and Paradox aren't available as file types in the Save In and Import dialog boxes. How do I import or export files to Lotus 1-2-3 or to Paradox?

You use the same Save As/Export command from the File menu to export data to Paradox or Lotus 1-2-3, and you can use the Get External Data command from the File menu to import these files. However, not all file types are listed in the Save As Type and Import list boxes by default. The standard installation of Access installs import/export filters for FoxPro, dBASE, Excel, RTF (Rich Text Format), text files, and earlier versions of Access. To add filters for Paradox or Lotus 1-2-3, you'll need to install them from the Office 97 ValuPack folder on the CD-ROM. If you have Access (or Office Professional, which includes Access) on CD-ROM, the disk contains the Office 97 ValuPack in addition to the Setup program. Open the \ValuPack\DataAcc folder on the CD, then double-click DataAcc.exe to run Setup for the Lotus and Paradox drivers.

? How can I get some addresses from Lotus Organizer into Access, when Access doesn't read the .ORG files produced by Lotus Organizer?

In Lotus Organizer, you'll need to use the Export command of the File menu to export the data either as a comma-separated values (.CSV) file, or as a dBASE (.DBF) file. You can then import this file into Access. You should be aware that Lotus Organizer stores the entire address (including the City, State or Province, and ZIP or Postal Code) as a single field. This makes separating the address data into separate fields a tedious affair. This is just an annoying trait of the way Lotus Organizer is designed.

Tip: Many experienced Access users report better success using the dBASE format instead of the comma-separated values format when importing Lotus Organizer files into Access tables.

?   **We need to export data on a weekly basis. Can we automate this process with a macro?**

You can automate the exporting (or importing) of data using a macro. Here are the steps you'll need to do this:

1. Open a new macro.
2. In the Action column, choose Transfer Database if you want to import or export from a database, Transfer Spreadsheet to import or export to a spreadsheet, or Transfer Text to import or export to a text file.
3. Under Action Arguments, set Transfer Type to Import or Export, as desired.
4. Fill in the remaining options under Action Arguments as desired.
5. Save the macro.

Once you've saved the macro, you can perform the import or export at any time by running the macro.

?   **How can I create a mail merge in Word, based on names and addresses in an Access table?**

The easiest way to do this from Access is to use the MS Word Mail Merge Wizard that's built into Access. You can get to this wizard from the Office Links toolbar button that's on the Database toolbar. Click the down arrow at the right side of the Office Links toolbar button, and choose Merge It with MS Word from the drop-down menu. Follow the directions in the wizard dialog boxes that appear, to select a new Word document or open an existing one. Once the document is open in Word, a Mail Merge toolbar will be added to the Word document window. You can then use the Insert Merge Field button at the left side of the toolbar to add fields from the Access table or query to the document. After adding the desired fields, you can use the Merge to New Document button on the Mail Merge toolbar to view the merged data, or you can use the Merge to Printer button on the same toolbar to print the form letters.

?   **Can I merge selected records from my tables into my word processor if I'm not using Word for Windows?**

Yes, Access can provide data that most Windows word processors can use as a data source in a merge file. (You'll need to refer to the documentation for your particular word processor to see how you create the merge document once you've exported the data.) Most Windows word processors can work with the RTF (Rich Text Format) file format in creating merge documents, so all you'll need to do is to export a query with your desired records to an RTF file. Use these steps:

1. Create a query that provides the desired records, in the sort order you want.
2. Right-click the query in the Database window, and choose Save As/Export in the shortcut menu which appears.
3. In the Save As dialog box that appears, leave the 'To an External File or Database' option selected, and click OK.
4. In the Save In dialog box that appears, choose Rich Text Format (RTF) under File Type.
5. Enter a name for the file in the File Name box.
6. Click Export to create the RTF file.

Open the RTF file in your Windows word processor, and use the appropriate techniques in your word processor to create the mail merge.

What does **ODBC** stand for?

ODBC stands for *Open Database Connectivity*. It is a powerful means of accessing data stored by a wide range of database management systems. Access uses ODBC drivers to manage information from different sources of data. The ODBC drivers that come with Access include ones for FoxPro, dBASE, Paradox, and Btrieve. You may also have other ODBC drivers on your system that came with other applications.

How can I link or import to tables stored on an **ODBC** server?

Before you attempt to link to an ODBC server, you must have the ODBC drivers installed on your system. (They are *not* installed as part of the default Access setup.) If necessary, rerun Setup to add the ODBC drivers. Once the

drivers are installed, you can use these steps to link
to tables stored on an ODBC server:

1. Make the Database window the active window.

2. Open the File menu, and choose Get External Data. From
   the submenu that appears, choose Import to import the
   ODBC server data into Access tables, or choose Link
   Tables to link to the ODBC server tables.

3. In the next dialog box that appears, select ODBC
   Databases in the Files of Type box.

4. In the Select Data Source dialog box, click the Machine
   Data Source tab to see the list of all ODBC sources for the
   ODBC drivers installed on your computer. Double-click
   the ODBC data source that contains the data you want to
   import or link. (If the ODBC data source requires you to
   log in, you will be prompted for a login and password.)
   Access connects to the ODBC source and displays a list of
   tables that you can import or link.

5. Click each table you want to import or link, and then
   click OK.

6. When done importing or linking the tables, click Close.

What is the **Office Links** toolbar button used for?

You can use the Office Links button on the Database toolbar
to export data quickly from a table, query, or report that is
selected in the Database window to a Word document or an
Excel worksheet. When you click on the arrow at the right
side of this button, you see the three menu options shown
here: Merge It with MS Word, Publish It with MS Word, and
Analyze It with MS Excel.

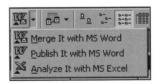

The Publish It with MS Word option launches Word (or
switches to it if Word is already running) and opens a new
document containing the data. The Merge It with MS Word
option launches a Mail Merge Wizard that helps you create

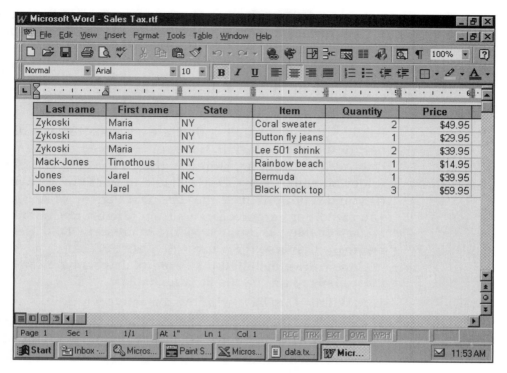

Figure 11-4: An Access table placed in a Word for Windows document

a mail merge document in Word, based on the data in the table or query. Finally, the Analyze It with Excel option launches Excel (or switches to it if Excel is already running) and opens a new worksheet page containing the data. Figure 11-4 shows an Access query after it has been exported to Word for Windows using the Publish It with MS Word option.

? In earlier versions of Access, I used the Output To command on the File menu to export Access tables and queries. What happened to this command?

The Output To command found in earlier versions has been replaced with the Save As/Export command. Just select the desired table or query in the Database window, open the File menu, and choose Save As/Export. In the next dialog box which appears, turn on the To External File or Database option, and click OK. You can then specify the file name and type of format for the exported file in the Save dialog box that appears.

How can I link or import **Paradox tables?**

Before attempting this, be aware that you must have the Paradox drivers installed; they are *not* installed as a default part of the Access installation. You will need to run the DataAcc.exe program, stored in the \ ValuPack \ DataAcc folder on your Setup CD-ROM, to add the Paradox drivers. (If you did not purchase the CD-ROM version of Access, you can order Paradox drivers from Microsoft. Contact Microsoft sales, and purchase the Microsoft ODBC Desktop Database Drivers kit for use with Office 97.)

Once you've installed the Paradox drivers, you can use these steps to link to the Paradox tables:

1. Make the Database window the active window.

2. Open the File menu, and choose Get External Data. From the submenu that appears, choose Import to import the Paradox data into Access tables, or choose Link Tables to link to the Paradox tables.

3. In the next dialog box that appears, select Paradox in the Files of Type box.

4. Click the arrow at the right side of the Look In box, choose the drive and folder where the Paradox tables are stored, and double-click the icon for the Paradox table. (If the Paradox table is password-protected, you will be prompted for the password.)

5. Repeat steps 2 through 4 for each Paradox table you want to link or import.

6. When done importing or linking to tables, click Close.

Note: If you link to a Paradox table that has a primary key, Access must be able to locate the Paradox index file (.PX) for the table, or you won't be able to open the linked table in Access. If you link to a table with memo fields, Access must be able to locate the associated memo field file (.MB) for the Paradox table, or you won't be able to open the table. Make sure these files are in the same folder as the Paradox table.

Also, if you link to a Paradox table and it has no primary key, you will be able to view the data in Access but not update it. To make the data updatable, go into Paradox and add a primary key.

? When I open my database, I see "Database name was created by a previous version of Microsoft Access. You won't be able to save changes to object definitions in this database." How do I edit my database?

You see this error message whenever you open a database that has been saved in an earlier version of Access. The message appears as a warning even after you choose to open the database in the first dialog box that you always see when opening an older Access database. You can edit the data in your tables, but you won't be able to make design changes to objects, such as table definitions, form and report designs, or query designs, unless you convert the database to Access 97 file format. To convert the database, use these steps:

1. Close any open database.

2. Open the Tools menu, and choose Database Utilities. From the submenu that appears, choose Convert Database.

3. In the dialog box that appears, select the database you want to convert and click OK.

4. In the next dialog box that appears, enter the name for the converted database and click Save.

Caution: If you enter the same name twice, Access replaces your old database with the updated one. Unless you have a backup of your database, try to avoid doing that, so that if you run into any problems with the converted database, you can always go back to the old one.

Note: When you save your converted database with the name of the original database to replace the original, Access doesn't actually replace the old database until it is finished converting. You need to have enough space on your hard disk to hold two complete copies of your database for this to work.

? **We have some data that's stored in Rbase that we need to convert to Access. How can we transfer the data?**

Rbase uses a rather unique format that is truly a world unto itself. You'll need to locate a copy of Rbase Express, a data export utility that was included with the Rbase system disks. Run the program, and use its menu options to export the Rbase tables to dBASE format. You can then import the resulting dBASE files into Access.

? **Can I export only selected records from a table?**

Yes, you can export selected records. However, you don't do so directly. To export selected records, you must create a query containing only those records. You can then export the query. Do this:

1. Design a select query that displays only the records you want to export.
2. Save the query.
3. Right-click the query in the Database window, and choose Save As/Export.
4. In the Save As dialog box that appears, leave the To an External File or Database option selected, and click OK.
5. Choose a desired export file format from the Save as Type list box.
6. Enter a file name for the exported file in the File Name box.
7. Make any other selections desired in the dialog box, and click OK.

? **How can I export a table or query as an Excel worksheet or as a FoxPro or dBASE database file?**

You can use the Save As/Export command of the File menu to export data from an Access table or query to most common file types. Use these steps to do this:

1. Select the table or query in the Database window.
2. Open the File menu, and choose Save As/Export.

3. In the Save As dialog box that appears, turn on the To an External File or Database option, and click OK.

4. In the Save dialog box that appears next, click in the Save as Type list box and choose a desired file format (various versions of FoxPro, dBASE, Excel, and other formats are listed).

5. Under File Name, enter a desired name for the exported file. (If you are exporting to a product that runs under DOS or Windows 3.*x*, remember to restrict your file names to 8 characters or fewer, with no spaces.)

6. Click Export to create the file.

WORKING WITH OLE AND DDE

? When I double-click an OLE object in my form, I see a message that says the file can't be opened. What do I do?

Access displays this message when it can't open the source file for an OLE object. Check these possibilities:

▷ Make sure the source file hasn't been renamed or moved. Click the object, open the Edit menu, and choose OLE/DDE Links. The Links dialog box that appears displays the original file name and path. If the file has been renamed or moved, click the link in the Links box, and click Change Source to reestablish the link.

▷ Make sure that the application needed to open the file is installed on your computer.

▷ If the application used to create the source file is already running, make sure it doesn't have any open dialog boxes.

▷ If it is a linked object, make sure someone else doesn't have it open for exclusive use on a network.

▷ Make sure that you have sufficient memory to open the other application. (Close down uneeded applications, if necessary.)

▷ If you are on a network, check with your network administrator to be sure that you have access rights to the directory in which the source file is located.

? **I want to see the content of my OLE object in my form or report, but all I see is an icon. How can I change this?**

The default display property for your object is set to an icon, rather than the contents of the object. Use these steps to change this:

1. Open the form or report in Design view.
2. Click the icon representing the OLE object.
3. Open the Edit menu, choose the appropriate object from the menu (for example, choose Bitmap Image Object for a bitmap), then click Convert from the submenu that appears. In the Convert dialog box that opens, turn off the Display as Icon check box.

? **Can I use OLE to paste an Access table into another application, such as Word or Excel?**

No, Microsoft Access is not an OLE server; it is only an OLE client. This means that you can put OLE data from other applications into Access, but you cannot put Access data in OLE form into other applications. If you try and paste Access data into another application, the data is copied—not embedded or linked by means of OLE. This means that the pasted data has no continuing link with Access.

For example, when you paste an Access table into Word for Windows, the data appears in a Word table within the document. Pasting an Access table into Excel copies the data in the table in the same column-and-row format that you see in a Datasheet view. (Figure 11-5 shows an Excel worksheet that contains data pasted from Access.) The data appears in these applications just as if you had entered it there. However, if the data is later changed in the Access table, it does not change in the Word or Excel document.

? **I have a Paintbrush image stored as a decorative object in a form. How can I prevent users from double-clicking the picture and editing it in Paintbrush?**

In this case, you have a picture placed in an unbound object frame, and you need to convert it to an image. Use these steps to do so:

1. Open the form in Design view.

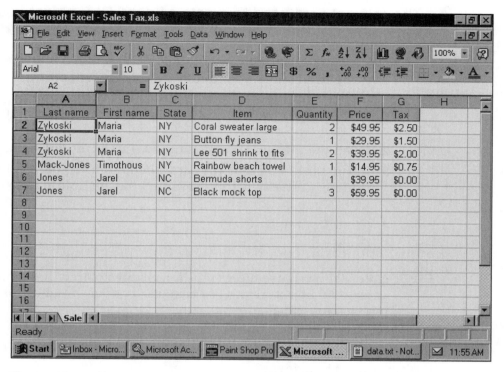

Figure 11-5: Data pasted from an Access table into an Excel worksheet

2. Click the image to select it.

3. Open the Format menu, and choose Change To. From the submenu that appears, choose Image.

4. When Access prompts that you cannot undo this operation, click OK.

When you use these steps, Access converts the unbound object frame to an image control. The image control is a static representation of the picture, and users won't be able to edit it in its original application.

Caution: You shouldn't use the above procedure with an object frame that contains video. If you convert an unbound object frame containing video to an image, just the first frame of the video remains, and users won't be able to play the video.

? The original data used to create a linked OLE object in my form or report has changed. How do I update the link?

You can use these steps to update an OLE link manually.

1. If the object is unbound, open the form or report in Design view, and click it. If the object is a bound object, open the form in Form view and find the record containing the object, then click the object.

2. Open the Edit menu and choose OLE/DDE Links.

3. In the Links box that appears, click the link you want to update. (You can select multiple links by holding the CTRL key as you click each link.)

4. Click Update Now.

5. Click Close.

Note: You can use these steps for pictures placed in unbound and bound object frames. Pictures used as backgrounds for forms are updated automatically.

? How can I play video or sound that's displayed in an OLE object field in a form?

If you store sound or video in an OLE Object field of a table, you can play the sound or video using the following steps:

1. Open the form containing the video or sound data.

2. Locate the record that contains the video or sound clip you want to play.

3. Open the Edit menu, and choose the appropriate command from the bottom of the menu. (For example, to play a video clip, you would open the Edit menu and choose Media Clip Object.)

4. From the submenu that appears, choose Play. When you do so, Access plays the sound or video.

chapter

12 Answers!

Access Macros

Answer Topics!

DESIGNING MACROS 300

How (and why) would I **create a macro**?

How can I **display a message** when a user enters an unlisted value in a combo box?

How can I use a macro for **importing or exporting of data**?

Is there a **length limit** for conditions?

How many **macro actions** can one macro have?

What is the **maximum number of characters** in a comment?

How do I **move the focus** to a control on a subform?

How can I change the **order** of actions?

Can I create a macro that exits Access and **shuts down Windows**?

Can a macro make sure that a **value entered in a form already exists**?

RUNNING MACROS 307

Can I assign a macro to a **key combination**?

Can I force a **message to contain multiple lines** in a dialog box?

Can I **prevent the message "Updating X records..."** from appearing?

Can I **prevent the opening screen** from appearing?

Can I display a message while a **query runs**?

Can I make a macro **run automatically** when I open a database?

Can I make macros **run conditionally**, depending on the data in a form?

Why doesn't my macro to **send keystrokes to a dialog box** work?

Why doesn't my macro to **send keystrokes to a form** work?

Can I use a macro to indicate when a record in a **table was last edited**?

How can I have a macro ignore a line while I **test the macro**?

How can I **troubleshoot** macros?

Can I run a **Visual Basic Function** from a macro?

Can I prevent **warning messages** resulting from a macro's actions?

Can I run another **Windows application** from a macro?

Access Macros @ a Glance

This chapter provides answers to questions that arise when you use macros. You can use macros as a guide for entering data and to make working with forms and reports easier. Macros may not be as comprehensive as Visual Basic for Applications (VBA) procedures, which provide full programming capabilities, but they are wonderful for less complex tasks.

If you are familiar with the design of macros in other applications like Microsoft Word and Excel, you should be aware that macros in Access are designed differently. Whereas you can create Word and Excel macros by turning on a recorder and performing a series of actions, in Access you design macros by specifying actions that you want the macros to perform in a design grid of a Macro window. If you haven't worked with Access macros in the past, you'll want to take a look at the following sidebar, "Macro Terms Revealed," to familiarize yourself with some basic terms you need to know.

Macro Terms Revealed

A macro uses some terms you may not recognize. To get the most out of this chapter's tips on macros, you need to understand these terms.

▷ **Action** A macro command that describes something you want the macro to do, such as opening a form or printing a report.

> ⊳ **Condition**   A logical statement in the Condition column next to an action that determines whether the action will be performed. When the condition is true, the action next to it is performed. Otherwise, the action is ignored. If you want the action to be controlled by the same condition that applied to the preceding action, enter ... (three dots) in the Condition column.
>
> ⊳ **Macro**   A set of actions to perform. Macros are stored either as individual database objects or as part of a macro group, which is a database object.
>
> ⊳ **Macro Group**   A collection of named macros stored as a single database object. You name macros within a macro group by displaying the Macro Name column and entering the name in this column. Only the first action in a macro needs a name. All of the other actions after the name and before the next name are part of that macro. To identify a macro in a macro group, enter the macro group name, a period, and the name of the macro.

DESIGNING MACROS

?   **How (and why) would I create a macro?**

A macro is a list of tasks that Access will carry out for you automatically, so you would want to consider creating a macro for any task you must carry out on a repetitive basis. These tasks include opening and closing forms, printing reports, and setting the values of controls on a form. Figure 12-1 shows a Macro window that contains macros saved in a macro group. Their names appear in the Macro Name column next to their first actions. When a macro window contains only one macro, rather than a macro group, the Macro Name column is empty and can be hidden. The optional Condition column has any conditions that determine whether to perform the action to the right. The Action column contains the instructions to perform. As you move between rows in the top half of the window, the bottom half of the window shows the arguments for the action.

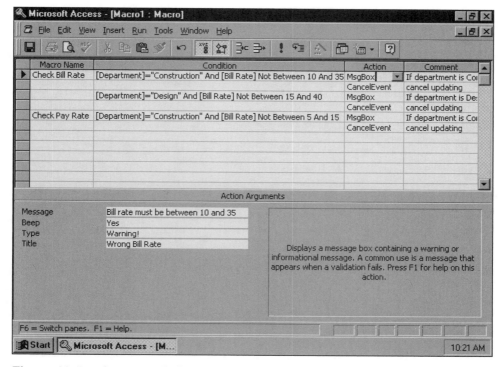

Figure 12-1:   A macro window containing macros saved as a macro group

You create macros from the macro panel of the database window. Start a macro with the following steps:

1. In the Database window, click the Macros tab.

2. Click the New button. When you do so, a new Macro window opens. The parts of a Macro window are shown in Figure 12-2; in the figure, an action has already been added, so action arguments for the action are visible.

3. In the Macro window, click in the first empty row under the Action column.

4. Type the desired action in the cell, or click the down arrow to open the list box and choose the desired action from the list.

5. Enter any desired optional comment in the Comment column, on the same line as the action.

6. Click in the lower portion of the dialog box (or press F6), and specify any desired action arguments.

7. Save the macro by opening the File menu and choosing Save.

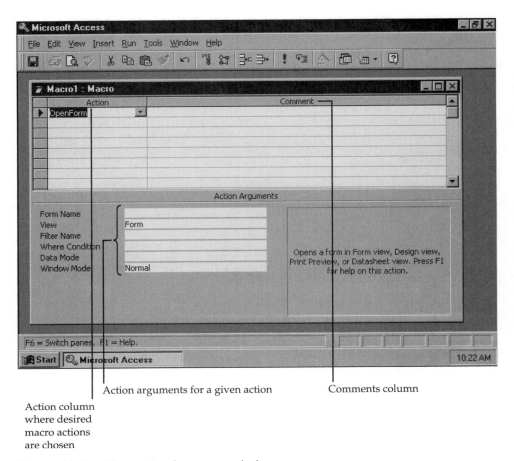

Action column
where desired
macro actions
are chosen

Action arguments for a given action

Comments column

Figure 12-2:   The parts of a macro window

❓ How can a macro **display a message** when a user enters an item in a combo box that is not in its list box?

To execute a macro when a user enters a new item in a combo box, you need to:

▷ Enter the macro name for the combo box's On Not In List property (on the Event tab of the Properties window for the combo box).

▷ Set the Limit To List property (on the Data tab) to Yes.

Once these two things are done, the macro will execute. The Not In List event occurs when a value is entered in the combo box that does not appear on its list while the Limit To List property is set to Yes.

? How can I automate the importing or exporting of data using a macro?

You can use the TransferDatabase, TransferSpreadsheet, or TransferText action to automate the importing or exporting of data. The TransferDatabase action can import or export data to and from other Access databases and from other popular database formats such as dBASE and FoxPro. The TransferSpreadsheet action can import or export data from various Excel and Lotus 1-2-3 spreadsheet formats. The TransferText action can import or export data as delimited or fixed-width text or as HTML files (you can also export text as Word merge files). When you create a new macro, choose TransferDatabase, TransferSpreadsheet, or TransferText as desired in the Action column. Then set the Action Arguments in the lower half of the Macro window as appropriate to the data you are trying to import or export. If you are unsure as to what entry you should make for any argument, you can click within that argument and then press F1 to obtain a help screen dealing with that specific argument.

? Is there a length limit for macro conditions?

A macro's condition can be up to 255 characters. If your condition is longer than this, use a VBA procedure instead.

? How many macro actions can I have in one macro?

Your macros may have as many as 999 actions. This limit applies to the contents of a Macro window, so macros within a macro group are limited to 999 actions for the entire group.

? What is the maximum number of characters I can have in a comment of a macro?

You can have as many as 200 characters of comment for each action in a macro. Use the comment to describe the purpose of the action.

? **How do I tell my macro to move the focus to a control on a subform?**

The GoToControl action moves the focus to a control, such as a subform control. This action accepts only one control name, *not* the full reference syntax of a control on a subform. You cannot use Forms![*Main form*]![*Control Name Of Subform*].Form![*Control On Subform*] as a Control name argument for the GoToControl action. However, subforms are considered just another control on an Access form. Therefore, add the following actions to your macro:

⇨ A GoToControl action that specifies the control name of the subform as the Control Name argument

⇨ Another GoToControl action that specifies the control name of the control within the subform as the Control Name argument

If there's another layer to this scenario, as in a subform within a subform, just add one more GoToControl action.

? **How can I change the order of my macro actions?**

You can insert new actions and rearrange existing actions within a macro as needed, using any of the following techniques:

⇨ To insert a new row in a macro, select the entire row below where the new row should be added. Then press the INS key or choose Rows from the Insert menu.

⇨ To delete an existing row, select the desired row, then press the DEL key or choose Delete Rows from the Edit menu.

⇨ To move an existing row, first click the row selector button to select it. Then drag the selected row to the desired position.

? **Can I create a macro that exits Access and shuts down Windows?**

If you just wanted to exit Access, you could handle the job with a single Quit action added to a macro. But since you also want to shut down Windows, you'll need to have a macro call some VBA coding. The VBA code will call a standard Windows API function that shuts down Windows—the equivalent of choosing Shut Down from the Start menu and clicking Yes in the dialog box. Use these steps:

1. Create a new Module (click the Modules tab in the Database window, then click New). Type the following code into the Declarations section of the module (just below the "Option Compare Database" and "Option Explicit" lines). Although the line appears on two lines here because of printing limitations, you should enter it as one long line in the Module window.

    Declare Function ExitWindowsEx Lib "user32" (ByVal uFlags As Long, ByVal dwReserved As Long) As Long

2. Type the following procedure into the Module window:

    ```
    Function LeaveWindows()
        Dim z As Long
        z = ExitWindowsEx(1, 0)
        Application.Quit acExit
    End Function
    ```

3. Save the module and close it. (You can give it any name you wish.)

4. Create a new macro. In the Action column of the macro, choose RunCode. Under Function Name in the Action Arguments, enter **LeaveWindows( )**.

5. Save the macro and close it.

You can now run the macro from anywhere in your Access application. When run, it will close Access and shut down Windows.

Tip: If you are running Access atop Windows NT Workstation and you want to shut down Windows but not log the user off, you can change the line of code that reads z = **ExitWindowsEx(1, 0)** to z = **ExitWindowsEx(0, 0)**.

Caution Exiting Windows by making calls to the Windows API can leave undeleted files in the Windows Temp directory. These files would then need to be manually deleted at some point to recover disk space.

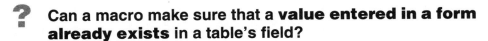

Can a macro make sure that a **value entered in a form already exists** in a table's field?

Yes, a macro can limit entries to a predefined list of options stored in a field. You do this by placing a condition in front of the macro's actions that tests whether the value is acceptable. When this condition is true, Access performs the actions that handle the new entry. When this condition is false, Access skips over the macro actions. The condition uses the DCount domain aggregate function to test whether the field has a matching entry. To add this condition:

1. Create the macro and add the actions that you want performed when the form entry does *not* match any existing entry in a table's field. For example, adding a CancelEvent action stops the updating process. This action combined with the condition lets you halt the updating unless the entry has a match in the field.

2. Click the Conditions toolbar button, or choose Conditions from the View menu to add the Conditions column to the Macro window.

3. Move to the Conditions column in the row containing the first macro action.

4. Enter the following condition:

   DCount("[*Field In Table*]","*Name of Table*","[*Match Field in Table*] = Forms![*Form Name*]![*Control On Form*]") = 0

   In this condition, *Field In Table* is the field name from the table to count entries. *Name of Table* is the table name containing the entry to match. *Match Field in Table* is the name of the field to match from the table. *Form Name* and *Control on Form* identify the form and control with the entry you are testing. This function returns the number of matching entries it finds from the table. If DCount cannot find a matching entry, this function equals 0. This makes the condition true, so Access performs the action next to the condition. You can change the =0 to >0 for conditions used with actions you want performed when Access *does* find a matching entry.

5. Type ... below this condition to repeat it for the other actions that are to be performed if the DCount function does not find a matching entry (or finds one, if ">0" was used).

6. Save the macro.

7. Attach the macro to the event you want to trigger the macro.

8. Use the form. When you make an entry and the event that triggers the macro occurs, Access tests the value you have entered as the condition for the macro's entry.

As an example, suppose you want a form's BeforeUpdate event to run a macro that rejects an entry in the form's FirstName control when it does not match any existing entry in the FirstName field in a table called Friends. You would attach a macro to the On Before Update property that has a CancelEvent action and the following condition:

DCount("[FirstName]","Friends","[FirstName] = Forms![Form1] ![FirstName]")=0

RUNNING MACROS

How can I assign a macro to a **key combination**?

Access macros can be assigned to specific key combinations. For example, you might assign to the CTRL-Y key combination a macro that prints the contents of the active window. You can assign a macro to a key combination by performing the following steps:

1. In the Database window, click the Macros tab, then click New to create a new macro.

2. If the Macro Names column is not visible, choose Macro Names from the View menu or click the Macro Names button on the toolbar.

3. In the Macro Names column, type the code representing the key combination to which you want to assign the macro. (See Table 12-1 for the acceptable key combinations.) Each key or key combination can call one set of macro actions in the macro group.

4. In the Action column, choose the actions you want to run when the key combination is pressed. You can select several actions in sequence by leaving the Macro Name column blank for the rows that follow the key combination.

Table 12-1:   Macro Key Combinations

Syntax	Meaning
Caret(^) followed by a letter or number (for example, ^P, ^6)	CTRL key plus that letter or number; hence, ^P would mean CTRL-P
{F1}	Any function key named inside the braces
^{F1}	CTRL plus any function key named inside the braces
+{F1}	SHIFT plus any function key named inside the braces
{INSERT}	INS key
^{INSERT}	CTRL-INS
+{INSERT}	SHIFT-INS
{DELETE} or {DEL}	DEL key
^{DELETE} or ^{DEL}	CTRL-DEL
+{DELETE} or +{DEL}	SHIFT-DEL

5. Repeat Steps 3 and 4 as needed to make any additional assignments, assigning an action or combination of actions to each key combination.

6. Choose <u>S</u>ave from the <u>F</u>ile menu to save the macro group. When prompted for a name, call the macro AutoKeys. The key assignments are stored for use when you save the macro, and they automatically take effect when the database is opened. Table 12-1 shows the key combinations used to assign keys to macros.

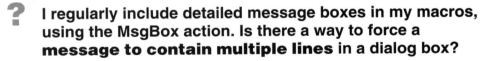 **I regularly include detailed message boxes in my macros, using the MsgBox action. Is there a way to force a message to contain multiple lines in a dialog box?**

You can force Access to divide a message into multiple lines with the line breaks where you want them by entering the Message argument text as an expression that includes the Chr( ) function with the ASCII values of 13 (for a carriage return) and 10 (for a line feed). You will need to begin the expression with an equals sign and surround the text with quotes. As an example, you could enter an expression like this one in the Message argument for the MsgBox action in a macro:

= "Forms cannot remain open for over ten minutes."& Chr(13) & Chr(10) & "Form has been closed automatically."

When the macro runs, the resulting message box contains multiple lines with a line break after the first sentence, like the one shown here.

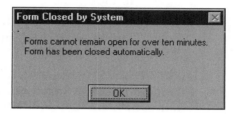

In a macro that updates a table, can I **prevent the message "Updating X records..."** from appearing?

Yes. Add the SetWarnings action to the macro. The default for this action is No. This action prevents showing system messages such as updating records and appending records. Access still displays error messages.

My Autoexec macro displays an opening screen for my application. Can I **prevent the opening screen** from appearing every time I open my database?

To keep an Autoexec macro from executing when you open the database, press SHIFT while you select the database to open.

Is there a way to have a macro display a "please wait" message while a **query runs?**

You can manage this by running the query from within a macro and having the macro display a small form containing the text of your warning message. The first macro action opens the form with the message, the second action runs the query, and the last action closes the form. Use these steps:

1. Create a new form that is not based on any table or query. Add a label to the form containing the message you want displayed as the query runs. In the All tab of the Properties window for the form, set the form's Scroll Bars property to Neither, the Modal property to Yes, the Popup property to Yes, and the Record Selectors and Navigation Buttons properties to No.

2. Save and close the form. Call it **Warning**.

3. Create a new macro. For the first action, choose Open Form. Under Action Arguments, set the Form Name to **Warning**.

4. For the second action of the macro, choose Open Query. Under Action Arguments, set the Query Name to the name of the query you want to run. Set the View and Edit options as desired for your query.

5. For the last action of the macro, choose Close. Under Action Arguments, set the Object Type to Form. Set the Object Name to **Warning**.

6. Save and close the macro.

When the macro runs, the form containing the warning message is displayed on the screen as the query runs. Once the query finishes running, the form closes. Note that if the computer running the query is very fast or the underlying table is not very large, the message may not remain on the screen long enough for the viewer to see it.

How can I cause a macro to **run automatically** when I open a database?

In Access, any macro that is named *Autoexec* runs when the database containing that macro is opened. To start any macro automatically, create the new macro and add the desired actions. Save the macro, and when prompted for a name, call it **Autoexec**. Thereafter, each time the database is initially opened, the macro runs automatically (unless the user holds down the SHIFT key while opening the database).

? How can I make macros run conditionally, depending on the data in a form?

You can do this by adding a conditional expression to the macro's design. To enter a conditional expression in a macro, perform the following steps:

1. If the Condition column is not visible in the Macro window, choose Conditions from the View menu, or click the Conditions button on the toolbar.

2. In the Condition column, enter an expression in the row where you want to establish the condition.

3. In the Action column, choose the macro action you want Access to perform when the condition is true.

? I have a macro that uses a SendKeys action to send keystrokes to a dialog box, but the keystrokes aren't being sent. What's wrong?

Dialog boxes suspend the operation of macros. Since this occurs by design in Access, you must place your SendKeys action prior to the action that opens the dialog box, and set the Wait argument to No to prevent any pauses in processing of the keys.

? I have a macro that uses a SendKeys action to send keystrokes to a form. The keystrokes are valid when typed manually, but when the macro runs, I hear beeping and I don't get the desired results. What's wrong?

This usually happens due to a timing conflict; the macro is sending the keystrokes before some other part of Access is ready to receive them. Open the macro in Design view, click in the SendKeys action, and set the Wait argument under Action Arguments to Yes. This will cause the macro to wait until the keystrokes are processed before moving on to the next macro action.

? **Can I use a macro to store a date and time in a field to indicate when a record in a table was last edited?**

You can use a macro to add a *timestamp* to records indicating the date and time of the last update by having the macro store the current date and time in a control of a form used to edit the records. The following steps assume that your table contains a date/time field called "Last Modified," and your form used to edit the field contains a corresponding control named "Last Modified."

1. Create a new macro. In the Action column, choose SetValue. Under Item in the Action Arguments area, enter the name of your form's control, surrounded by brackets. For example, assuming the control is named Last Modified, you would enter **[Last Modified]** under Item.

2. Under Expression, enter **Now( )** and note that you should *not* precede the expression with an equal sign.

3. Save the macro and name it **Last Modified**.

4. Open the form used to edit the table in Design view.

5. Choose Properties from the View menu to display the Properties window for the form.

6. On the Event tab, set the Before Update property to the name of the macro (in this example, **Last Modified**).

7. Save and close the form.

When you use the form to edit a record, the value of the current date will be stored in the field once you move to another record. If it isn't important for users to see the contents of the Last Modified field, you can go into Design view for the form and set the Visible property for the control to No. The control won't appear, but the macro will still store the current date to the field as edits are made.

? **How can I have a macro temporarily ignore a line while I test the macro?**

You can disable any line by putting a condition in front of it that is always false. Choose Conditions from the View menu, or click the Conditions button on the toolbar. Type **0** into the conditions for the lines you want to ignore. An action executes only if the condition evaluates as true. The zero, which equals false, prevents the macro from executing that particular line. Remember that this affects *only* the line to which you added the 0 (and subsequent lines that have ... in the Condition column). When you no longer want this line ignored, remove the 0.

How can I **troubleshoot** problems I'm having with my macros?

You can use a number of different techniques to find the cause of problems in the design of your macros, including the following:

⮞ *Action Failed Dialog Box*   Whenever a macro halts due to an error, Access displays the Action Failed dialog box (an example is shown here).

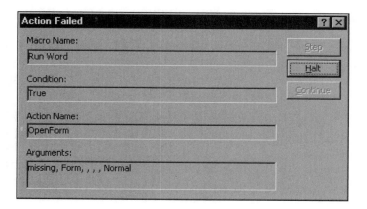

The Action Failed dialog box contains the name of the macro that was halted, the value of any expression in the Condition column at the time the macro stopped, the Action Name of the action where the macro halted, and the arguments for the action. You can use this information to narrow down the source of the problem, and click Halt to stop the macro.

⮞ *Single Stepping*   You can run a macro one step at a time to analyze what happens during each step. Open the macro in Design view, then open the <u>R</u>un menu and choose <u>S</u>ingle Step (or click the Single Step button in the toolbar). Close the macro, then run it. As the macro executes its first step, you will see the Single Step dialog box, shown here.

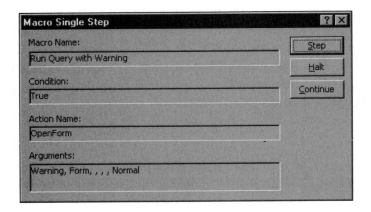

You can click the Step button each time you want to proceed to the next step of the macro. When you are done using the single-step process to test the macro, open the macro in Design view and again choose Single Step from the Run menu to turn off the Single Step feature.

▷ *Using the MsgBox Action*   If you suspect that a value of a control may be causing a problem at some point within the macro, you can add a MsgBox action that displays the value of that control at any point in the macro. Add a MsgBox action where desired among the steps of the macro, and for the Message argument, enter the name of the control you want to check. For example, if you wanted to show the value of a control named Amount Due in a form named Billing, you would enter the expression

=**Forms![Billing]![Amount Due]**

in the Message argument.

❓ How can I run a **Visual Basic Function** from a macro?

To run a VBA function from a macro, add a RunCode action to the macro. In the Function Name argument, enter the name of the desired function.

? **Is there a way to prevent the warning messages and dialog boxes that may appear as a result of a macro's actions?**

You can suppress the warning messages that may appear while your macro runs. At the start of the macro, add a SetWarnings action, and set the Warnings On argument to No. This action is the equivalent of telling Access to press ENTER whenever a warning message box appears. If you use this technique, you may want to add another SetWarnings action at the end of the macro, with the Warnings On argument set to Yes, to turn the warnings back on.

? **How can I run another Windows application from a macro?**

To run another application, add the RunApp action to your macro. In the Command Line argument, enter the command needed to start the program.

Tip: If you don't know the precise wording (including the path) for a command line, and an icon exists on the desktop for the program you want to run, right-click the program's icon and choose Properties from the shortcut menu. Click the Shortcut tab in the dialog box that appears. You'll find the text of the command line highlighted in the Target box. While it is highlighted, you can press CTRL-C to copy the command line, then switch back to Access, go to the macro in Design view, click in the Command Line argument, and press CTRL-V to place the command line in the argument.

chapter

13 Answers!

Access Charts

Answer Topics!

Access Charts
@ a Glance

Access provides the ability to produce charts in forms and reports, based on numeric data stored in your tables or accessible through your queries. Access makes use of Microsoft Graph, an application provided with Access and with other Microsoft Office 97 products, to create charts that appear as objects within the forms or reports. The questions in this chapter are divided into two areas:

➤ **Working with Charts** This portion of the chapter answers questions about the basic creation and formatting of charts.

➤ **Troubleshooting** This part of the chapter provides answers to problems that arise when using charts in Access forms and reports.

WORKING WITH CHARTS

 How do I create a chart?

The easiest way to create a chart is with the aid of the Chart Wizard. The Chart Wizard presents a series of questions and, depending on your answers, will either summarize the data from all the records in a single chart or create a record-based chart that changes as you move from record to record. Figure 13-1 shows an example of a chart in an Access form.

 Note: To use the Chart Wizard, you must have Microsoft Graph installed on your system. Microsoft Graph is supplied with Access and with Office 97 Professional, but it is not installed with Access by default. You may need to rerun Setup to add Microsoft Graph.

You can use these steps to add a chart to an existing form or report:

1. Open the form or report in Design view.
2. Open the Insert menu and choose Chart.

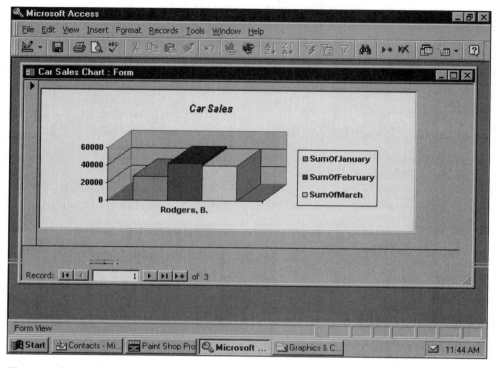

Figure 13-1:   A chart placed in an Access form

3. In the form or report, click where you want to place the chart. In a moment, the first Chart Wizard dialog box appears.

4. Follow the directions in the Chart Wizard dialog boxes to create a chart based on the fields you select within the underlying table or query.

5. Save the form or report, and switch to Form view or to Report Print Preview to see the finished chart.

And you can use these steps to create a new chart from scratch:

1. In the Database window, click the Forms tab if you want to create a form containing a chart, or click the Reports tab to create a report with a chart.

2. Click New.

3. In the dialog box that appears, select the desired table or query that will supply the data for the chart.

4. Click Chart Wizard, then click OK.

5. Follow the directions in the Chart Wizard dialog boxes to create a chart based on the fields you select within the underlying table or query.

6. Save the form or report. Switch to Form view or to Report Print Preview to see the finished chart.

I don't like my chart's colors (chart type, fonts). How can I modify the chart?

You make modifications to charts by editing them within Microsoft Graph. (Microsoft Graph is the mini-application that's used to create and edit charts within Access as well as within Microsoft Word and Microsoft PowerPoint.) Open the form or report containing the chart in Design view, and double-click the chart. In a moment, a Microsoft Graph window opens containing a representative chart as shown in Figure 13-2. Also, the menus change to reflect the options of Microsoft Graph. Note that as you work in Microsoft

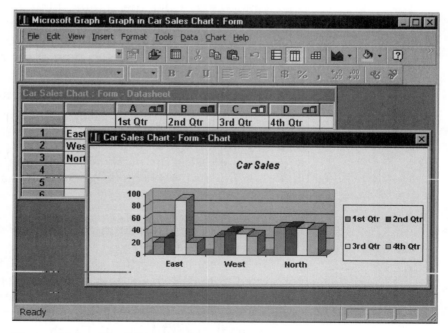

Figure 13-2:   The Microsoft Graph window

Graph, you see sample data, not the actual data from your underlying table or query.

▷ To change the color of markers in a chart, first select the marker (make sure all six selection handles appear on the data marker you wish to format), then right-click it and choose Format Data Point from the shortcut menu that appears. Click the Patterns tab in the next dialog box, and click a desired color to select it, then click OK.

▷ To change the fonts used for labeling along an axis or a title or the chart's legend, first right-click the label or title or legend that you want to change, then choose Format from the shortcut menu that appears. (The menu will provide an option called Format Axis, Format Legend, or Format Chart Title, depending on what object you selected.) Click the Font tab in the next dialog box, choose the desired fonts, then click OK.

▷ To change the type of chart (for example, from a bar chart to a line chart), open the Chart menu and choose Chart Type. Click the Standard tab in the dialog box that appears (if it isn't already selected). At the left side of the dialog box, click the desired chart type. Then click the desired sub-type at the right side of the dialog box, and click OK.

When done making the desired changes to the chart, open the File menu and choose Exit and Return to leave Microsoft Graph and return to the form or report. (The command's precise wording will be "Exit and Return to *your object*," where *your object* is the name of your form or report.) When you view or print the form or report, the changes will appear in the chart.

Tip: There are more formatting options available in Microsoft Graph than this chapter can reasonably cover. However, you can get detailed help that is specific to charts while you are editing a chart. Get into Microsoft Graph using the steps described above, then open the Help menu and choose Contents and Index. The help screens that appear will provide specifics on the use of Microsoft Graph.

TROUBLESHOOTING

? Why can't I put my chart's **columns in the order** I want?

You can't change the actual order of the columns within Microsoft Graph; this is determined by the order of the fields providing the data in your underlying table or query. You could modify the query, moving the fields around so that they fall in the desired order, and rerun the Chart Wizard to build a new chart. But there is another way to do this without discarding the existing chart. You can change the order of the data in the Row Source property for the form or report containing the chart. Use these steps:

1. Open the form or report containing the chart in Design view.

2. Click the chart to select it, then open the View menu and choose Properties to display the Properties window for the chart.

3. Click the Data tab, then click in the Row Source property.

4. Click the Build button to the right of the property. A Query Builder window for the Row Source property opens, like that shown in Figure 13-3.

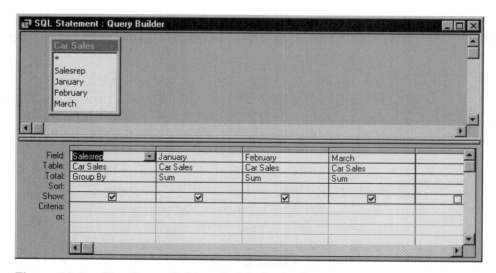

Figure 13-3:   The Query Builder window for the Row Source property of a chart

5. In the window, rearrange the fields in the order that you want them to appear as the markers in the chart, from left to right.

6. Close the query and save the changes.

When you redisplay the form or open the report, the chart columns will appear in the proper order.

❓ Why does my chart appear **dimmed or blank?**

This problem occurs when the Row Source property for a chart is no longer valid. (Typically, this happens because the underlying query has been renamed or deleted.) Use these steps to check that a chart's Row Source property is still valid:

1. Open the form or report containing the chart in Design view.

2. Click the chart to select it, then open the View menu and choose Properties to display the Properties window for the chart.

3. Click the Data tab, then click in the Row Source property.

4. Make sure that the Row Source property box contains a valid entry. Make any needed edits to the entry, and save the form or report.

❓ Why can't I change the names of the **labels** on my chart?

When you use Microsoft Graph to change the wording of any labels for chart axes, they get overwritten by the names of the fields in the table or query that supplies the data. If you want axis labels that are different from your field names, you'll need to change the query specified by the Row Source property of the chart. Use these steps:

1. Open the form or report containing the chart in Design view.

2. Click the chart to select it, then open the View menu and choose Properties to display the Properties window for the chart.

3. Click the Data tab, then click in the Row Source property.

4. Click the Build button to the right of the property. A Query Builder window for the Row Source property opens, like that shown earlier in Figure 13-3.

5. In the query, enter the name you want followed by a colon in front of the actual name of the field. For example, if you want a field named Jan to read as January 97 in the chart, enter **January 97:Jan** as a name in the query field.

6. Close the query and save the changes.

When you redisplay the form or open the report, the label will contain your desired wording.

chapter

14 Answers!

Access and the Internet

Answer Topics!

Access and the Internet
@ a Glance

The major difference between Access 97 and its immediate predecessor (Access 95) lies in the added capabilities for working with the Internet. Access 97 provides features for publishing data to static HTML and dynamic HTX/IDC and ASP formats, ready for uploading to your web server. Access 97 also introduces the concept of *hyperlinks* to Access databases. Users can click on hyperlinks to jump to other files, to locations within other Office 97 documents, or to web sites on the Internet or on a company's intranet.

This chapter answers questions that arise when you are using the features of Access designed to link to the Internet or to a corporate intranet. Questions throughout the chapter fall into these three areas:

▷ **Working with Hyperlinks** In this part of the chapter, you'll find answers to questions about hyperlinks, which let you jump to other files or to Web sites from within Access.

▷ **Access and the Web** Here you'll find answers to questions about the Web features of Access in general, and how you can produce files that can be published on the Internet or on an intranet.

▷ **Troubleshooting** This portion of the chapter will help you quickly overcome problems that arise in working with data on the Web, in using links, and in exporting files for uploading to web servers.

WORKING WITH HYPERLINKS

? **How do I create hyperlinks as part of a table design?**

Access 97 adds a new field type, *Hyperlink,* to the field types that are available during the table creation process, so adding a hyperlink to a table is as simple a matter as choosing Hyperlink from the list of available data types. Open the desired table in Design view, click in the Field Name column, and enter a name for the field. Then choose Hyperlink from the drop-down list. After saving the table's structure, you can open the table in Datasheet view and enter the desired addresses in the Hyperlink fields of the table.

Once the hyperlink field exists in the table, you can insert hyperlink addresses in the field by clicking in the field

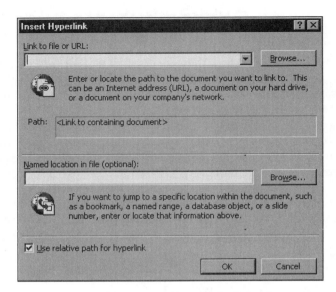

Figure 14-1:   The Insert Hyperlink dialog box

and choosing Hyperlink from the Insert menu, or clicking the Insert Hyperlink button in the toolbar. This causes an Insert Hyperlink dialog box to appear (Figure 14-1), which you can use to specify the hyperlink address. (An alternative method of entering the address is to type the URL or filename and path into the hyperlink field.)

Tip: Hyperlinks can also be used to jump to locations in other Office 97 documents or to files created with other Windows applications as well as to Web sites. For example, you could use hyperlinks to jump to a slide in a PowerPoint presentation, to a bookmark in a Word document, or to a named range in an Excel worksheet. You can also use hyperlinks to jump to a file created with other Windows applications. When you identify a file as the location for the hyperlink, a jump to that file causes it to be opened by the Windows application associated with the file type.

How can I **delete a hyperlink** that's stored in a table?

You can delete the entry in a Hyperlink field of a table by performing these steps.

1. Open the table or query containing the hyperlink field, or open a form that displays the data.

2. Locate the hyperlink entry in the record that you want to delete.

3. In the cell of the Datasheet or in the control of the form, right-click the entry, and choose Cut from the shortcut menu that appears.

? When I click in a hyperlink field to edit the link, Access launches my browser and takes me to the link. How can I edit a hyperlink instead of jumping to it?

If you want to edit the entry that's stored in a hyperlink field, you can't just click in the field. Since Access is designed to use hyperlinks as jump points, clicking in the field always results in a jump to the link. To edit the link, right-click the entry, choose Hyperlink, then choose Edit Hyperlink from the shortcut menus. In a moment, you see the Edit Hyperlink dialog box, shown in Figure 14-2.

In the upper half of the dialog box, you enter the valid jump address. (This can be a URL for a Web site, or it can be a filename for a file stored locally or on an attached network.) Optionally, in the lower half of the dialog box,

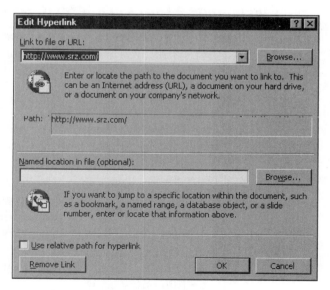

Figure 14-2:   The Edit Hyperlink dialog box

you can enter a location within another Office 97 document that you want to jump to, such as the name of a Word bookmark, a named range in an Excel worksheet, or the number of a slide within a PowerPoint presentation.

? What is a **hyperlink**?

A hyperlink is a link from Access to a Web site, a location in another file on your hard disk or on the local area network, or another object in the Access database.

Hyperlink fields in Access tables accept entries that are in the form of URLs or UNCs. The URL, for *Uniform Resource Locator,* is the standard way of naming locations on the Internet and on private intranets. A Web site address such as **http://www.microsoft.com** is a URL. The UNC, for *Uniform Naming Convention,* is the standard way of identifying file locations under Windows. UNC addresses include paths to files on an attached hard disk, such as **G:\Data\Documents\Smith\sales98.xls**, or on other computers on the local area network, such as **\\server2\vpath1\Smith\sales98.xls**.

? Can I create a **label** in a form to serve as a hyperlink?

You can add a label to a form so that the label can be used as a hyperlink. If a user of the form clicks on the label, Access then makes the jump to the link. Use these steps to add a label that serves as a link:

1. Open the form in Design view.

2. Open the Insert menu and choose Hyperlink, or click the Insert Hyperlink button in the toolbar. The Insert Hyperlink dialog box appears, as shown earlier in Figure 14-1.

3. In the "Link to File or URL" entry at the top of the dialog box, enter the desired address for the hyperlink. (You can click the Browse button at the right to open a dialog box where you can browse for the location of a file.) If the link is to another object in the current Access database, leave this entry blank.

4. If the link is to a Web site, leave the "Named Location in File" entry blank. If the link is to a location in another Office 97 document and you want the link to lead to a location in the document other than its beginning, enter the exact location (the name of the Word bookmark, a named range in Excel, or the PowerPoint slide number). If the link is to another object in the current database, enter the object type followed by the object name (such as **Table Clients** or **Form Sales98**).

5. Click OK. Access adds a label to the form, with the text of the label containing the address for the link.

6. Right-click the label, choose Properties, and click the Format tab in the Properties window that opens.

7. Change the Caption property to your desired text, and make any desired changes to the size and fonts used for the label.

8. Save the form by choosing Save from the File menu.

After saving the form, you can test the link by switching to Form view and clicking on the label.

? How can I add a picture to a form so that users can click on the picture to follow a hyperlink?

Using an existing graphic (such as a Windows Paintbrush bitmap or an icon), you can add a picture to a form to serve as a hyperlink. When users click on the picture, Access makes the jump to the link. Use these steps:

1. Open the form in Design view.

2. In the Toolbox, click the Image Control tool. (If the Toolbox isn't visible, choose Toolbox from the View menu to display it.)

3. In the form, click where you want to create the picture.

4. In the Insert Picture dialog box that appears, locate the desired picture file and click OK to add the picture to the form.

5. With the Image control selected, choose Properties from the View menu to open the Properties window for the control.

6. Click the Format tab and enter the desired address for the hyperlink in the Hyperlink Address property. (You can click the Build button, which appears at the right after you click in the property, to open a dialog box where you can browse for the location of a file.) If the link is to another object in the current Access database, leave this entry blank.

7. If the link is to a Web site, leave the Hyperlink Subaddress property blank. If the link is to a location in another Office 97 document, and you want the link to lead to a location in the document other than its beginning, enter the exact location (the name of the Word bookmark, a named range in Excel, or the PowerPoint slide number). If the link is to another object in the current database, enter the object type followed by the object name (such as **Table Clients** or **Form Sales98**).

8. Save the form by choosing <u>S</u>ave from the <u>F</u>ile menu.

After saving the form, you can test the link by switching to Form view and clicking on the image.

ACCESS AND THE WEB

?   **How can I display a Web page on a form?**

If you have Internet Explorer 3.0 or above installed on your system, you can display Web pages within forms by adding a Web Browser control to the form. (The Web Browser control is an ActiveX control. It is not provided with Access but is installed automatically as part of the installation of Microsoft Internet Explorer.) Figure 14-3 shows the use of a Web Browser control within an Access form.

Use these steps to add a control that lets you display a Web page:

1. Open the form in Design view.

2. In the toolbox, click the More Controls tool to open a menu that contains all ActiveX controls installed on your system.

3. In the menu of ActiveX controls, choose the Microsoft Web Browser control.

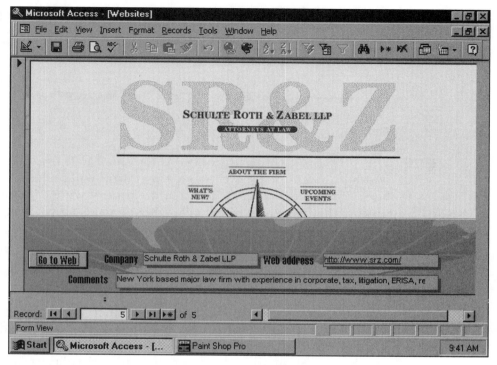

Figure 14-3:   A Web Browser control used to display a Web page within a form in Access

4. In the form, click where you want to place the control. A rectangle appears, representing the Web Browser control.

5. Size and move the control to the desired location in the form.

Once the control exists, you can use the *Navigate* method for the control to jump to desired Web sites. You do this using Visual Basic for Applications (VBA). The syntax for the method is *ControlName.***Navigate** *"Resource-location"*, where *ControlName* is the name of the Web Browser control and *Resource-location* is the URL for the Web site. As an example, you could place a button in the form that, when clicked, would open Microsoft's Web site in the control. Assuming you named the Web Browser control "MyBrowser", the code

attached to the On Click property of the command button
would look like this:

```
Private Sub Command1_Click

    MyBrowser.Navigate "http://www.microsoft.com"

End Sub
```

▪▪▪▪▪▪   *Tip:*   If the Web Browser control is too small to show the full
width or height of the Web page, the control will include scroll
bars. But it is usually best to make the control wide enough to
display the full width of the average Web page, so your users
aren't forced to resort to unneeded scrolling.

❓ What are the differences between **file formats** that Access can produce for publishing to the Web?

The Publish to the Web Wizard can produce Web pages in
static form or in dynamic form. Web pages that are saved
in static form are saved under the HTML file format. They
can be used with all Web servers, but they display static
data—when data in the tables or queries change, the HTML
files produced are not updated automatically to reflect any
changes. Dynamic Web pages can be saved to HTX/IDC
(Internet Database Connector) format or to ASP (Microsoft
Active Server Pages) format. These pages automatically
reflect any changes made to the underlying Access tables
or queries, but they are not compatible with all Web servers.
The dynamic files require the Microsoft Internet Information
Server with the IDC Add-In, the Microsoft Personal Web
Server, Microsoft Windows NT Workstation with Peer Web
Services, or another Web server that is fully compatible with
the HTX/IDC or ASP file formats.

❓ How can I save a table, query, form, or report in **HTML** format?

The Publish to the Web Wizard (available by choosing Save
as HTML from the File menu) works well when you want
to publish a collection of database objects to the Web. But if
you want to save a single database object in HTML format,

use the Save <u>A</u>s/Export option of the <u>F</u>ile menu. You can use these steps:

1. In the Database window, select the desired table, query, form, or report.

2. Open the <u>F</u>ile menu and choose Save <u>A</u>s/Export.

3. In the Save As dialog box which appears, leave the "To an External File or Database" option selected, and click OK.

4. In the Save dialog box, which appears next, choose the location and enter a name for the file in the "File name" box. In the "Save as type" box, change the selection to HTML Documents.

5. Click Export to create the HTML file in the specified location.

 ### How can I **publish my Access database** to the Internet?

Access 97 includes a Publish to the Web Wizard. You can use the Publish to the Web Wizard to publish a collection of tables, queries, forms, and reports so that you can upload the data to the Internet or to a company's intranet. This wizard can be started by means of the Save as <u>H</u>TML option of the <u>F</u>ile menu. You can use these steps to publish the database for uploading to the Internet or an intranet:

1. Open the desired database.

2. Choose Save as <u>H</u>TML from the <u>F</u>ile menu. In a moment, the first page of the Publish to the Web Wizard appears, explaining the purpose of the wizard.

3. Click Next, to display the second dialog box of the Publish to the Web Wizard, shown in Figure 14-4.

4. Using the different tabs of the dialog box, turn on the check boxes for the desired tables, queries, forms, and reports that you want to publish. When done selecting the desired objects, click Next.

5. Follow the directions in the successive dialog boxes that appear. Access will ask where the files should be stored, what types of files should be created (static HTML or dynamic HTX/IDC or ASP), and whether a home page

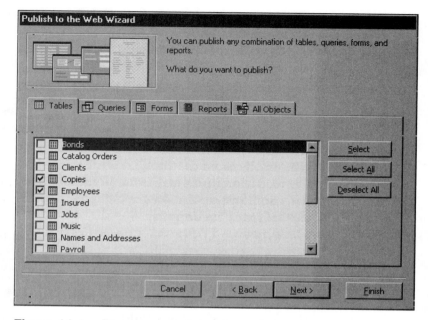

Figure 14-4:   The second dialog box of the Publish to the Web Wizard

linking the items together should be included in the files produced by the wizard.

When you finish answering questions presented by the wizard, Access creates the files necessary to produce your Web pages. You can then upload the files to your Web server.

TROUBLESHOOTING

When trying to open a Web page saved in IDC format, I get an error message saying "Error HTTP/1.0 Access Forbidden." What's wrong?

This error occurs if you don't have Read or Execute permission for the virtual directory on the Web server where the files are stored. Contact the webmaster for the server and request that you be given access rights to the appropriate directory on the server.

? After I use the Publish to the Web Wizard to create Dynamic HTX/IDC or ASP files on our Web server, I get the message "Data source name not found" when I try to view the Web page. Why is this happening?

There are two possible reasons for this error. Either you did not create a System DSN data source on the Web server, or the dynamic files you created in Access for the Web server contain an incorrect data source name. You can use these steps to check the data source name or to add a new one:

1. Go to your Web server, and double-click the ODBC icon in the Control Panel.

2. In the Data Sources dialog box, click System DSN.

3. If you don't see the name of the System DSN you used in the Publish to the Web Wizard, click Add.

4. Click Microsoft Access Driver, then click Finish.

5. Fill in the entries in the ODBC Microsoft Access 97 Setup dialog box that appears. Note that the name you enter in the Data Source Name box is the same name that you must use in the Data Source Name box shown in the Publish to the Web Wizard of Access.

6. Click OK to close the ODBC Microsoft Access 97 Setup dialog box.

7. Click OK to close the ODBC Data Source Administrator box.

8. If the Data Source Name you entered on the Web server differs from the name you entered in the Publish to the Web Wizard, restart the Publish to the Web Wizard and rebuild your Web pages, entering the correct Data Source Name when asked.

? When I click a hyperlink, an error message appears. What's wrong?

This problem occurs when, for one reason or another, Access cannot locate the resource that's specified by the hyperlink. If the destination is in another file, the file may have been renamed or moved. Use My Computer or Windows Explorer to check for the existence of the file.

If the file has been renamed or is in a different location, you'll need to change the hyperlink accordingly. To edit the hyperlink, right-click the hyperlink, and choose Hyperlink then Edit Hyperlink from the shortcut menu.

If the resource is on the Internet, check to make sure you have access to the Internet. If you can reach the net, the server where the resource is located is probably busy or unavailable.

If the resource is on your company's intranet, check your network connections to be sure your company's Web server is accessible. You may want to check with your network administrator to ensure that you have access rights to the resource.

When I try to export an action query as HTML, I get the message, "an action query cannot be used as a row source." What's wrong?

This behavior is an intentional design trait of Access. You cannot export action queries to any of the Web server file formats (HTML, IDC, or ASP). To work around this, use the action query as a data source for a make-table query. Run the make-table query to create a new table, then export the table as HTML.

When I export a form with a subform as HTML, only the data from the main form appears in the HTML document. What happened to the data from the subform?

With forms exported as HTML, this is an intentional limitation of design. When forms containing subforms are exported as HTML, only the records visible in the main form are exported to the file. To get around this, create a relational query that contains all the data you need, then export the query to an HTML file.

Why are my subforms blank when browsing Active Server Page (ASP) files under Windows NT Workstation?

This is a known bug that occurs when using Internet Explorer 3.0 or 3.01 running on Windows NT 4.0. Under Windows 95, when Active Server Page files contain a subform, the subform gets displayed in a separate instance of Internet Explorer, but under Windows NT 4.0 the second instance of Internet Explorer needed to display the subform fails to launch. At the time of this writing, there is no workaround other than to use a different platform than Windows NT 4.0 for displaying the subform data at the Web page.

?   I use a table containing hyperlinks to jump to different links. As I do this repeatedly, my system response slows to a crawl. What's wrong?

This is a trait of the way hyperlinks call needed applications, particularly other Microsoft Office 97 applications such as Word, Excel, and PowerPoint. When you click a series of hyperlinks in succession, all the programs needed to open those resources are loaded into memory. As you click another hyperlink, the previous program is not automatically released from memory. And if you jump to multiple locations on the Internet from the hyperlinks in your Access database, your system may load multiple instances of your Web browser. (We confirmed this behavior with both Microsoft's Internet Explorer 3.01 and with Netscape Navigator 3.0.) You'll need to keep track of your system resources visually by glancing at the Windows 95 Taskbar. If there are instances of applications that you no longer need, close them by right-clicking each application's icon in the Taskbar and choosing Close from the shortcut menu.

chapter

15 Answers!

Access
and Visual
Basic for
Applications

Answer Topics!

How can I **convert macros** to VBA code?

Can VBA **create a form or report**?

Can I use VBA to **create a table**?

Why doesn't my **Database window** show a new TableDef object in the list of tables?

Can I **declare the type of data** returned by a function?

Can I stop an **infinite loop**?

Why does Access ignore a control's **input mask** after I add a VBA function to assign its value?

Can I continue a **line of code** that is very long?

Can I carry out a **macro action** from within a VBA procedure?

Can I **print a single procedure** in a module?

Can I **protect my VBA code** from being read or changed?

Can I set the **Record Source** property of a form at run time?

Can I **step through my Function procedure** to find errors?

I have trouble with **syntax in VBA**. Is there an easy way to write code?

Can I **test the functions** before using them?

Can I view **two procedures at once**?

Can I replace a form name with the contents of a **variable**?

Access and Visual Basic for Applications @ a Glance

Visual Basic for Applications (VBA) is a programming language that can be used as a part of Access applications. Blocks of VBA code are saved as procedures in modules. You can run these procedures separately or as part of other database objects. The answers provided in this chapter all deal with VBA and are divided into the following areas:

➡ **What Is...?** This section provides answers regarding important definitions for various objects you'll work with as you write VBA code.

➡ **Using VBA with Access** In this portion of the chapter, you'll find answers to questions about performing various operations through the use of VBA code.

WHAT IS...?

❓ What is an **event**?

An *event* is a specific occurrence that takes place on or inside of an Access object. Events in Access include mouse clicks on buttons, the focus moving into or out of a control, forms opening or closing, or a section of a report being formatted for printing. Events are generally the result of the user doing something to an Access object. Most VBA programming revolves around events and how the Access environment should react to those events.

❓ What is an **event procedure**?

An event procedure is a Sub procedure associated with a particular event property of a form or report. When the particular event occurs, Access calls the event procedure. All the event procedures for a form or report are saved with the form or report. Access assigns each event procedure a specific name that indicates the control and the event to which the procedure is assigned. For example, the event procedure in Figure 15-1 is the procedure run when you click the button named Command21.

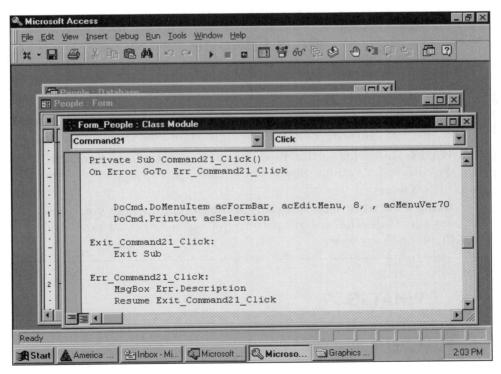

Figure 15-1:   An event procedure assigned to an event on a form

? What is a **function**?

A function is a specialized program that returns a value. When the function is called by an Access object, it performs a calculation of some sort and returns a value to the object that called it. Access provides a large number of built-in functions; for example, the =Now( ) function returns the current date and time. To construct custom functions that Access doesn't provide, VBA code is commonly used. For example, you could use VBA code to provide a function that would return the date of the first Monday after any given date, or a function that would accept a length and width in feet and return the number of square yards of the measured area.

When you use functions, you provide the function with information in the form of *arguments*. Arguments can be thought of as specific definitions for the function. They provide the additional information VBA needs to handle the task exactly as you prefer. The arguments follow the name of the function, and they are enclosed in parentheses.

? What is a **module**?

Modules are named collections of VBA code. In Access 97 you can have *standard modules* and *class modules*. *Standard modules* contain code that should be available to other procedures throughout your database. *Class modules* are used to contain definitions for new objects. The modules that are stored as part of forms or reports are class modules, while the modules that are visible in the Modules tab of the Database window are standard modules. Each module has a declarations section, which stores information such as user-defined data types, global constants, global variables, and references to external procedures in a dynamic link library (DLL). The rest of the module contains Function and Sub procedures. The information in the declarations section is available to all of the procedures in that module.

You can store all of your VBA code in one module or in several different ones. A form or report can have its own module to store the procedures it uses. This module gathers all the procedures for a form or report into one location. However, a form or report can also perform procedures that are in a separate module.

? What is a **recordset**?

Recordsets represent data from a base table or the result of a query. Access has three types of recordsets: tables, dynasets, and snapshots.

? What is the difference between a **Sub procedure and a Function procedure**?

A *Sub* procedure is a routine that carries out an operation. Unlike a Function procedure, a Sub procedure cannot return a value. *Function* procedures can return values and be used in expressions. Function procedures can be used at any other place where you would use one of Access' built-in functions. Function procedures include a statement that assigns a value to the function's name. Figure 15-2 shows both a Function procedure and a Sub procedure.

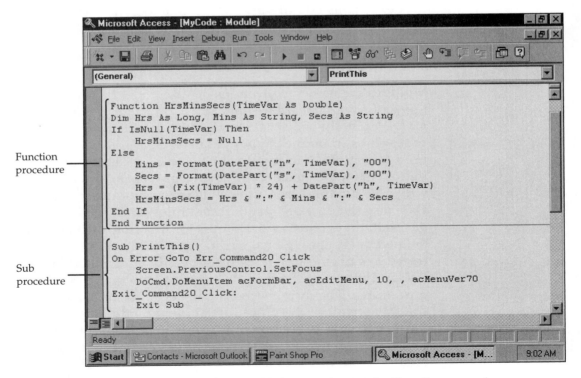

Figure 15-2:   Module window showing a Sub procedure and a Function procedure

Tip: The easy way to remember the difference is whether the procedure returns a value. If it does, it is a Function procedure. If it doesn't, it's a Sub procedure.

What is the **Variant data type?**

The Variant data type is a special kind of data type in VBA. Unlike the other data types, which can hold only a certain data format, Variant variables can hold numbers, strings, dates, and nulls. Variant is the default data type when VBA is used within Access, and it is useful in making your module more flexible. Its advantages are that you do not need to declare a data type and that you can switch from one type to another. The disadvantage is that it may use more memory.

You use the Variant data type when you are not sure which data type you will be working with, or when you know that a variable will have more than one type of data.

Macros or VBA?

One question that's common to those who are beginning to extend the limits of Access by programming in VBA is whether to use VBA or to use macros for a specific task. Access is unique among the Office 97 products in that it provides two ways to handle many complex programming-type tasks: through the use of macros, or with the use of VBA. Since many tasks can be performed equally well with macros or with VBA, some guidelines may help in deciding which approach to use with your specific tasks.

Macros work well when you need to automate the opening and closing of forms and the automated printing of reports. Macros also provide an easy way to prototype simple to moderately complex applications in Access quickly. And there are some tasks that *require* the use of macros, such as an action that is to be carried out when a database is initially loaded. (Of course, that macro action could be the running of a VBA procedure.)

Visual Basic is a better choice when you want tight control over your application or when you want a minimum of clutter. Any complex application built entirely with macros will have a Database window with a number of complex macros, and it can be hard to keep track of which macro is used for what purpose. VBA code, on the other hand, can be integrated directly into the design of your queries, forms, and reports, resulting in a database that is less cluttered with objects and easier to maintain.

VBA is also required when you want to create functions that perform specialized tasks beyond the range of what's possible with the functions built into Access. And you can use VBA to respond to error messages that might otherwise confuse the users of your application.

Finally, VBA is the choice when you want to perform complex operations outside of Access, while under the control of an Access application. You can use a macro to run a Windows or DOS program, but you can't do much else. With VBA, you can read and write files at the operating system level; you can use Automation or Dynamic Data Exchange (DDE) to communicate with other Windows applications such as Microsoft Word and Microsoft Excel; and you can call functions stored in Windows dynamic link libraries (DLLs).

USING VBA WITH ACCESS

❓ Where can I **add the functions** that I have written?

You can place the functions you create in the same places where you use any of the built-in Access functions, in several locations throughout your databases. These locations include:

- ➤ The Control Source property of an unbound text box on a form or report, where it provides the contents of the text box.

- ➤ An event property of a form or report. For example, to have a procedure be performed when the user clicks a command button, assign the procedure to the button's On Click property.

➪ The Field/Expression column of the Sorting and Grouping dialog box used to sort and group data in a report.

➪ The Field line in a query's QBE grid, where it provides the entry for that field in the query's datasheet.

➪ The Criteria line in a query's QBE grid, where it tells Access which data to choose with the query.

➪ The Update To line in an Update query, where it supplies the new table entry made by the query.

➪ The Condition column of a macro, where it chooses when to perform a macro action.

➪ The Expression argument of a SetValue macro action, where it sets what the item argument equals.

➪ The Function Name argument in a RunCode macro action.

➪ Another Function or Sub procedure.

How can I **convert macros** in my forms to VBA code?

Access 97 can convert macros on forms and reports to VBA code. To convert your macros to code, open the form in Design view. Open the Tools menu, choose Macro, and choose Convert Form's Macros to Visual Basic.

Can a VBA procedure **create a form or report**?

Yes. The way to create a form or report by using VBA is to use the CreateForm or CreateReport function. These functions create a form or report that is empty except for what the template places on the design document. (The template is simply an existing form or report that is used as the model for the new form or report.) The syntax for these functions is

CreateForm([*database*[, *formtemplate*]]**)**
CreateReport([*database*[, *reporttemplate*]]**)**

Database is the name identifying the database that contains the template. *Formtemplate* or *reporttemplate* is the name of the existing form or report that is used as the template.

Note that if you omit *database*, Access uses the current database. If you omit *formtemplate* or *reporttemplate* (or if the named template is missing), Access uses the form or report template specified on the Forms/Reports tab of the Options dialog box. (You can get to this by choosing Options from the Tools menu.) Once the procedure creates the form or report, other VBA statements can add controls and make property changes. The statements create forms and reports that are minimized, so you may want to add a **DoCmd.Restore** statement after creating the form or report to open it.

As an example, the following code, attached to the On Click property of a command button, creates a new report when the button is clicked. The new report's sections are based on an existing report named Sales.

```
Private Sub Command0_Click()
    Dim MyReport As Report
    Set MyReport = CreateReport(, "Sales")
    'Create the report.
    DoCmd.Restore            ' Restore report.
End Sub
```

? Can I use VBA to **create a table?**

You can manipulate TableDef objects using VBA to create tables on the fly, under the control of your VBA code. You use the Dim statement to declare your TableDef and Field variables; then you assign a name to the TableDef variable and field names to the Field variables. Finally, you use the Append and Refresh methods of the TableDef object to add the fields to the table object and store the table in the current database. The following code provides an example of how this can be done.

```
Private Sub Command15_Click()
    ' Declare variables.
    Dim MyDb As Database, MyTable As TableDef, MyField
    As Field
    ' Assign the current database to the MyDb variable.
    Set MyDb = CurrentDb
```

```
    ' Create the new table and assign it to the
    ' MyTable variable.
    Set MyTable = MyDb.CreateTableDef("Orders98")
    ' Create three text fields and assign them to
    ' variables.
    Set MyField = MyTable.CreateField("OrderID", dbText)
    MyTable.Fields.Append MyField
    Set MyField = MyTable.CreateField("ItemName", dbText)
    MyTable.Fields.Append MyField
    Set MyField = MyTable.CreateField("SalesRep", dbText)
    MyTable.Fields.Append MyField
    ' Append the fields to the table object and store
    ' it in the database.
    MyDb.TableDefs.Append MyTable
    MyDb.TableDefs.Refresh
End Sub
```

The code is attached to the On Click event for a command button on a form. When the button is clicked, the code creates a new table called "Orders98", containing three text fields called "OrderID", "ItemName", and "SalesRep". (If you create and run this code, you'll need to switch to any other tab in the Database window and then switch back to the Tables tab to see the new table.)

❓ Why doesn't my **Database window** show the TableDef object in the list of tables?

Access does not automatically refresh the Database window when you create TableDef objects. To see the newly created TableDef object in the Database window, choose another list of objects, such as queries, and then switch back to the list of tables. The Database window then refreshes its list, and the TableDef object appears.

❓ How can I **declare the type of data** returned by a function?

You can declare the data type that a function returns by specifying the desired data type, preceded by the word

As, at the end of the statement containing the function. For example, if you wanted Access to use a function called Sales( ) to return a value and you wanted that value returned as a currency amount, you would use this syntax:

Function Sales(*amount*) As Currency

My code is stuck in an **infinite loop**. How do I stop it?

Press CTRL-BREAK to stop executing a procedure.

Why is Access ignoring my control's **input mask** after I added a VBA function to assign a value to the control?

If you use VBA or a macro to assign a value to a control or field that has an input mask, Access ignores the input mask. Therefore, include the effect of the input mask in the VBA code or macro.

I have a **line of code** that is very long. Can I continue it on the next line?

No. There is no continuation character in VBA.

Can I carry out a **macro action** from within a VBA procedure?

Yes. Access provides a special object type, *DoCmd*, that can be used to carry out macro actions from within a VBA procedure. You use one of the available methods for the DoCmd object to perform the desired macro action. The syntax for the use of the DoCmd object is

DoCmd.*method*[*arguments*]

where *method* is the name of the method that describes the macro action, and *arguments* are the arguments for the macro action, if any are used. As an example, you could add the OpenReport method of the DoCmd object to create code that would carry out the OpenReport macro action, opening a report. The following line of code in a procedure would open a report named Quarterly Sales:

DoCmd.OpenReport "Quarterly Sales"

I want to print a procedure. When I print the module, all of the code in the module prints. How can I print a single procedure in a module?

Open the module and drag through the entire block of code you want to print to select it. Then choose Print from the File menu. In the Print dialog box that appears, click Selected Records, then click OK.

How can I protect my VBA code from being read or changed by others?

You can save your database as an MDE file and then distribute the MDE file for use by others. When a database is saved as an MDE file, all editable source code is removed from the database. Your VBA code will still run, but it cannot be viewed or edited. In addition, users will be unable to open or modify forms or reports in Design view. You can use the following steps to save a database as an MDE file:

1. Close the database you want to save, if it is open. (If you are on a network, all other users must be out of the database.)
2. Open the Tools menu and choose Database Utilities, then choose Make MDE File.
3. In the Database to Save as MDE dialog box that appears, choose the database you want to save as an MDE file, then click Make MDE.
4. In the Save MDE As dialog box, specify a name and a location for the MDE file, and click Save.

Caution: When saving a database file as an MDE file, be sure you keep an original copy of the database. You can't change the design of any objects in an MDE file, so if you need to make changes to the code or to forms or reports in the database, you will need the original database to do so.

How can I set the **Record Source** property of a form at run time?

Use the Me property to specify the current table or query for the Record Source property. An example is shown here:

Me.RecordSource = "*New Record Source*"

New Record Source represents the table or query that the form or report opened with this setting will use.

Note: You can also do this in a macro by adding the SetValue action. For the Item argument, enter **Forms![***Form Name***].RecordSource**. For the Expression argument, enter the table name, query name, or SQL statement.

How can I **step through my Function procedure** so that I can find errors?

You can execute a Function or Sub procedure one line at a time. To do this, add *breakpoints* to your procedure. Breakpoints tell Access to stop executing the code at the line of code where the breakpoint has been added. After Access stops executing the code, you can choose to execute the lines one line at a time. To place a breakpoint on a line of your code, use these steps:

1. Move to a line in the procedure where you want to place the breakpoint.
2. Click the Toggle Breakpoint button in the toolbar, or open the <u>D</u>ebug menu, and choose <u>T</u>oggle Breakpoint.
3. Open the Debug window by clicking the Debug button in the toolbar or by choosing <u>D</u>ebug Window from the <u>V</u>iew menu.

4. Type **?** *FunctionName*( ) and press ENTER, where *FunctionName* is the name of your function. Any arguments to the function are placed between the parentheses. For a Sub procedure, don't enter the parentheses. The line of code containing the breakpoint is highlighted in the module window, and the Step Into and Step Over buttons, shown here, become active in the toolbar.

5. Click the Step Into or Step Over button to step through the procedure. Step Into executes one line at a time. Step Over does too, except that a call to a subroutine or function is treated as a single step.

As an example, Figure 15-3 shows the entry in the Debug window that runs the HrsMinsSecs Function procedure. After encountering the line containing the breakpoint, Access performs the remainder of the procedure one line at a time. The line of code with the circle to its left indicates

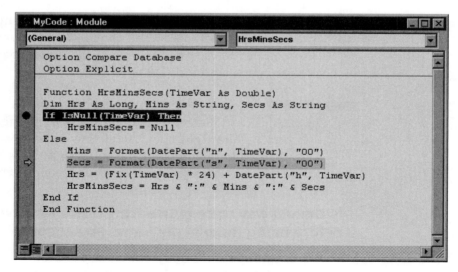

Figure 15-3:   Showing a procedure as Access performs it one step at a time

the setting of the breakpoint. The highlighted line of code with the arrow to its left is the one that Access performs when you click the Step Into button.

Note: When you are done testing, you can use the Clear All Breakpoints option of the Debug menu to get rid of your breakpoints.

I have trouble with **syntax in VBA**. Is there an easy way to write code?

The online help provided by Access is a great source for finding correct syntax. First, search the online help for the command, function, method, or action you want to use. Open the Help menu and choose Contents and Index. Click the Index tab in the dialog box that appears. Type the command, method, function, or action into the text box, then double-click the desired matching entry in the list box. Once you have displayed the help topic about that command, function, method, or action, click Example under the topic heading. Help will display an example of VBA code like the one shown in Figure 15-4. You can use the mouse to drag through any desired code in the example to select it, and press CTRL-C to copy it to the Clipboard. Then switch back to the module window containing your code, and press CTRL-V to add the sample code to your module. Remember to change the arguments in the pasted code to reflect your actual database.

Tip: You can copy code from one procedure to another with the Clipboard. Select the code to copy by dragging the mouse across it. Then right-click the mouse and choose Copy. Next, switch to where you want the code, right-click where you want the code added to the procedure, and choose Paste.

Is there a way to **test the functions** that I've created before using them in my forms and reports?

You can use the Debug window (Figure 15-5) to execute any VBA statement. To view the Debug window, open your module, then open the View menu and choose Debug Window. To test a function, in the lower half of the window,

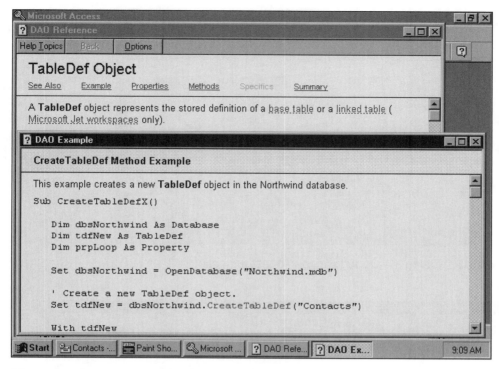

Figure 15-4: An example of VBA code in a help screen

use the Print method (the question mark) followed by the function. For example, you might test a function called HrsMinsSecs, designed to take a serial time value and return the equivalent hours, minutes, and seconds, by entering **? HrsMinsSecs(1.7235)** into the Debug window. Figure 15-5 shows the results of such a test.

Can I view **two procedures at once?**

Yes. Choose Split from the Window menu. Access divides the Module window in half. At this point, both halves of the window show the same procedure. You can switch to either half to show another procedure. You can drag the split bar that divides the two halves up or down to change how much of the window each part uses. The Split command is a toggle, so you can again choose Split from the Window menu to remove the split when done. Figure 15-6 shows a Module window split between two procedures.

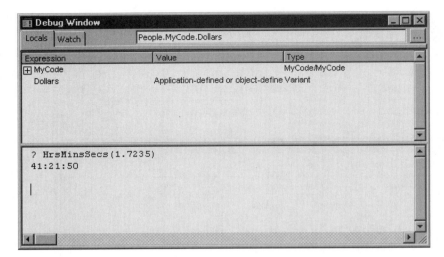

Figure 15-5:   Using the Debug window to test a function

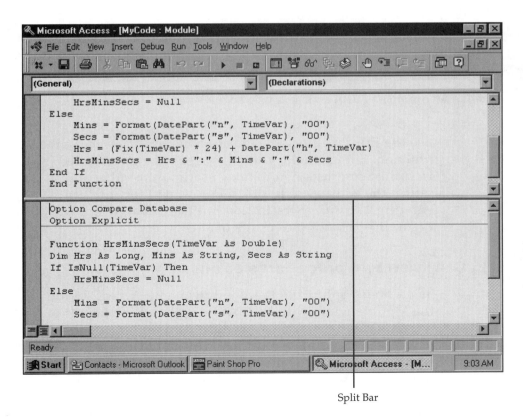

Split Bar

Figure 15-6:   A module showing two procedures split across a window

Tip: The split bar appears at the top of the right scroll bar for the Module window when the window isn't split. Dragging this split bar down is another way to split a window.

How do I replace a constant form name in my code with the contents of a **variable**?

You can replace Forms![*FormName*] in your code with a variable name. The following example shows how to do this, using MyVar as the name of the variable that will equal an acceptable form name.

```
Dim MyVar as String
Let MyVar = "FormName"
```

Now you can replace **Forms![*FormName*]** with **Forms![(MyVar)]** each place it occurs in the code. To refer to a different form, just use another Let statement to assign its name to MyVar.

Miscellaneous Questions

Answer Topics!

How can I convert a number to its **ordinal equivalent**?

Why do I continually get **Out of Memory** errors?

Can I **print a Word document** from within Access?

Can I use a **printer** that's not in my list?

Can I **round my numbers** to so many decimal places?

Can I find the **size of a text file** in bytes?

How can I **speed up my Access database** on a network?

Can I use a **SQL statement as the record source** for a form or report?

How can I **view the query** for a report or form?

Why are the **Wizards dimmed**?

Miscellaneous Questions
@ a Glance

This chapter addresses some of the miscellaneous problems you may encounter with Access that don't fit neatly into the other chapters of this book. Because these answers represent a potpourri of solutions that don't necessarily deal with any single subject, they are not grouped under subheadings; instead, you'll find them all in one section, arranged in alphabetical order by the key phrase in the question. Keep in mind that if you can't find an answer here, you can also check Access' online Help system. Once you familiarize yourself with it, Help can provide you with all sorts of useful tips, tricks, and solutions.

Using the Microsoft Knowledge Base

In addition to the built-in help screens, Microsoft provides an excellent source of answers to technical questions at no cost, if you have access to the Internet. The Microsoft Knowledge Base is a searchable database with solutions to problems and usage tips for all Microsoft applications. To get to the Knowledge Base, launch your Web browser and enter this address:

http://www.microsoft.com/kb

This address takes you to the first page of the Microsoft Knowledge Base, shown in Figure 16-1.

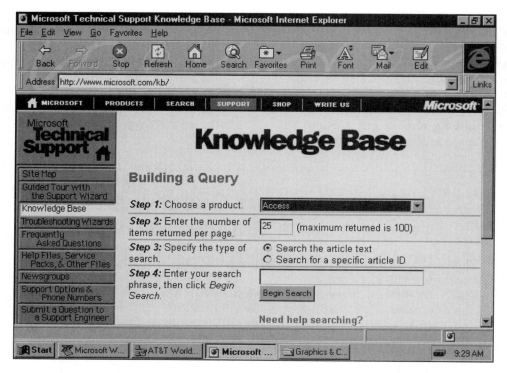

Figure 16-1:   The first page of the Microsoft Knowledge Base

In the Step 1 list box of the Knowledge Base, choose Access. Under Step 2, enter the maximum number of responses per page that you would like to see. Leave the Step 3 options set to the default of "Search the article text"; then enter a search phrase in the Step 4 text box. Click the Begin Search button, and the Knowledge Base will respond with one or more pages of articles that contain your search phrase text. You can click on each article name to display that article within the Knowledge Base.

? How do I **capitalize the first letter** of each word in a text field?

You can create a function procedure that capitalizes text. Then you can use this function as if it were one of Access' built-in functions. To create this procedure, type the following into a module:

```
Function Capitalize (Word As Variant) As String
Dim Temp As String, C As String, OldC As String, X As Integer
If IsNull(Word) Then
    Exit Function
Else
    Temp = CStr(LCase(Word))
    OldC = " "
    For X = 1 to Len(Temp)
      C = Mid(Temp, X, 1)
      If C >= "a" and C <= "z" and (OldC < "a" Or OldC > "z") Then
        Mid(Temp, X, 1) = UCase(C)
      End If
      OldC = C
    Next X
    Capitalize = Temp
End If
End Function
```

In the query or Control Source property, change the field name to
=**Capitalize(**[*text field name*]**)**

> For example, if an Address field of the current
> record contains "245 apple valley way", then
> =Capitalize([Address]) returns 245 Apple Valley Way.

? Can I create a Function procedure that will calculate a person's age?

> Yes. If you know a person's date of birth, you can create a
> function procedure that will subtract the person's birthday
> from today's date and convert the number of days between
> the two dates into years. You can create this procedure by
> typing the following into a module:

> ```
> Function HowOld(DOB As String) As Long
> Dim Birthday As Double
> Birthday = CVDate(DOB)
> HowOld = Fix(DateDiff("d", Birthday, Date) / 365.25)
> End Function
> ```

> With this procedure, DOB represents the date of birth. You
> can use this function just like you use Access' built-in

functions. For example, a control in a form can have a Control Source property of HowOld([Date of Birth]). If Date Of Birth equals 7/5/66 and today is 7/14/98, this control displays 32.

❓ How can I **change the folder** that Access defaults to when I choose <u>O</u>pen Database from the <u>F</u>ile menu?

Open the <u>T</u>ools menu and choose <u>O</u>ptions. When the Options dialog box appears, click the General tab. In the Default Database Folder box, enter the full path for the desired folder, including the drive letter.

❓ How can I speed up a report or form based on a **crosstab query**?

Using fixed column headings improves the performance of forms and reports based on crosstab queries. To create fixed column headings, display the Properties window for the query. (Open the query in Design view, right-click in any blank space in the query, and choose <u>P</u>roperties from the shortcut menu that appears.) In the Column Headings property, type the heading entries for the crosstab query, separated with commas. Supplying the column headings works only if the query has the same column headings every time you run it.

❓ How can I display the most **current data** while viewing data on a network?

When you're using a database that's shared with others on a network, Access automatically updates the data at regular intervals, based on the Refresh Interval setting. (Choose <u>O</u>ptions from the <u>T</u>ools menu and click Advanced to change this value.) You can force Access to display the current data at any time by opening the <u>R</u>ecords menu and choosing Refres<u>h</u>. Note, however, that this updates data that already exists in the datasheet or form; it doesn't display new records that have been added since you opened the query or form. To display new data, requery the records by pressing SHIFT-F9.

Is there a way to change the default font for the entire database, not just for the datasheets? On my monitor, I find the default font used by Access to be hard to read.

You can try changing your default font settings for Windows. Use these steps:

1. In the Windows Taskbar, click Start and choose Settings, then choose Control Panel.

2. In the Control Panel window that opens, double-click Display.

3. Click the Appearance tab.

4. In the Item list, click Menu.

5. Using the Font arrow, increase the font size. (For example, if the font size is 8, try a value of 10.)

6. Click OK.

7. Repeat step 5 for other items in the Item list.

Note: The choices you make will affect other Windows applications, so you should check the appearance of other software after making changes in the Control Panel.

Whenever I use the binoculars in any toolbar or the equivalent Find command of the Edit menu to search for a record, I usually must change the Match entry in the Find dialog box to Start of Field. Is there a way to change the default search behavior of Access?

You can do this at the Options dialog box. Open the Tools menu and choose Options, then click the Edit/Find tab in the dialog box that appears. Turn on the Start of Field Search entry under Default Find/Replace Behavior; then click OK. (You will need to exit and restart Access before this change takes effect.)

I have two date fields. How can I find the difference between them?

To find the difference between two dates, you simply subtract them, as in =**[First Date Field]** − **[Second Date Field]**. You can enter this expression as a calculated field in a query, as a calculated control in a form or report, or as a calculation in a Visual Basic for Applications (VBA) procedure.

This calculation returns the difference between the dates as the number of days between the two dates. You can also use the DateDiff( ) function, which returns a part of the date depending on the interval you provide for the function's first argument. Table 16-1 lists the possible interval entries. As an example of this function at work, you can enter =**DateDiff("yyyy"**, [*First date field*],[*Second date field*]**)** as the Control Source property for an unbound control in a form or report. To display a different interval, replace "yyyy" with another entry from Table 16-1.

Table 16-1:   Possible Intervals for the DateDiff Function

Interval	Result
"yyyy"	The number of years difference between the two dates
"q"	The number of quarters difference between the two dates
"m"	The number of months difference between the two dates
"d"	The number of days difference between the two dates
"w"	The number of weekdays difference between the two dates
"ww"	The number of weeks difference between the two dates
"h"	The number of hours difference between the two dates
"n"	The number of minutes difference between the two dates
"s"	The number of seconds difference between the two dates

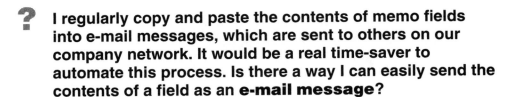

I regularly copy and paste the contents of memo fields into e-mail messages, which are sent to others on our company network. It would be a real time-saver to automate this process. Is there a way I can easily send the contents of a field as an e-mail message?

If you have any MAPI-compatible mail client (such as Microsoft Exchange or Microsoft Outlook) installed and configured to send mail from your workstation, you can do this from within Access. You can do it with a minimal amount of VBA programming; a few lines of code attached to a button on a form is all it will take. You use the SendObject method, which sends data from Access in the form of an e-mail message. Figure 16-2 shows a form

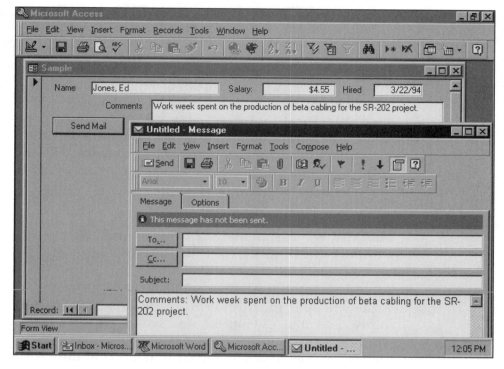

Figure 16-2: An e-mail message resulting from VBA code attached to a form's button

containing a memo field with a command button added to send an e-mail, along with the e-mail message window that appears when the button is clicked.

You can use these steps to add a button that sends a field's contents in the form of an e-mail message:

1. Open the form that contains the field you want to send in Design view. Note the name of the text box containing the desired field.

2. In the Toolbox, turn off the Control Wizards if they are turned on.

3. Use the Command Button tool in the Toolbox to add a command button to the form.

4. Right-click the button and choose Properties from the shortcut menu.

5. Click the Events tab in the Properties window that appears.

6. Click in the On Click property; then click the Build button that appears at the right edge of the property.

7. Double-click Code Builder in the window that appears.

8. In the Module window that opens, enter the following code between the "Private Sub" and "End Sub" lines, which Access adds automatically. In the second line of code, substitute the name assigned to your text box for the name "Comments". Note that in the DoCmd statement the commas represent arguments that are intentionally omitted, and the exact number of commas shown are required.

Dim MailMsg As String
MailMsg = "Comments: " & [Comments]
DoCmd.SendObject , , , , , , , MailMsg

9. Close the Module window and save the form.

When you open the form in Form view, locate a desired record, and click the button, Access will launch a message window using your installed e-mail package, and the contents of the field will appear in the text of the mail message. Note that the SendObject method of VBA is successful only if either of the following is true:

> You have a MAPI-compatible e-mail application installed on your system.

> You have a VIM-compatible e-mail application and you have installed and set up Mapivim.dll, a Windows dynamic-link library that allows the use of VIM-compatible e-mail systems with Microsoft Office applications.

See the documentation for your e-mail package or talk to your Network Administrator for more specifics.

When entering data in a form, why do I get the **error message** "Microsoft Access can't find the macro '.'"?

Someone has inadvertently typed one or more spaces into an event property for a control on the form or into an event property for the form. You'll have to open the form in Design view, look in the Properties window, find the property that contains one or more spaces, and delete them.

If the error occurs when you open the form, check the On Load, On Open, or On Current properties for the form, and check the On Enter property for the first control in the form that gets the focus. If the error occurs as you move into a control or change data in a control, check the On Focus, Before Update, and After Update properties for the control. If the error occurs when you try to save a record, check the Before Update and After Update properties for the form. If you still can't find any extra spaces, go to each property that is blank and press the DEL key.

How do I know when to use the **exclamation point or the period** in an expression?

You use the exclamation point before anything you can name yourself and a period before anything that Microsoft Access names. For example, form names, report names, and control names have an exclamation point before them. Properties have a period.

My computer has the APS (Advanced Power Management System) feature built in. When it switches to suspend mode after inactivity and I restart it, Access displays the message "This program has performed an **illegal operation** and will be shut down." Why is this happening?

This problem occurs on hardware with the APS feature when Access has been installed using the Run From Server option of the Setup program. A Run From Server installation of Access results in most program files used by Access being stored on the network file server. When the APS power management feature puts a computer into suspend mode, network server connections are lost. When you bring the computer out of suspend mode, Access crashes because it has lost the connection with program files that are needed for normal operation. The only ways to avoid this are to disable the APS suspend feature (see your computer's operating manual for details) or to install Access locally (on your hard disk) using the Typical or Custom installation of the Setup program. Also, note that if you connect to the network regularly, it is not a wise idea to use the APS feature of your computer. It will cause problems with all types of Windows software that rely on communicating with files stored on the network.

? How can I prevent a user from **locking a record** for an excessive period of time?

Access doesn't provide any table or form property for "maximum record lock interval", but you can simulate the effect by making your forms used for editing data close automatically after long periods of time. You can use the On Timer property of a form to close a form after a set period of time, keeping users from leaving the form open. By including appropriate VBA code, you can display a message box that tells users why the form was closed. Use these steps:

1. Open the form in Design view, or if the form is already open, choose Select Form from the Edit menu.

2. Open the View menu and choose Properties.

3. Click the Event tab in the Properties window that appears.

4. In the Timer Interval property, enter a value in milliseconds that you want the form to remain open. (One second = 1,000 milliseconds, so if you wanted to limit a form's being open to a maximum of ten minutes, you would enter 600000.)

5. Click in the On Timer property, then click the Build button at the right of the property.

6. Double-click the Code Builder in the dialog box that appears.

7. In the Module window that opens, enter the following code.

```
Private Sub Form_Timer( )
    DoCmd.Close
    MsgBox("Maximum editing time exceeded. Form closed.")
End Sub
```

8. Close the module window.

9. Save the form.

When you open the form in Form view, it automatically closes after the specified time period, and the message is displayed.

One drawback to this technique is that if a user leaves a form open for a long period of time and then begins editing, the form may close while the user is in the midst of the editing process. If you use this approach, it's up to you to warn your users that your forms close automatically. You also may want to provide another form without the timer event strictly for the purpose of adding records, since the addition of multiple records might not be completed within a specific time period. In the Data tab of that form's Properties window, you could set the Allow Edits property to No and the Allow Additions property to Yes, so users could use that form only for adding records.

I've written an application in Access that I need to provide to multiple users. Is there a way to do this without purchasing a copy of Access for each user?

You can do this with the run-time version of Access 97. The run-time version is a part of the Office 97 Developer's Edition, and it includes a Setup Wizard that will package your application along with an Access run-time executable (.EXE) file that allows users to run your application without purchasing Access. Users will not be able to create objects or change the design of any objects in your database, but they will be able to run your application. You can find more specifics about the run-time version of Access 97 in the documentation for Microsoft Office 97, Developer's Edition.

Can I start Microsoft Word and open a Word document from an Access application?

You can do this, and it won't take any excessive amount of VBA programming. All you'll need is a macro containing a RunApp action. You can include the name of the document, including the path, as an argument for the Command line in the macro. Create a new macro, and in the Action column, choose RunApp. In the Command Line box under Action Arguments, enter the following:

winword *"c:\ myfolder\ docname.doc"*

where *c* represents the letter of your drive, *myfolder* is the folder name, and *docname.doc* represents the name of your Word document.

•••••• *Tip:* You can have the macro run when a button is clicked, by choosing the macro's name in the On Click property of the command button.

? How can I convert a number to its **ordinal equivalent?**

You can create a Function procedure that takes a number and converts it to a string with text like "st" or "th" after it. To create this function, type the following into a module:

```
Function Ordinal(Num As Double)
Dim NumPart As String
'NumPart to contain the number's suffix
Ordinal = Num 'Assign the value of Num to Ordinal
If Num > 0 Then 'Add a cardinal suffix when Num > 0
    NumPart = Right(Num, 1)
    'Get the last digit from Num
    Select Case Val(NumPart)
    'Choose which suffix based on the last digit
    Case 1
      Ordinal = Num & "st"
      'When Num = 1 Ordinal equals Num and "st"
    Case 2
      Ordinal = Num & "nd"
      'When Num = 2 Ordinal equals Num and "nd"
    Case 3
      Ordinal = Num & "rd"
      'When Num = 3 Ordinal equals Num and "rd"
    Case Else
      Ordinal = Num & "th"
      'When Num = 4 Ordinal equals Num and "th"
    End Select
End If
If Val(Right(Num, 2)) > 10 And Val(Right(Num, 2)) < 14 Then
    Ordinal = Num & "th"
    'Replace 11st, 12nd and 13rd with 11th, 12th, & 13th
End If
End Function
```

In the query or control source property, where you would usually refer to just the field, enter the following:

=**Ordinal**([*field name*])

This works only for numbers greater than zero. Any number less than 1 entered into the function is returned without modification. As examples of this procedure's output, =Ordinal(1) returns "1st", =Ordinal(14) returns "14th", and =Ordinal(-23) returns "-23".

? **I have 32MB of RAM installed. Why do I continually get Out of Memory errors when no programs other than the Microsoft Office Shortcut Bar are running while I am using Access?**

This message appears not only when you run low on overall memory, but also any time you run low on system resources. This was a far more common problem in Windows 3.*x*, but with complex Access applications it is possible to tax the resources under newer versions of Windows as well. If you're sure you have no other applications open, check for a large number of graph objects that may be open due to charts present in your forms or reports. Microsoft Graph, the mini-application used to create charts within Access, is quite a resource hog. If you open multiple charts, you can quickly deplete all available resources.

? **How can I print a Word document from within Access?**

You can handle this trick with a small amount of VBA coding. If you need to print the document in response to an event, open a new module and create the code as a Function procedure. Then name the function in the property for the desired event. If you need to print the document as a result of clicking on a command button, add the code between the "Private Sub" and "End Sub" lines that Access automatically places behind the On Click property for the button. What follows is an example of the code you'll need. Substitute your actual file name and path for the example of **C:\ My Documents\ letter1.doc** shown in this code.

```
Private Sub Command10_Click()
      Dim WordObj As Object
      Set WordObj = CreateObject("Word.Application")
      WordObj.Documents.Open "C:\My Documents\letter1.doc"
      WordObj.PrintOut Background:=False
      WordObj.Quit
      Set WordObj = Nothing
End Sub
```

≡ *Note:*   The above code assumes that you are using Word 97
or Word 95. You cannot use this code with earlier versions of
Word, because earlier versions use WordBasic rather than VBA
as the programming language.

❓ How can I use a **printer** that's not in my list of available printers?

If the printer that you want to use doesn't appear in the
Printers list box, you'll need to install it. Click the Start
menu on the Windows taskbar, choose Settings, then choose
Printers. Double-click the Add Printer icon, then follow
the instructions that appear in the Add Printer wizard. (If
you are running Access atop Windows NT Workstation, see
your Windows NT Workstation documentation for details
on adding new printers.)

❓ How can I **round my numbers** to a specific number of decimal places?

You can create a Round function that rounds a number to
a set number of decimal places. If you have used rounding
functions in spreadsheet applications, you are already
familiar with how to use this one. To create this function,
type the following VBA code into a module:

```
Function Round(Value As Variant, Decimals As Integer)
If Decimals >= 0 Then
```

```
Else
    MsgBox ("Invalid amount of decimal places supplied!")
    Round = Value
End If
End Function
```

You can use this procedure just like Access' built-in functions. In the query or control source where you would usually refer to just the field, enter the following:

= **Round**([*number field name*],*x*)

where *x* represents the number of decimal places to use for rounding. For example, Round(123.45678,2) will return 123.46, and Round(87.654321,3) will return 87.654.

? Can I find the **size of a text file** in bytes?

You can create a procedure in VBA that opens text files and then uses the LOF function to return the file's size in bytes. A procedure that performs this on a text file named CONSTANT.TXT might look like:

```
Function Size_Of_File( )
Dim Filesize As Integer
Open "CONSTANT.TXT" For Input As #1
Filesize = LOF(1)
Close #1
Size_Of_File = Filesize
End Function
```

? How can I **speed up my Access database** on my company's network?

There are a number of different steps you can take. Try any or all of these tips to improve performance of your databases.

➢ Run the Performance Analyzer to suggest possible improvements in the design of your various database objects. Open the Tools menu and choose Analyze, then choose Performance from the next menu to run the Performance Analyzer. In the next dialog box that appears, use the tabs to display the various database objects, and click the check boxes to select the desired objects to analyze. If the Performance Analyzer is able to make any suggestions for improvements in design, the suggestions will appear in dialog boxes.

➤ Place only the tables on the network server. Store the other database objects (queries, forms, reports, macros, and modules) on the users' local hard drives, and attach from the local databases to the tables stored on the network server. This technique improves performance, because only the data needs to be retrieved across the network.

➤ Avoid record-locking conflicts by adjusting the Refresh Interval, Update Retry Interval, Number of Update Retries, and ODBC Refresh Interval Settings. Open the Tools menu and choose Options, then click the Advanced tab, and change any of the desired settings.

Can I use a **SQL statement as the record source** for a form or report?

Yes, a form or report can get its data from a SQL statement. The form or report includes the same records as a query designed with the same SQL statement. You can type the SQL statement in the Record Source property of a form or report. You can also click the Build button at the end of the property's field to open a Query Builder: SQL Statement window. Here you can use the QBE grid to create a query and view the results of its SQL statement. When the correct records are selected, close the window. Access places the SQL statement that represents the query into the Record Source property.

What's an easy way to **view the query** that a report or form is based on?

While in Design view for the form or report, open the Properties window and click the Data tab. If you click in the Record Source property, a Build button appears, marked only by an ellipsis (a set of three periods). If you click it, the query the report or form is based on opens in Design view.

⁇ Why are the form and report **Wizards dimmed** so that I can't select one?

If you can't access the Form Wizard or the Report Wizard, the wizards have not been installed. Rerun Setup from your CD-ROM or System Disk #1, and click Add/Remove in the Setup dialog box. (If you are installing from Office 97 Professional, you will need to select Microsoft Access when presented with the dialog box containing a list of available programs.) When presented with the dialog box containing the list of options available with Access (shown here), turn on the Wizards check box, then click OK, then click Continue to install the wizards.

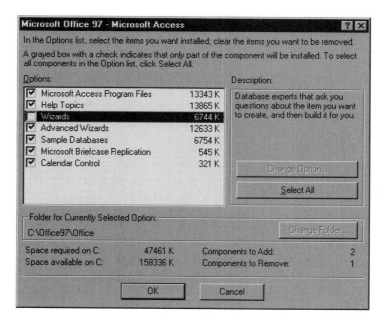

Index

Action Index

If you want to...	You'll find help here...
Create a relationship when one field is an AutoNumber field	80
Create a report	210
Create a report based on a form	179
Create a report manually	212
Create a report that uses different numbers of columns for different sections	222
Create a report with the Report Wizards	210
Create a shadow box on a form's controls	191
Create a startup form	8
Create a table	43
Create a table using VBA	346
Create an AutoKeys macro	26
Create an import/export specification	283
Create an index based on a single field	52
Create an index based on multiple fields	53
Create hyperlinks as part of a table design	325
Create mailing labels	236
Create tabbed forms	170
Cross-tabulate numeric data	136
Customize a toolbar	24
Decide whether to use a Memo field or an OLE Object field for a large amount of text	49
Decide whether to use a text field or a Memo field	48
Declare the type of data returned by a function	348
Delete a batch of records using a query	110
Delete a hyperlink	326
Delete a primary key	51
Delete a relationship	83
Delete all records in a table	73
Delete duplicate records	74
Design better databases	40
Disable a line in a macro	312
Disable certain keyboard keys	26
Disable the Datasheet view for a form	174
Display a bitmap on a command button	253
Display a calculated field as dollars and cents in a query	145
Display a calculated field in Scientific format	124
Display a field using the format assigned in the table	125
Display a photo in an OLE Object field in a form	192
Display a text label on a form as reverse video	189
Display a total of values from a subform on the main form	203
Display a warning message while running a query	309

To **speak to the support experts** who handle more than one million technical issues every month, call **Stream's** Microsoft® Access® answer line! Trained specialists will answer your Microsoft Access questions including setup, built-in networking, printing, multimedia, Microsoft Exchange Mail client and Wizards.

Have all your questions been answered?

1-800-866-7166 $34.95 per problem (Charge to a major credit card.)

1-900-555-2008 $34.95 per problem (Charge to your phone bill.)

Visit our web site at www.stream.com.

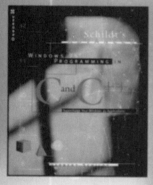

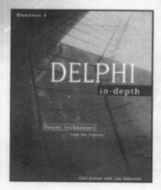

ORDER BOOKS DIRECTLY FROM OSBORNE/McGRAW-HILL

For a complete catalog of Osborne's books, call 510-549-6600 or write to us at 2600 Tenth Street, Berkeley, CA 94710

☎ Call Toll-Free, *24 hours a day, 7 days a week, in the U.S.A.*
U.S.A.: 1-800-262-4729   **Canada: 1-800-565-5758**

✉ Mail *in the U.S.A. to:*
McGraw-Hill, Inc.
Customer Service Dept.
P.O. Box 182607
Columbus, OH 43218-2607

Canada
McGraw-Hill Ryerson
Customer Service
300 Water Street
Whitby, Ontario L1N 9B6

Fax *in the U.S.A. to:*
1-614-759-3644

Canada
1-800-463-5885
Canada
orders@mcgrawhill.ca

SHIP TO:

Name

Company

Address

City / State / Zip

Daytime Telephone *(We'll contact you if there's a question about your order.)*

ISBN #	BOOK TITLE	Quantity	Price	Total
0-07-88				
0-07-88				
0-07-88				
0-07-88				
0-07-88				
0-07088				
0-07-88				
0-07-88				
0-07-88				
0-07-88				
0-07-88				
0-07-88				
0-07-88				

	Shipping & Handling Charge from Chart Below	
	Subtotal	
	Please Add Applicable State & Local Sales Tax	
	TOTAL	

Shipping & Handling Charges

Order Amount	U.S.	Outside U.S.
$15.00 - $24.99	$4.00	$6.00
$25.00 - $49.99	$5.00	$7.00
$50.00 - $74.99	$6.00	$8.00
$75.00 - and up	$7.00	$9.00
$100.00 - and up	$8.00	$10.00

Occasionally we allow other selected companies to use our mailing list. If you would prefer that we not include you in these extra mailings, please check here: ☐

METHOD OF PAYMENT

☐ **Check or money order enclosed** (payable to Osborne/McGraw-Hill)

☐ AMERICAN EXPRESS   ☐ DISCOVER   ☐ MasterCard   ☐ VISA

Account No.

Expiration Date

Signature

In a hurry? Call with your order anytime, day or night, or visit your local bookstore.

Thank you for your order

Code BC640SL